Masterpieces of the Imaginative Mind: Literature's Most Fantastic Works
Part I

Professor Eric S. Rabkin

THE TEACHING COMPANY ®

PUBLISHED BY:

THE TEACHING COMPANY
4151 Lafayette Center Drive, Suite 100
Chantilly, Virginia 20151-1232
1-800-TEACH-12
Fax—703-378-3819
www.teach12.com

ISBN 1-59803-291-7

Eric S. Rabkin, Ph.D.
Arthur F. Thurnau Professor of English Language and Literature, University of Michigan

Eric S. Rabkin is the Arthur F. Thurnau Professor of English Language and Literature at the University of Michigan in Ann Arbor. Born (1946) and raised in New York City and educated at Stuyvesant H.S., Cornell University (A.B., 1967), and the University of Iowa (Ph.D., 1970), he joined the Michigan faculty as an assistant professor in 1970, became associate professor in 1974, and full professor in 1977. His current research interests include fantasy and science fiction, graphic narrative, the quantitative study of culture, traditional literary criticism and theory, and academic computing.

As a teacher, Dr. Rabkin is especially known for his large, popular lecture courses on science fiction and fantasy and for his many teaching innovations. He has received the University Teaching Award (1990), the LS&A Excellence in Education Award (2000), and the Golden Apple Award (2006), given annually by the students for the outstanding teacher at the University of Michigan.

As an administrator, Dr. Rabkin has filled many roles at the University of Michigan. He was co-founder and first director (1976–1982) of the university-wide Collegiate Institute for Values and Science; Associate Dean for Long Range Planning for the College of Literature, Science and the Arts (1979–1983); College Minority Affairs Officer; Interim Chair of the Department of Linguistics and, simultaneously, Interim Director of the English Language Institute (1982–1984). As the University's Acting Director of Academic Information Processes (1997–1998), he helped lead improvement and innovation in the development and uses of academic information technology both intramurally and extramurally. He currently leads the faculty/student collaborative Genre Evolution Project (http://www.umich.edu/~genreevo).

Dr. Rabkin has more than 160 publications, including 31 books written, co-written, edited, or co-edited, including *Narrative Suspense* (1973); *The Fantastic in Literature* (1976); *Science Fiction: History, Science, Vision* (with Robert Scholes, 1977); *Teaching Writing That Works: A Group Approach to Practical English* (with Macklin Smith, 1990); *It's a Gas: A Study of*

Flatulence (with Eugene M. Silverman, 1991); *Stories: An Anthology and an Introduction* (1995); and *Mars: A Tour of the Human Imagination* (2005).

Dr. Rabkin has lectured widely to both general and academic audiences on fantasy, science fiction, fairy tales, humor, American literature, literary theory, culture studies, pedagogy, composition, administration, and information technology. He has had lecture tours in the United States, Europe, and Australia and, from 1990 through 1996, offered a regular commentary on language and culture topics on WUOM-FM radio.

The professor has served as a consultant to more than 60 publishers, journals, and other organizations and is the founder of *Write On Target*, a corporate communications consulting firm.

Dr. Rabkin's awards include a fellowship from the American Council for Learned Societies (1973), research funding from the American Philosophical Society (1991), and the University of Michigan Distinguished Faculty Achievement Award (2005).

He lives in Ann Arbor with his wife, Elizabeth Rabkin, a retired elementary-school teacher. They have two children, David Ivan (b. 1970) and Rachel Ann (b. 1975), and two grandchildren.

Table of Contents
Masterpieces of the Imaginative Mind:
Literature's Most Fantastic Works
Part I

Masterpieces of the Imaginative Mind:
Literature's Most Fantastic Works

Scope:

Walter Benjamin wrote that "[t]he fairy tale, which to this day is the first tutor of mankind, secretly lives on in the story. The first true storyteller is, and will continue to be, the teller of fairy tales." Fairy tales, of course, are fantastic. Despite the sophisticated preference the 20th century showed for realism, the vast majority of the greatest works of literature, from ancient myths and epics to modern Nobel Prize–winning novels, rely on the fantastic.

This course has two parts; the first discusses the fantastic in its many varieties, and the second, its most important modern variety, science fiction.

The discussion of the fantastic covers many specific works and many general theoretical frameworks for understanding those works. We begin with fairy tales, how they came to be gathered and published, how they reflect the world in which they are told, and what they say about human psychology. They suggest the function of narrative in our pre-literate heritage. The world of fairy tales is fantastic—animals talk there—but not true fantasy, because once in the fictional world, its rules are known and stable. Sophisticated writers, such as E. T. A. Hoffmann, reworked fairy tales by making them ever more fantastic, changing the ground rules as we read, and thus, produced true fantasy, stories that challenge our ability to understand not only the stories themselves but potentially everything in human existence. Hoffmann's own favorite story was "The Golden Pot," which he subtitled "A Modern Fairy Tale."

Edgar Allan Poe's stories fall into several fantastic genres. He called one of those *tales of ratiocination*, but we would divide them into detective stories (such as "The Purloined Letter") and science fiction (such as "The Descent into the Maelstrom"). Some seem to straddle genres, such as "The Pit and the Pendulum," which could be read as horror or as science fiction. By examining a series of Poe's works, including some of his poems, we can see that similar materials can be handled less or more fantastically. Thus, true oral fairy tales and basic detective stories are both about midway on a continuum of the fantastic between the most sober, stable realism and the most mind-challenging fantasy.

Using and refining these theoretical insights, we can see how Lewis Carroll's *Alice* books give us both true fantasy and an understanding of why we often associate the fantastic with children's literature. H. G. Wells's science fictions show the seriousness possible when the fantastic is used for political and philosophical inquiry. Franz Kafka's works use the fantastic to convey the alienation of the modern world of inhumane institutions. Virginia Woolf and Alain Robbe-Grillet use the fantastic to attempt to free us from the unconscious constraints imposed by, respectively, patriarchal society and shared linguistic habits. J. R. R. Tolkien tells almost Arthurian tales, but in a new, more fantastic way, to provide both psychological and spiritual consolation, a function common in much children's literature, including that by Beatrix Potter and Dr. Seuss. Finally, however, the extreme application of the fantastic in the development of any given genre leads to thoroughly modern myths and magical realism in such Postmodern writers as Italo Calvino and Laura Esquivel.

The second part of this course discusses the fantastic genre that is most important today, science fiction, and traces its development from its precursors in the ancient world, including Plato's *Republic* and Lucian's *Icaromenippus*, to such 17th- and 18th-century works as Cyrano's *Other Worlds* and Jonathan Swift's *Gulliver's Travels*. Science fiction claims plausibility for its fantastic elements against a background of science. Where some writers of Gothic romance, such as Ann Radcliffe, had added a fantastic twist to their novels by ending them with a naturalizing explanation, Mary Shelley in *Frankenstein* moved that explanation to the beginning of the work and, thus, produced the world's first true science fiction novel.

As a variety of Romantic literature, we see science fiction develop in the stories of Nathaniel Hawthorne and Edgar Allan Poe. With Jules Verne, science fiction becomes a literature of conquest. But almost in reply, H. G. Wells uses science fiction to criticize imperialism. Both writers fall to some extent within the oldest tributary of the mainstream of science fiction, utopianism, which descends in four great historic movements from the ancient world to the Christian Renaissance to the Industrial Revolution to the modern industrial state. Like some utopian fiction, such as More's *Utopia*, science fiction, with its astronomical leaps of perspective and focus on the power of the individual's acquiring knowledge, naturally raises questions normally dealt with by religion. Science fiction, especially in America, also has a pulp fiction heritage that influenced its choice of themes and politics. Ray Bradbury bridged the pulp and high cultures, and Robert Heinlein mastered the new, more thoughtful, yet still popular form. Isaac Asimov and Arthur C. Clarke, working at the same time, tried to retain some utopian hopes. But as the world globalized, so did science fiction, and the cultural diversity and feminism of Ursula K. Le Guin ascended. Finally, science fiction began to experiment in the same way mainstream literature had for three-quarters of a century and quickly produced the New Wave, then cyberpunk. On reflection, we see these experimental reactions to our information age as simultaneously new science fiction and threads in the fabric of Postmodernism. With Nobel Prizes awarded to such writers as Gabriel García Márquez (*One Hundred Years of Solitude*) and José Saramago (*Blindness*), the fantastic, both in general and as science fiction, has regained its place at the center of storytelling. We live in a science fictional world.

Lecture One
The Brothers Grimm & Fairy Tale Psychology

Scope:

Half a century before the unification of Germany, two very unusual scholarly brothers named Grimm, fervent nationalists and great philologists, set out to demonstrate the classic roots of the German language and its function as a treasury of fundamental human culture. In pursuing this aim, they gathered folk tales that supposedly came down from antiquity. These powerful stories do teach morals but not the morals we may expect. Nonetheless, the Grimm brothers' collection unexpectedly swept through the world and made folklore a new field of study. To understand how such tales as "Hansel and Gretel," "Little Red Riding Hood," and "Rapunzel" project such transnational power, we need to understand how they appeal symbolically and psychologically both to the archetypal grandmother teller and to child audiences of many ages.

Outline

I. The fantastic drives works, such as "Cinderella" and *Frankenstein*, whose characters have escaped their pages to share our lives. In this course, we will explore the fantastic in literature and culture.

    A. Although we naturally will touch on ancient works, such as the *Odyssey*, we will focus on works from the beginning of the 19th century onward, because from this point on, we can use solid knowledge of each author's life and culture to understand the texts.

    B. Although the theoretical frameworks we will develop to discuss the fantastic often apply universally, we will focus on works from Western culture because our familiarity with that culture allows us to probe its works most deeply.

    C. These lectures are distributed into two parts.

        1. The first part focuses on the broad range of fantastic literary genres, from fairy tales to magical realism. It both offers analyses of specific works and develops general theoretical frameworks for understanding the significance of those works and of the fantastic.

    2. The second part focuses on science fiction, arguably the most important of the fantastic genres in our time.

II. There is no better place to begin a study of the masterpieces of the imaginative mind than with the works of two scholarly brothers, Jakob (1785–1863) and Wilhelm (1786–1859) Grimm, who set out to demonstrate the significance of German culture half a century before there was a unified German state. To do so, they sought to demonstrate their culture's ancient roots.

    A. Although Jakob was a bachelor and Wilhelm married, the brothers lived and worked together their entire lives.

    B. They were pioneering philologists who discovered the very first law of phonological change, what we now call Grimms' law. This demonstrated the connection between German and the classical European languages.

    C. Although they were not the first to record fairy tales, their method intended to demonstrate the antiquity of those tales by reproducing them from supposedly oral sources.

        1. Earlier collections, such as those of Charles Perrault (1628–1703), were aimed at courtly readers.

        2. The Grimms' collection was known as *Kinder- und Hausmärchen*, that is, *Children's and Household Tales*. The Grimms thought that tales passed from teller to teller, rather than from writer to writer, would give a "natural" insight into the oldest sources of culture, thus making the "folk," such as contemporary German peasants, even more important culturally than the writers of antiquity.

III. The Grimms' insight that folk tales, or fairy tales, are prehistoric is now universally accepted.

    A. Fairy tales are "the first tutor of mankind" according to Walter Benjamin (1892–1940), the pioneering culture critic.

        1. Benjamin identified fairy tales by their conventional ending: "and they lived happily ever after."

        2. Most people today, including such folklorists as Max Lüthi, identify fairy tales by their conventional beginning: "once upon a time."

3. The plurality of the Grimms' retold stories is revealing in that they have no common ending, but they do have a common beginning: "in olden times, when it was of use to wish for something."

4. We can see both the antiquity and the conventional consolation of fairy tales in "Rapunzel."

B. Fairy tales are ubiquitous.

1. Such works as the Stith Thompson Motif Index (created by a professor at Indiana University, which still has a leading folklore department) record the existence of common folktale elements, as well as whole stories, even in cultures with no ancient connection.

2. "Cinderella," for example, occurs with different footwear and different causes of the heroine's orphan state, but the framework of the story is universal.

C. It is correct to say that fairy tales teach morals. This is true for those shaped by oral transmission through generations and for those, like many of Aesop's fables, that may have been invented by a professional storyteller rather than through an oral process over generations.

1. In "Cinderella," diligence is rewarded.

2. In "The Three Spinsters," however, the "moral" is that beauty is better than honesty.

3. The morals of fairy tales "tutor" us, whether or not we accept those morals as good.

IV. Fairy tales work with a fundamental, familiar, familial psychology.

A. Fairy godmothers (and mothers in general) are marked by their desire to feed you. Witches, the anti-mothers, would eat you.

B. Fairy tales collectively represent a world in which females exist in only three states: asexual girlhood, sexual adulthood, and post-menopausal old age.

C. Many fairy tales deal with common issues, such as the anxiety one may feel in anticipating moving from the comparative simplicity of childhood to the demanding world of adulthood. We can see variations of that theme for audiences of different ages by comparing "Little Red Riding Hood," "Sleeping Beauty," and "Snow White."

   D. An analysis of the backstory of "Hansel and Gretel" helps us understand why that tale is a mainstay of our common culture.

      1. The archetypal child listener is motivated in part by the promise of being able to work out certain perhaps unconscious feelings of guilt and/or abandonment, symbolically.

      2. The archetypal grandmother teller is motivated in part by the opportunity to express safely her perhaps unconscious ambivalence toward someone who will supplant her.

   E. By offering a satisfying symbolic experience for all concerned, fairy tales have remained essential parts of human culture from before recorded history.

Essential Reading:

Grimm, Jakob, and Wilhelm Grimm. *Household Stories of the Brothers Grimm.*

Supplementary Reading:

Lüthi, Max. *Once Upon a Time: On the Nature of Fairy Tales.*

Perrault, Charles. *Perrault's Fairy Tales.*

Questions to Consider:

1. What are the differences between making up a story for a child and telling a child a story you already know?

2. What roles do traditional stories play in how you view the world?

Lecture One—Transcript
The Brothers Grimm & Fairy Tale Psychology

Hello, my name is Eric Rabkin, and I'm delighted to welcome you to this course on the fantastic. Fantasy often has a bad reputation. Something is a "mere" fantasy. Why we can't do that, because it's just a fantasy. Or in Freudian psychology, his problem is that he has that fantasy. But in fact, the fantastic drives us forward. We dream of what we may accomplish. We dream of a possible new world, and we shape our lives and the world around us accordingly. Who doesn't like a Cinderella story? If not the version that you learned as a child, then perhaps Julia Roberts in *Pretty Woman*. And, when we want to express our fears—for example, of genetically modified foods—we call then "Frankenfoods." Cinderella and Frankenstein's monster are characters that have walked off the pages of their books, and they share our lives. This course will explore the fantastic in literature and culture.

Although we will naturally touch on ancient works like the *Odyssey*, with its gods and endless, endless encounters with strange and marvelous beings, we will focus on works from the beginning of the 19th century onward for three reasons. First, this is the beginning of a mass reading public; in a sense, in other words, our era. Second, this is the beginning of the segmentation of the publishing industry by markets, which makes it possible to look at different varieties of work and see to whom they are expected to appeal. Third, from this point on, we can use solid knowledge of each author's life and culture in understanding the texts. Although the theoretical frameworks that we will develop to discuss the fantastic often apply universally, we will discuss works primarily from Western culture because our familiarity with that culture allows us to probe its works most deeply.

These lectures are distributed into two parts. The first part focuses on the broad range of fantastic literary genres, from fairy tales to Magic Realism. This isn't just a broad range historically, but a broad range generically. In fact, detective stories are, according to W. H. Auden, "those works that indulge the fantasy that hidden guilt may be revealed." Many different genres are, to one extent or another, fantastic; and the fantastic develops through time. We'll develop a theoretical framework for understanding the significance of the fantastic in general, and look at specific works from a whole range of those fantastic genres. The second part of the course will focus on science fiction. Why? Because in our world, shaped as it is inevitably by the constant development of science and technology. Forced, as we are, to live in a world whose material conditions make our lives different—and hence our perceptions different—the only literature that genuinely engages those forces that change us is the literature of science and technology; that is to say science fiction. For us, science fiction is the most important of the fantastic genres.

But first, we need to understand the fantastic in general, and there is no better place to begin a study of the masterpieces of the imaginative mind than with the works of two scholarly brothers, Jakob and Wilhelm Grimm. These fellow set out to demonstrate not something about fairy takes, which is what they are most known for now, but rather the significance of German culture. They did this half a century before there was a unified German state. What they wanted to do was demonstrate the antiquity and significance of German culture—that is, German language culture—although the German speakers were distributed among many different political domains. To do this, they sought to demonstrate the ancient roots of their culture.

Although Jakob was a bachelor and Wilhelm married; Jakob very active and Wilhelm relatively frail; Jakob always traveling around the world and Wilhelm staying home, the brothers lived and worked together their entire lives, and only Wilhelm had children. They were, in fact, before they set out collect fairly takes—folk tales— pioneering philologists. Philology is the study of language development. In particular, they developed the very first law of phonological change. Phonology is that branch of philology that concerns itself with the sounds of language. We all know, if we know several Romance languages, that there are similarities. We know that it's *trois* in French for three, and *tre* in Italian. And if we know several Germanic languages, we know it's *three* in English, and it's *drei* in German.

What the Grimm brothers discovered was that a certain class of sound changes regularly when it goes from the ancient languages to Germanic languages, but does not change when it goes to the Romance languages. That class of sound is called a voiceless plosive. A voiceless sound is a sound that does not engage your voice box. *Sss*; when you say that sound, you feel no vibration in your larynx.

Mmm; when you say that sound, you do feel a vibration in your larynx, your voice box. *Sss* is voiceless; *Mmm* is voiced. Voiceless stops are sounds produced by stopping the air and then releasing them; *Ppp, Kkk*. What the Grimm brothers discovered is that voiceless stops—in Latin, for example—remain voiceless stops in Romance languages, but become voiceless fricatives—that is, sounds produced by friction—in Germanic languages. The Latin *pater* becomes the French *père*, the Spanish *padre*, but the English *father* and the German *fater*.

Voiceless stops become voiceless fricatives in Germanic languages, but remain voiceless stops in Romance languages. There are three such sounds: *Ppp, Ttt, Kkk*. Those sounds change, so we get *pater* through; and, for example, *cornu* becomes *corn* in English, but remains "corn," or a sound like corn; *casa*, becomes *house*. We have those regular changes. Why? No one knows. But what it proves is that we can make a direct line from German, right back to the ancient classical languages. In the same way, the Grimm brothers said we have stories, stories we were all raised on, stories that were transmitted orally, and these stories passed from grandmother to grandchild. These stories must have been the ones that are most powerful in our culture. They must go all the way back.

There had been collections of fairy tales, folk tales, household stories, before the Grimm brothers. Charles Perrault did a famous collection at the end of the 17th century, but his stories were really re-workings of stories that were well known; intended by their literary elegance to appeal to courtly readers. The Grimm brothers ostensibly wanted the true oral tale, and they sent their students—they were university professors—and they themselves out into the field, theoretically at least, to collect true oral tales. In fact, that is not quite what they did, as we will discuss in the next lecture, but they were supposedly getting true oral tales. When they gathered them together, they called them *Kinder- und Hausmärchen—Children's and Household Tales*. They didn't mean this to be children's literature; they meant this to be the literature that gets told to children in the household context. In an agrarian society, when you can no longer work the fields, what is your use? The grandmother—who may feel bitter because time has passed her by—can at least tend to the children who are not yet strong enough to go out and work the fields. She tells them stories, and these are those stories.

The Grimms' insight that folk tales or fairy tales are, in some sense, prehistoric has now been universally accepted. Their tales swept the European world, and were almost instantly translated into many languages. Fairy tales, as the pioneering culture critic Walter Benjamin has said, are "the first tutor of mankind." Benjamin identified fairy tales by their conventional ending, "and they lived happily ever after." But I think most people today would identify fairy tales, more likely, by their conventional beginning, "once upon a time." As soon as we hear that, we know we're in the land of fairy tales. We make a fantastic change, and we expect talking animals and golden-haired princesses. If you read all of the Grimms' tales, you'll see that they begin in different ways, but they do tend mostly to have a single beginning, although they have wildly different endings. The beginning is, *"In den alten Zeiten, wo das Wünschen noch geholfen hat..."* "In the olden times when it was of use to wish for something..."

We can understand what that means in a perfectly good, absolutely archetypal, and well-known fairy tale like "Rapunzel." It begins, "There once lived a man and his wife who had long wished for a child, but in vain." So here we have the situation. We have the wishes. Will it be worth wishing after something? Indeed, what they have is a beautiful garden nearby, which the old wife can see from her window, and she develops a passion for the rampion that is growing in that garden. But the garden belongs to an old witch who has forbidden anyone to enter it. Still, she must have it. And her husband, who loves her dearly, one night climbs over the garden wall and comes back with the rampion. The woman is delighted; she feels wonderful, and sends him again the next night. The next night, the witch finds the old man and demands, with "angry eyes," to know what has gone wrong.

The eye imagery is crucial throughout "Rapunzel." Eye imagery is crucial throughout the world of fairy tales. "I *see* what you mean. I have a *perspective* on this problem. What a *brilliant* idea that is, or am I being *obscure*? Can you *see* this through the *cloudy* presentation? Don't *look* at the world through rose-colored glasses." The association of sight imagery with knowledge is universal. Knowledge, even at the linguistic level, is related to conception; conception of the mind, conception of the body. The witch looked at the old man with angry eyes, and he said, "please be merciful rather than just," and explains why he has gone into the garden to satisfy his wife's urge for the rampion. "If it is all as you say," the witch replies, "you may have as much rampion as you like, but I shall have the child that comes from it."

What child? No one has said a word about a child except for the opening line that said for a long time, the husband and wife had yearned for a child. The world of fairy tales takes much for granted. The witch understands that these are pregnancy cravings. The word for rampion, which is English, in German is *rapunzel*. Rapunzel represents the vegetative power, the fertility that the mother has, but the witch does not. But the witch, like an anti-god, has her garden, and she must keep people out as God keeps Adam and Eve and their descendants out of the Garden of Eden. Ultimately, the witch takes Rapunzel, and at about the age of puberty, puts her in a tower, which has no doors or windows down below, but only one window at the very top. It is clearly a phallic symbol.

She lives there, Rapunzel does, and the witch comes to see her daily, climbing up Rapunzel's ever-lengthening golden hair. She calls out, "Rapunzel, Rapunzel, let down your golden hair." We know what "let down your hair" means; it means get loose. It may even mean take down your hairdo and get ready to go to bed. One day, a prince comes by and hears this, and sees the witch scamper up. After the witch leaves, he calls, "Rapunzel, Rapunzel, let down your golden hair," and he scampers up. Soon thereafter, when the witch comes again, Rapunzel says why is it that you come up so slowly and the prince comes up so rapidly? Prince? What prince? The next time the prince comes, the witch has lowered the hair, tied to a nail—she's cut it off Rapunzel's head, a classic way of abusing fertile-aged women for having conspired with the enemy. As the prince gets to the top of the window, she pushes him, and he falls down onto the brambles down below; the thorns of which put out his eyes.

Then the witch abandons Rapunzel in a waste and desert place, meaning a place of no fertility. Years pass, and the blind prince is wandering through the world. Rapunzel sees him. She throws herself on his neck. She cries piteously. The liquid, the tears from her eyes—water, a sign of fertility in all cultures. Go away for the weekend. Come back and add water to your plants. Go unpack and look at how your plants have suddenly gotten happy. Of course water is a sign of fertility. The tears, the water from her eyes, fall into the prince's eyes. His sight is restored, and the last scene we see is the two of them walking off so that he can go back to his kingdom, where he will become the king, with Rapunzel as his queen, and the twin boy and girl they have borne as the prince and princess. Twin boy and girl? Where did they come from? They came from that time up in the tower.

In other words, what we have here is a story of female competition for the power of fertility. In fact, because of the use of the term Rapunzel, we know that this story actually goes all the way back to vegetation gods, to the time before writing when, indeed, the great gods were female gods, before they had been supplanted by male gods. There are three key times for a woman in Grimms' tales: there's the asexual time of girlhood; there is the sexually active time of adulthood, and there is the post-menopausal time of old age. The witch is in old age. The mother in "Rapunzel" is fertile; Rapunzel grows through these ages. These continuing motifs, these pieces of story that occur in story after story, lend a kind of continuing power to fairy tales. We know that the Grimms' version is already Christianized. The thorns that put out the prince's eyes are like the crown of thorns that Jesus wears. But the underlying structure is clear, and we know that there's a competition among females.

There is something called a Motif Index, created by Stith Thompson, a pioneering folklore professor at Indiana University, that traces the recurrence of these motifs from culture to culture. "Cinderella" gives us a terrific example of that. "Cinderella" is the story of a girl who is under the domination of her stepmother and her ugly stepsisters. She wants to go to the ball so that she can meet her prince, but the stepmother says well, you have to do housework, and takes a bunch of lentils and throws them into the cinders of the fireplace— Cinderella; *Aschenputtel* in German. If she can retrieve those, then she can go to the ball. In fact, birds come down and pick out those lentils for her, and she can put them back in a bag and gets to go to the ball, with the famous episode of the glass slipper and so on.

To show you the staying power of this series of motifs, we need to ask, for example, where did that glass slipper come from? In Charles Perrault's version of "Cinderella," "*Cendrillon*," we have "*souliers de vair*." "*Vair*" is, in fact, a comparatively rare word in French—*V-A-I-R* —and it is exactly the same word in English; but in English, even rarer—*V-A-I-R*. It means squirrel fur. She was wearing "*souliers de vair*," "slippers of squirrel fur." However, the word in French, *verre*, means a "cup" or a "glass." It doesn't mean the material glass, which is *cristal*, but it means a glass as in a glass of water, *verre*. Therefore, English readers pronouncing the French story out loud, saw Cinderella as wearing "*soulier de verre*," glass slippers. Clearly, you can't wear glass slippers. They don't have the flexibility to make it possible to dance in them at all. That particular detail is delightful, and we've kept it all this time. But we've only been able to keep it because it fits into the large story.

How is it that Cinderella has these ugly stepsisters to deal with? I'm not sure, but the Greek version of the story—and I don't read Greek, but I've read the French translation of it—is called "*Cendrillon et les Soeurs Cannibales*," "Cinderella and the Cannibal Sisters." Her mom is dead because she's been eaten by these girls. She also has a fairy godmother. Where does that come from? I think it's reasonable to suppose that she is the spirit of the mother that is dead. Fairy tales teach us morals. We like to say that. "Cinderella" teaches the moral that diligence is rewarded.

One of my favorite tales is "The Three Spinsters." In "The Three Spinsters," we have a girl who will not do any housework. She is the opposite of Cinderella, and she is lying with her head on a window, looking out into the street, as her mother behind her is yelling at her to get busy. The queen, walking by, hears the yelling and goes upstairs and asks the woman why she's berating her daughter. Not wanting to admit that her daughter is lazy, the woman says my daughter will just work and work and work all the time. She cannot be stopped. She's always spinning; she's always producing things. The queen says well, if that's as it is, let me take her with me. I may want her as a wife for my son. So the girl goes off to the castle. There she was with her head on the window again because the queen has left her with half a room full of flax to be spun into linen, and she's not up for it.

But three ugly women go by, the three spinsters of the title. One of them has a big hanging lip. One of them has a splatted thumb, and one of them has a big splay foot. They say they'll do the spinning, but if there's a wedding, they must be invited as if they were the relatives. The girl readily agrees, and in fact, night after night, they spin for her ever-larger amounts of flax, and she is given in marriage to the prince. The wedding occurs, and in come these three uglies.

The prince says, "Who are they? The princess says, "These are my cousins." "How did they get to look that way?" "Well, the one with the big lip was always trying to wet the thread. The one with the big thumb was always trying to spin out the thread. The one with the splay foot is always trying to work the treadle." "Well, if that is as you say, the prince says, "you will never spin again." The moral of the story? It's better to be a beautiful, lazy liar than diligent. In other words, fairy tales do teach us morals, but not necessarily the morals we think they should tell.

Fairy tales work in a fundamental, familiar, familial psychology. The fairy godmothers are marked—and mothers in general—by their desire to feed you. Witches are the anti-mothers, and they would eat you. In a true oral folktale, no one ever says, "I love you;" they just give you food. No one ever says, "I hate you;" they just give you poison. Fairy tales collectively represent a world in which females exist, as I said, in these three states; asexuality, sexuality and post-sexuality. The ideal state is the familial state before sexuality, as with the twins at the end of "Rapunzel." Many fairy tales deal with common issues; for example, the anxiety that one might feel having to contemplate moving to a new stage of life with a greater sense of responsibility. We can see that by looking at a series of folk tales that deal with, essentially, that same structure.

"Little Red Riding Hood"—"Little Red Cap," as the Grimm brothers call it—is a story about a girl; asexual, but at the point of menses— she's known by her red cap—that her mother in the village, a fertile female, sends with bread and cakes—that Red keeps under her apron, thinking about the impending sexuality—to feed her old grandmother in the woods. "Do not tarry along the way," the mother says. But Red, of course, does because she's stopped by a wolf. We, even today, use the word "wolf" to refer to a sexual predator. The wolf says, "Why are you running along so fast? Look at all the wonderful flowers around you." Flowers, as anyone in an agricultural society would know, are the sex organs of plants. Red stops. She looks at the flowers, and she starts gathering them. We are told that she does not stop until her arms are so full that she can't hold anymore. Then, only when she has no longer the physical capacity to gather flowers, does she get back on the path and go to her grandmother's hut where, as we all know, she finds herself confronting a very odd-looking grandmother. In fact, it's the wolf, which has eaten the grandmother.

Now the huntsman comes along, and he has a rifle. He could kill the wolf, but for some reason he thinks, what if there's someone alive in there? And so, he takes a pair of scissors and cuts open the wolf's belly—we have a kind of reverse birth—out comes Red; out comes granny. Red takes some rocks, puts them into the cavity of the wolf's belly, and sews them up. Then the wolf, trying to escape, leaps onto the roof of the house, but falls down through the chimney into the cooking pot and is boiled to death. Red, in other words, kills the wolf. In Charles Perrault's version, however, the huntsman comes in and just finds the wolf; Red dies. The explicit moral that Perrault puts at the end of the tale is, "and so little girls should always obey their mothers." In other words, the child, thinking of going out on her own, thinking of becoming more adult, thinking of being the feeder, thinking of having sexuality, fails to follow her mother's instructions and pays for it with her life.

This is a compensation, symbolically, for those fears. It says just obey your mother. You will be safe if you just obey your mother. What kind of a child needs that lesson? Maybe a six-year-old. But in "Little Red Cap," it says, "I will never go into the forest again as long as my mother forbids it. Here, Red has escaped. As long as my mother forbids it. Okay, so this maybe an eight-year-old. She knows it's dangerous, but Mom is her guide. In the version that's illustrated by Arthur Rackham, the child says, "I will not go into the woods again until I am ready." So the new order is expected in some safe future. This is perhaps for a ten-year-old.

"Rapunzel" is, in a sense, the same story, right? It's the little girl who had to pay and wait until eventually she can have her own sexuality. But there, the problem isn't caused by the child's foolishness; it's caused by the mother's carelessness. The new order of that child's sexuality and adult responsibility matures as the old order dies. We do not have a narration of the time between the prince coming to the tower and the prince finding Rapunzel again. In "Sleeping Beauty," the girl falls backward when she pricks her finger on a spindle at the age of 15. And in "Snow White," we have a 17-year-old who is made to fall into sleep by the poison of her envious stepmother. In other words, we have here half a dozen different stories, all giving the same psychological, symbolic problem;

working it through, but with slightly different endings, to help us deal with problems.

"Hansel and Gretel" is a terrific story for understanding these psychological compensations. "Hansel and Gretel" was a story in which a stepmother has said, "We don't have enough food. Let's abandon the children in the forest." The woodcutter/gardener father agrees. Hansel has heard that this is the plan. So, as they go off into the woods, he leaves a trail of—not breadcrumbs, which we always remember—he leaves a trail of flints. And then they turn around and come right back. The next day, they're abandoned again, but this time Hansel has left a trail of breadcrumbs, and the birds pick up the breadcrumbs. They wander in the forest lost, and they see a wonderful house of gingerbread and other goodies. They find themselves with a witch. The witch says that she wants to feed them, but in fact she claps Hansel into a cage and means to fatten him up so that she can eat him. She is the anti-mother.

Gretel is set to housework. Every day, though, she gives Hansel an old chicken bone. And when the almost blind witch comes by to feel whether or not Hansel is getting fatter, he holds out the chicken bone. Eventually, the witch says, "Well, even if you're not getting any fatter, it's time to eat you." She tells Gretel to fire up the oven. Gretel feigns inability. The witch does it instead. Gretel pushes the witch in. The witch is killed in the oven. Immediately, Gretel releases Hansel, and they go back. They find their way home almost instantly, sleep overnight in the forest, and get on a swan's back to be carried across the river. The last scene we see is them with their father; the stepmother, in their absence, conveniently having died.

Consider the backstory. Like Cinderella's fairy godmother, I would like to suggest that this is a story about illicit desire. Children often want to supplant their parents. Stereotypically, girls want to supplant their mothers to marry their fathers; boys supplant their fathers to marry their mothers. We don't have to go into sexuality and think of real killing. The fact is children often want to be more important in the eyes of their parents than the other parent's position makes that possible for them. Consider a Gretel who wished her mother were dead. That is unreasonable; it can't even be thought of. Okay; but then there's a stepmother who comes along. Well, you could want a stepmother dead; especially one who would abandon you in the forest. But the stepmother gives pleasure to the father. You can't really want him dead. So you go into the forest and meet a true anti-mother, the witch. She deserves to die. When you kill her, her double, the stepmother, is already conveniently dead. And so, on her return, Gretel is at peace with her father, and has saved her brother. In short, the story allows a symbolic compensation for having had the thought to kill one's mother.

Grandmothers may be quite bitter about their waning powers. They may want to hurt, in some sense, their grandchildren. They can tell them horrifying stories, but they know that their stories are shaped in such a way that the child will win in the end. Take a child and throw it in the air; catch it, and listen to it scream in delight. The heightened terror is what allows for the heightened sense of security. By offering symbolic experience that satisfies both the teller, the grandmother, and the told, the children, we see that fairy tales deal with persistent human experience; have done so from before the beginning of reported literature, and continue to do so down to the present.

Lecture Two
Propp, Structure, and Cultural Identity

Scope:

Vladimir Propp, studying Russian folk tales, was able to demonstrate the astonishing structural universality of what we call fairy tales but only when they are truly oral compositions. Using Propp's work, we see that the Grimms manipulated the stories they published. Those that most violate Propp's structure, such as "The Table, the Stick, and the Ass," are also among the least successful. But those that follow the structure, even when they reveal highly literary influences, such as "The Frog Prince," nonetheless retain great power. Proppian analysis foreshadowed powerful studies that illuminated such national epics as *The Odyssey* and *Beowulf.* Seeing how diverse values can be conveyed using the same underlying structure, we can understand the implicit morals fairy tales teach about gender roles, power fantasies, and the importance of Hamlet's ghost, as well as the contribution of the Grimms toward the millennial fantasy of Nazism.

Outline

I. Vladimir Propp (1895–1970), in *The Morphology of the Folk Tale* (1927), reported one of the most astonishing discoveries in all of cultural studies, the universality of the structure of true oral folk tales. These were precisely the kinds of stories the Grimm brothers had purported to publish.

   A. Propp's discovery included four "theorems."

      1. The functions of characters serve as stable, constant elements in a tale, independent of how and by whom they are fulfilled.

      2. The number of functions known to the fairy tale is limited.

      3. The sequence of functions is always identical.

      4. All fairy tales are of one type in regard to their structure.

   B. Propp's work has been tested successfully around the world.

1. With one fascinating exception, Propp's theorems hold true across cultures.

2. The one exception is that multiplied elements, such as the number of tests the hero must meet, varies from two in East Asia to four in South Asia and Native America to three in Europe and North Africa. But this regular variation reveals a complete universality within oral traditions and a regular variation across oral traditions.

C. Propp's work laid the foundation for the study of the founding tales of diverse cultures.

1. Albert Lord's *The Singer of Tales* (1960) demonstrated the oral composition of the original *Odyssey* and *Beowulf.* By showing how functions create a framework that can be clothed with standard verbal formulae, such as "wine-dark sea," Lord also showed how we can identify the marks of the scribal hand in the versions we have of those ancient tales.

2. Using Lord's insight into scribal manipulation and Propp's discovery of universal structure, we can see that the most successful Grimm fairy tales follow oral tradition. Thus, highly modified works, such as "The Table, the Stick, and the Ass," although clever, are largely forgotten, while conforming works, such as "The Frog Prince," succeed despite having ancient literary antecedents.

II. A common feature of true fairy tales is the exploration of the role of authority.

A. For males, such as the Gallant Tailor, a happy ending is lying your way to become a king.

B. For females, such as Rapunzel, Cinderella, and the princess in "The Frog Prince," a happy ending is marrying the prince who will become king even if that means being forced, like the princess, to yield to the authority of father and husband.

C. Other authority, for example, that of the witch in "Rapunzel," can be flouted, because the heroine, like the tailor, has youth. Even though Rumplestiltskin makes and wins a fair bargain with the princess, he loses because he is old and lonely while she is young and lovely.

D. The exploration of the role of authority is common in fantastic works that are influenced by fairy tales. While Cinderella has no doubt about relying on her fairy godmother in a work intended to be told to children, Hamlet is endlessly torn about how to deal with the exhortations of his ghost father, who appears in the opening scene of the play. Clearly, the same fantastic elements may be used differently for different audiences.

III. The Grimm brothers quite consciously built their tales on the framework of universal narratives in order to establish a common culture.

   A. The Grimm brothers sought to demonstrate the fundamental significance of a single German-language culture, thus helping lay the groundwork for the wars that led to the creation of a single German state.

   B. That single culture had many features we question today.

      1. Beautiful people deserve better fates than ugly people, other things being equal.

      2. We can see the sexism of these tales by comparing the effects of Hansel's actions with those of Cinderella's.

      3. We can see the anti-Semitism of the Grimms by examining one of their favorite tales, "The Jew Among the Thistles," and its foreign sources.

IV. The Grimm brothers rightly saw that fairy tales could be a source of national, cultural identity. Today, every nation raises its children on versions of their stories, for better and for worse.

Essential Reading:

Grimm, Jakob, and Wilhelm Grimm. *Household Stories of the Brothers Grimm.*

Supplementary Reading:

Heaney, Seamus. *Beowulf: A New Verse Translation.*

Lord, Albert. *The Singer of Tales.*

Ovid. *Metamorphoses.*

Propp, Vladimir. *Morphology of the Folktale.*

Questions to Consider:

1. Why do you think popular memory of "The Frog Prince" is so different from the Grimms' version?

2. On balance, do you think traditional stories, such as "Cinderella" and "The Gallant Tailor," are good or bad for our culture?

Lecture Two—Transcript
Propp, Structure, and Cultural Identity

Vladimir Propp was a member of a group of very important critics called "The Russian Formalists," and he studied a book called *The Afanas'ev's Collection of Russian Folk Tales.* The term "folk tale" is, for Russians, the same as the term "fairy tale" for many speakers of English. In 1927, he published a book called *The Morphology of the Folk Tale*, based on this study, and reported one of the most astonishing discoveries in all of cultural history. He discovered the universality of the structure of true oral folk tales or, as we would say if they were truly orally composed, fairy tales. These were precisely the kinds of stories the Grimm brothers had purported to publish.

Propp's discovery included four "theorems"—that's his term for what he discovered. First, he says, the functions of characters serve as stable, constant elements in a tale, independent of how and by whom they are fulfilled. This is really an astonishing statement. According to his introduction, he read these tales in order. There are about 400 in the Afanas'ev Collection, and by the time he had finished reading the first 10, he already had every one of these functions found. The rest of the reading merely confirmed that these common elements, these things that characters do, happen again and again and again.

The second theorem is that the number of functions that is known to the fairy tale is limited. That is to say, you can't just keep making them up. In fact, there are 32, a large number, but not larger, for instance, than the number of prepositions that we know how to use quite easily as native speakers of English.

The third theorem is that the sequence of functions is always identical. The fourth theorem is really the inference one can make from the first three—that all fairy tales are of one type in regard to their structure. Let me see if I can make this clearer.

Propp says we have this set number of maximum functions. One of them, absentation, is obligatory. In fact, several of them are obligatory; you must have them. Absentation is the child leaving the parent or the parent dying or the child wandering off. In some way, the viewpoint character becomes absent from the authority figure, who should have been protecting the viewpoint character. Absentation is an obligatory function, and there are many.

There are other functions that are optional. You can have them or not have them. But, if you have them, think of them as numbered, from absentation right through to the ultimate consolation; if you have them and think of them as numbered, whichever functions occur—whether they are obligatory or optional—will occur in their order.

Now, there are some small exceptions to this. For instance, the leaving home—departure—and return are optional; but if there is a departure, there must be a return. In addition, some functions, according to Propp, can triplicate. So, there is the function, for example, of testing the protagonist. But, in some tales, instead of the protagonist having one test, the protagonist has three tests.

It turns out that Propp was wrong in one tiny detail. It is not universally true that those functions triplicate. Had Propp said that these functions multiply, he would have been universally correct. It turns out that in Western culture, functions that can multiply triplicate; in southern Asian and Native North American cultures, functions that can multiply quadruplicate; and in East Asian cultures, they duplicate. But within those cultures, the number, the multiplier, is constant, and in all other regards, Propp turns out to be right. For true oral tales, there is a single known function. There is, in other words, in the basis of fairy tales, something that tells us about the basic narrative structure that all human beings share, regardless of how far apart their cultures may be.

Propp laid the foundation for the study of the founding tales of diverse cultures. Albert Lord, an American professor, in a famous book called *The Singer of Tales,* demonstrated how one could have oral composition of works such as the *Odyssey* and *Beowulf.* He showed, taking a hint from this notion of functions from Propp, that you could have a complicated narrative in which one knew only the basic nuggets, as it were, of the story in order. But, then, one could have standardized verbal formulae, such as the "wine-dark sea" or "wily Odysseus."

Oral tales were collected in the Balkans. Lord went and listened to people apparently sing epics, things that would take nights around the campfire to recount. All the people sitting around believed that the singer was giving the same tale verbatim that they had heard on other occasions previously, but Lord was able to actually tape record these, transcribe them, and discovered that while the nuggets were the same and the formulae were the same, within the structure that the rhythm of the singing created, the singer was able to make variations from telling to telling of the same tale. They struck the hearers as being the same, but they were not identical; they were merely the same in nuggets, like Propp's functions, and formulae, certain verbal structures.

Using Lord's insight into scribal manipulation—that is, how the written-down versions have changed what the oral composition was—and Propp's discovery of universal structure, we can see that the most successful of Grimms' fairy tales followed the oral tradition. We could compare one that does not with one that does to make this clear. If we read a highly modified, scribally changed tale, such as "The Table, the Stick, and the Ass," we'll see why it is that while we all know the name "Cinderella" or "The Frog Prince" or "Rapunzel," we don't think so quickly of "The Table, the Stick, and the Ass." This tale is one in which a father has a goat, and he sends each of his sons—it's triplicated—one after another to bring the goat out to pasture. In each case, the goat lies and says that she has not been properly fed, and the father becomes angry and eventually drives his sons away.

When the sons are away, each of them has an adventure—a journey and then a return. In each adventure, each son is tested, and each one passes the test and acquires a magical table that can lay out food; a magical stick that can beat people, thence protect you; and a magical ass that can spit out gold coins. They feel quite good, and, as always the case in fairy tales, it's the youngest son that saves the day. He comes back with the most important of these, and frees his brothers, who have been kept in a village nearby because the people were angry at their magical activities. He brings his brothers back home to the father, and they explain what really happened with the goat. The father becomes angry at having been fooled by the goat, and drives the goat out. The goat, then, has adventures—three.

The goat has been shaved by the father as a sign of her disgrace. She is attacked by different animals, and by the third attack, that of bees, she is driven off forever, and that's the end of the story.

So, is it a story about a goat? Is it a story about fathers and sons? In fact, you can think of this as three separate stories. There is the story of the goat who makes believe she won't eat. There's the story of the sons who come, ultimately, to be able to have power and return and take over their home, and then there's the story of the goat, which is being punished by the other animals. By interconnecting these, by submerging one within the other, what the Grimm brothers did with the tales that they collected was to produce a story that they may have liked literarily, but it violates the fundamental Proppian structure. We can see the work of the scribal hand destroying the elegant simplicity of the Proppian structure.

Now, by comparison, we have "The Frog Prince." "The Frog Prince" also turns out to be a learned story. "The Frog Prince," by the way, is a story that most of us tend to remember about kissing a frog and having him turn into a prince. It begins with the princess, who goes out into the woods to play with her golden ball. She is so beautiful that the very sun stops and looks down at her in admiration. The sun, being the oldest symbol of a monotheistic God, the golden ball being the symbol of God—as well as, of course royalty—and she throws it up in the air and she's playing catch with it, but she misses it and it falls down into a well of water so deep that she cannot even see it. A frog nearby says, "I will take you back your ball if you will be my playfellow, let me eat at your plate, and sleep in your bed." She agrees. He goes down into the water and comes back out with the ball. We remember, of course, that water is a sign of fertility; frogs, because they can move from one realm to another, suggest the possibility of one kind of life transforming into another. But she really doesn't want the frog, so she takes the ball and runs away. The frog hops after her. This is a retelling, in an interesting way, of the story of Atalanta, the story of a girl, a princess, who would not be willing to marry, despite her father, the king, telling her that she must, unless a man could come along who could beat her in a foot race. Hippomenes is the beneficiary of the mercy of a goddess, who tells him where he can find the golden apples of the Hebrides. He takes those golden apples, and as he runs through the forest he drops first one, then another—triplicate—and Atalanta keeps stopping to pick up one after the other. So Hippomenes beats her back to the castle and, though she does not want to marry, the king says she must. All right, she must. As it turns out, marriage agrees with her, and she's glad she had to submit to authority.

In the case of "The Frog Prince," the frog hops back and comes into the castle after the princess. The king says, "What is this?" The princess explains what the frog is doing there, that she has made this promise, but the frog is ugly. The king says, "No. No. You must fulfill your promise." So he hops up on the table and eats out of her plate—he's trying to be her playmate as well—and then, after the meal, he hops after her to her bedroom. She takes one look at the frog, and in the Grimms' version, she picks him up and flings him against the wall, where he smashes and falls down, instantly transformed into a handsome prince. Seeing the prince in her bedroom, this all looks a little different to the princess, and they live happily ever after.

Now, the story here follows an exact Proppian structure. It begins with the absentation of the princess from the king. It has a test. It has a magical gift. It gives us both departure and return—and so on. Even though we can see, because of its connection with the ancient Roman Ovid, and his description of the story of Atalanta, that this is a scribal change of the oral tale, it makes no difference. The tale persists and its meaning stays with us. So, as long as we keep this structure, we know we can hang tremendously powerful meanings on them.

Authority, who can tell you what to do, is clearly important in fairy tales. In "Rapunzel," for example, the witch has authority, but she can be flouted because the heroine has fertility and the witch does not. In "The Gallant Tailor," we have a youth, a young man, who's a liar, like the girl in "The Three Spinsters." He kills seven flies with one shot, and is so puffed up with his own bravery that he embroiders a saying on his own belt that says, "Seven with one blow." He's taken to be a great killer, and he lies his way into a position in which ultimately he becomes a king. Why is he allowed to do that? Because he has youth.

There's the story of "Rumplestiltskin." A miller's daughter claims to be able—she's lying, but she wants to be on the good side of the prince—to be able to spin straw into gold. She can't, but along comes a spirit of the woods, Rumplestiltskin, who says, "Well, I'll do it for you if you like." But, like the witch in "Rapunzel," when you have a child, the child must be mine.

He does spin the straw into gold. She does marry. She does have a child. But, then, she is unwilling to repay her part of the bargain. However, when she says she would rather have something living than all of the things that are valuable that are not living, he relents and says, "All right. You can keep the child if you can guess my name." Of course, he has a very unusual name, but one of the princess's—the queen to be—the princess's servants follows him into the woods, and hears him giving his own little speech about what his name may be. Actually, on the first two times that he comes back to the princess, she gets it wrong, but there's triplication. On the third time, she has now been told what his name really is. She says his name, and he is so angry that he stamps his foot into the ground and drives himself into the ground, where he dies.

Why is it fair for Rumplestiltskin to die for doing exactly what he said he would do, and even giving the princess a second chance? It's not fair. The morals of fairy tales aren't that the world is fair. The morals of the fairy tales are that if you're youthful, strong, beautiful, and all the things that that stands for—meaning beloved of your parents—that you will succeed, and others will not. Authority can be flouted if you have the power to do so. If not—as the princess in "The Frog Prince" did not until she became married to a prince and able to move up herself—you had best listen.

When Cinderella has no doubt about her fairy godmother helping her, we understand that. It's a godmother. But in works of imagination intended for adults, for example, in *Hamlet*, the situation is not nearly so clear. Remember, the opening scene of *Hamlet* shows Hamlet on the battlements of the castle confronting the ghost of his father, who tells him how uneasily he rests because he's been murdered. And most of the rest of the play has Hamlet trying to figure out how, in what way he can, if, indeed he should, avenge the death of his father. The fairy godmother comes to help the child; the ghostly godfather comes to tell the child what he must do. In the adult work, the imagination is equally strongly involved. But understanding what do to with it is no longer so simple, because the world of adults is not as simple as we, at least, would like to have children be able to believe their world may be.

The Grimm brothers consciously built their stories on this universal structure. Their aim was to establish a German culture. The German culture ultimately led to a German state. What do these tales tell us?

They tell us that beautiful people deserve better fates than ugly people, all things being equal. They also tell us that the world is a sexist domain. Consider the difference between the story of Hansel and Gretel and the story of Cinderella. In the story of Hansel and Gretel, most people don't recall that there are really two trips that the children make into the woods after Hansel has heard that their stepmother wants to abandon them because there is not enough food to eat. On the first trip, Hansel leaves a trail of flints, and they follow those flints back. On the second trip, they leave a trail of bread crumbs. However, the birds eat the bread crumbs. It's because the birds eat the bread crumbs that the children are left in the woods, where they encounter the female witch, who has an attractive house made of food, but the food is only a lure because she wants to make the children into food herself.

Why is it that the flints worked and the bread crumbs did not? We have the answer by looking at "Cinderella." In "Cinderella," after the stepmother throws the lentils into the ashes, the birds come down and pick the lentils out for Cinderella. They don't eat them, though they could eat them as easily as they could eat bread crumbs. Cinderella is female, and food is the domain of females, universally, in Grimms' fairy tales. Flints are used to strike fire in a rifle. That is the domain of males. In "Little Red Cap," or "Little Red Riding Hood," as it's more usually known in English, the huntsman comes and aims his gun at the wolf, but thinks someone may be alive in there. When he picks up scissors to cut open the wolf's belly, he's using a female implement, and when Red and her grandmother come out, we have an ironic kind of birth, where they, then, become the fertile, powerful figures, and undo that birth when Red sews the stones into the wolf's belly. We have male domain and female domain, and if males do what males should do, they will succeed; if females do what females should do, they will succeed; but if they try to work in each other's domains, they will fail.

The Frog Prince is not a frog. Our memory that a kiss turns the frog into a prince is false. Not only is there no kiss, but rather an act of violence, but the frog, we need to understand, had already been a human being. The frog is not turned into a prince; he is turned back into a prince. The sign of his fundamental humanity is that he speaks. And, in fact, in the world of fairy tales, we have equally well a set of distinctions, just like that between male and female, that lets us know what should count as human and what should not, so that sometimes we will have talking animals in the same tale in which other animals do not speak. There is one tale in which a mute horse is slaughtered by his rider to feed a society of ants, the king of whom begs him for help. We know that those who are of us deserve our help; those who are not can be used.

The world of Grimms' fairy tales is, in fact, somewhat brutal. As we look at these tales, we have to understand that they can be used to shape many morals. Males, in general, are better than females. The way in which Cinderella achieves her consolation is not only by moving up socially, but by submitting to the authority of a man. We know that the higher social orders are better than the lower social orders. We even know that life in the city is better than life in the country. With all of this being integrated into tales that hang on a fundamental structure that all human beings share, the question arises, what can you do with this?

The Grimm brothers, of course, decided to "make Germany," as it were. In their own lifetime, besides publishing three volumes of stories that together came to somewhat over 200, they also published a single version of their tales, a small select group, and their favorites. In that group they had a tale called, "The Jew Among the Thistles." This particular tale is one that was dropped out in the late 19th century when people published one-volume additions of *Grimms' Fairy Tales*, and then was brought back in again during the Nazi period, and has since been expunged, again, from one-volume additions of Grimm, although you can find it easily in the complete works.

The story of "The Jew Among the Thistles" goes like this: There was, we are told, an upright, hardworking, kind-hearted servant who gives a dwarf the only money that he has. The dwarf rewards him by giving this kind-hearted, upright servant a magic fiddle that can set anyone who hears it dancing. The Jew—not even a Jew, but in the Grimms' telling, the Jew—happens upon the servant and tries to cheat him. The servant throws him into a briar patch and starts fiddling. The Jew has no choice but to dance, and he dances and dances until his beard is torn, his clothing and flesh are streaming with tatters, and he calls out in a phrase that the Grimm brothers seemed to think was quite fun to listen to, "*Oy Vey*," which, of course, is German [sic Yiddish].

The servant leaves the Jew, goes into town, but the Jew comes after him and complains to the Justice that he has been tormented by that lad. There is a trial, and the lad is convicted. As he is standing on the gallows, he begins to fiddle again, and the Jew begins to dance, and everyone sees that, in fact, the Jew did something wrong, and for that the lad is led off the gallows and the Jew is put in his place and killed.

Now, we've seen often in Grimms' fairy tales that our idea of justice may not be everybody's idea of justice, that an attempt to cheat that fails ultimately leads to a happy idea that the attempted cheater should be killed seems entirely wrong, while the actual robbery that the upright servant performs by taking away the Jew's money with him goes unpunished.

However, the Grimm brothers didn't really collect oral folk tales. The Grimm brothers were professors, and we all know how professors rely on the help of friendly graduate students. They sent their graduate students out to the farms to try to collect tales, and their graduate students wrote them down as best they could. There were no tape recorders in those days; in fact, shorthand hadn't yet been invented. The Grimm brothers themselves went to the neighborhood they lived in and talked to a number of housewives, middle-class housewives, who told them the stories they remembered. Jakob was in charge of this collection activity. He then took versions of the stories and gave them to Wilhelm, who went through the repetitions that we would naturally expect, and tried to come up with single versions of the tales, which he then made to sound good and published them.

Now, he didn't just use these not-actually-orally collected tales. He also used other existing sources of tales, such Charles Perrault's late 17th century version of fairy tales, and we have found in the Grimm brothers' library, a volume of Italian folk tales, within which there is a story, not of the Jew among the thistles, but the friar among the thistles. The Grimm brothers took a story that they already knew, and instead of having it be a story that attacked the authority, the perverted authority in the teller's view, of the Church, used it to attack Jews.

The Grimm brothers took fundamental realities of human imagination and used them to create stories that last through all of human history in such a way that, collectively, they teach sexism; they teach class stratification; and, in fact, taught anti-Semitism. But they did this in such a way as to bind together a nation. The power of the imagination is limitless.

Lecture Three
Hoffmann and the Theory of the Fantastic

Scope:

E. T. A. Hoffmann was a polymath of the Romantic era. As a writer of fantastic fiction, he shows us how the fantastic functions at the narrative levels of style, theme, character, and plot. His works exemplify the fantastic both as a psychological affect generated by art and as true literary fantasy (works that fully exploit the fantastic). Hoffmann's true fantasies, such as "The Golden Pot," demonstrate the crucial intellectual power of structural ambiguity, while the lives of his characters, as in "Councillor Krespel" and "The Doubles," suggest the centrality of art as a psychological tool. In such works as "The Sandman" (which Sigmund Freud used to explicate his own theory of the role of psychological fantasy in art), and "Ritter Gluck," Hoffmann offers a Platonic aesthetic theory that connects his own work with Homer's and with our reading experience.

Outline

I. Ernst Theodor Wilhelm Hoffmann (1776–1822) was a Romantic polymath.

  A. Hoffmann had a restless desire to create.

    1. He produced significant work as an author, a government legal councillor, a music critic, a caricaturist, and a composer.

    2. He changed his own middle name, Wilhelm, to Amadeus to honor Wolfgang Amadeus Mozart.

    3. *The Tales of Hoffmann*, however, is not by Hoffmann. It is an opera (1881) by Jacques Offenbach based on Hoffmann's "The Sandman," "Councillor Krespel," and "The Lost Reflection."

    4. Pyotr Ilyich Tchaikovsky's ballet *The Nutcracker* (1892) uses Alexandre Dumas's adaptation of Hoffmann's "The Nutcracker and the Mouse King."

  B. The terms *romance* and *romantic* have six related definitions that bear on the study of the arts.

1. Romance *languages* are those descended from Latin, the language of Rome, a city northern Europeans viewed as exotic, mysterious, and flamboyant.

2. Romantic *content* is erotically or otherwise heightened over the merely natural. This use of the term *romantic*, like *fantastic*, is often opposed to *realistic*.

3. Romantic *attitudes and themes* stress the importance of the ego and strong emotion.

4. The Romantic *period in art*, for English speakers, conventionally begins with the publication of Wordsworth and Coleridge's quite personal *Lyrical Ballads* (1798).

5. The canonical Romantic *poets* in English are Wordsworth, Coleridge, Shelley, Keats, and Byron. German Romantic writers include Goethe and Hoffmann.

6. The Romantic *structure in art*, particularly in literature, characterizes works that realize their own ideals, such as Longus's *Daphnis and Chloe*.

C. Art itself is a central subject in Hoffmann's stories.

1. The title character of "Councillor Krespel" is odd and self-indulgent yet fantastically successful as his own architect who proceeds without a plan; however, his egotistical indulgence in music has fatal consequences for his daughter.

2. The main characters in "The Doubles" are ensnared in a world of art come to life but find peace from this disturbing reality by renouncing emotion for religion or for art itself.

II. The fantastic in literature is a psychological affect created by the quick, complete reversal of fundamental assumptions held by the reader at a given moment as the reading proceeds. Put more technically, the fantastic is the affect generated by the diametric, diachronic reversal of the ground rules of the narrative world.

A. In "Ritter Gluck," these reversals happen at all four levels of narrative that conserve diachronic information (that is, information that extends through time): style, thematic development, character development, and plot.

B. Hoffmann called "The Golden Pot, or a Modern Fairy Tale," his own favorite of his stories. Like "Ritter Gluck," it concerns art and ends in permanent structural ambiguity. These works are true literary fantasy.

III. Hoffmann's works give us insight into the psychology of fantasy.

    A. Hoffmann portrays art in his own stories as both a fantastic compulsion and as a practical tool in our lives, as in "Councillor Krespel" and "The Doubles."

    B. In "The Uncanny" (1919), Sigmund Freud (1856–1939) grounded his own theory of the fantastic in his analysis of Hoffmann's "The Sandman."

        1. Art is motivated by trauma.

        2. Art arises from the unconscious.

        3. Art is compensatory.

        4. Art is repetitive.

    C. Hoffmann believed in depth psychology, which posits the existence of an underlying unconscious (or subconscious) mind that can be more powerful than the conscious mind.

        1. Hoffmann's psychology in such works as "The Sandman" supports the tripartite model of the psyche promulgated by Freud.

        2. Hoffmann's psychology in such works as "The Doubles" supports the quadripartite model of the psyche promulgated by one of Freud's most prominent disciples and later antagonists, Carl Gustav Jung (1875–1961).

IV. Hoffmann's own artistic compulsions, however, also support a Platonic theory of art.

    A. Art is a matter of inspiration—or compulsion—from above, as suggested in "Ritter Gluck." Hoffmann's works themselves served as inspirations to others.

    B. Art is a matter of striving for ideal forms, as suggested in both "The Doubles" and "The Sandman."

    C. For Hoffmann, and for many of the world's great imaginative artists, the achievement of art depends upon both embracing and disciplining the fantastic.

Essential Reading:

Hoffmann, E. T. A. *The Tales of E. T. A. Hoffmann.*

Supplementary Reading:

Freud, Sigmund. *The Uncanny.*

Jung, Carl Gustav. *Man and His Symbols.*

Plato. *The Collected Dialogues of Plato.* See especially "Ion" for the theory of aesthetic inspiration, "Sophist" on the truth of the fantastic, and "The Republic" for utopianism.

Questions to Consider:

1. When is fantasizing positive in our lives; when negative?

2. When are the effects of fantasizing in art positive in our lives; when negative?

Lecture Three—Transcript
Hoffmann and the Theory of the Fantastic

Ernst Theodor Wilhelm Hoffman, E. T. A. Hoffman, was a Romantic polymath. He had a restless desire to create. In fact, he produced significant work as an author of fiction, a government legal councilor, a music critic, a caricaturist, and a composer. He changed his own middle name, Wilhelm, to Amadeus, to honor Wolfgang Amadeus Mozart, and, hence, E. T. A. Hoffmann. But *The Tales of Hoffmann* are not by Hoffmann; *The Tales of Hoffmann* is an opera by Jacques Offenbach based on three of Hoffmann's stories, "The Sandman," "Councilor Krespel," and "The Lost Reflection." Tchaikovsky's ballet, *The Nutcracker*, uses Alexandre Dumas's adaptation of Hoffmann's "The Nutcracker and the Mouse King." In other words, Hoffmann not only produced in many, many areas, he was influential in many, many areas, most of them, that is, the artistic ones, full of imagination. He is what we would call a Romantic polymath.

The terms "romance" and "romantic" have six related meanings that bear on the study of the arts. They are the Romance languages, Romantic content, Romantic attitudes and themes, the Romantic period in art, the Romantic poets, and the Romantic structure in art. Let me explain each of these in turn because, as we will see, imaginative works are always, in some sense, Romantic.

First, the Romance languages are those descended from Latin, the language of Rome, hence French, Spanish, Italian, Romansh, Romani, Portuguese, and so on. But northern Europeans viewed Rome as exotic, mysterious, flamboyant, so the Romance languages are not nearly a set of languages, but languages that convey a certain affinity to whatever exoticism, mystery, and flamboyance they mean.

The second, Romantic content, tells us something about that. Romantic content is erotically charged, or in some other way heightened over the merely natural. This use of the term "Romantic," like the term "fantastic," is often opposed to the term realistic. It was a Romantic idea; it was a realistic idea. There are also Romantic attitudes and themes. These stress the importance of the ego and strong emotion.

The Romantic period in art, at least for English speakers, conventionally is said to begin with the publication of Wordsworth and Coleridge's quite personal volume called *Lyrical Ballads* in 1798. What Coleridge and Wordsworth said they were about was recording the real language of the people. Anyone who reads their poems knows that people don't really speak that way, but they speak much more that way than was the language of the preceding period, the balanced cadences of the neo-classic period.

The canonical Romantic poets in English are, of course, Wordsworth and Coleridge, and also Shelley, Keats, and Byron. In the Germanic culture, the key Romantic writers are Goethe and Hoffmann.

Then there is the Romantic structure in art, particularly in literature. Romantic structure indicates a work in which the ideals that are posited—sometimes only by implication at the very beginning—are fulfilled by the end. Now, let me try to exemplify this, going all the way back, for example, to the classic tale *Daphnis and Chloe* by Longus. In the first chapter, an infant boy is found abandoned on an island, and he has with him a little golden scepter. In the second chapter, a little infant girl is found abandoned on the other side of the island, and around her waist is a little golden chain. They will be found by shepherds; they will be raised, but we already know, because of the golden tokens with which they're found, and the parallelism of their discovery, that Daphnis and Chloe are going to turn out to be of royal birth, they will come together, and ultimately they will marry. Of course, along the way, their true identities have to be discovered. When they fall in love, the course of romance may not be smooth—in fact, pirates kidnap Chloe, and Daphnis has to retrieve her—but, in the last chapter of the book, the two of them together go off into the cave of Hymen, the god of marriage. In other words, they "come together." From the very beginning, we can see that the ideal for these characters is that they will be joined in some high estate, and the end is simply the ratification that this original understanding of the ideal was true.

When I use the word "ideal" in this sense, I don't necessarily mean ideally good. I mean ideal in the same way that Plato uses the word ideal—that is, something perfect. So we have, for example, in American literature, a work like *The Jungle,* in which, at the beginning, we see that the character, the poor, down-trodden immigrant, is likely to have his condition go from bad to worse. And, indeed, as we go through the book, his condition goes from bad to worse to worse to worse to worse. At the end of that book, suddenly the author, Upton Sinclair, has the main character enlightened, and he says, "Ah, yes. Workers of the world unite. "Chicago"—that's where it's set—"will be ours," and, in theory, it's a happy ending. In fact, most readers feel that the ending is simply tacked on, that the real story is the story of the degradation of Jurgis, the main character, by the packing industry, the meat packing industry, in which he works. We can have ideals that are bad; we can have ideals that are good. The point is that they are, in some sense, ideal.

Realistic works of literature do not necessarily fulfill opening ideals. We don't know at the beginning of *The Sun Also Rises* by Hemmingway how the story will end, but we know at the beginning of *Daphnis and Chloe* that they will come together. Most works, in fact, are Romantic. Despite the critical preference for realism since the late 19th century, in fact, most of the works in the world are imaginative and often Romantic because people are satisfied by having their predictions confirmed.

So, we have six uses for the term Romantic: Romantic languages; Romantic content; Romantic attitudes and themes—oh that ego—the Romantic period in art, when that ego is justified, validated, and expressed in the language of the people; particularly by the Romantic poets fulfilling Romantic structures in art. Indeed, most of the imaginative works that we would discuss will, in fact, will seem to be, in one way or another, Romantic.

Hoffmann was a Romantic polymath. Art is a central subject in Hoffmann's own stories. The title character of "Councilor Krespel" is odd, self-indulgent, yet, it turns out fantastically successful as his own architect. Notice the Councilor Krespel is, as Hoffmann was, a legal councilor. He is able to work as an architect with a plan just as Hoffmann was a caricaturist. In this story, Councilor Krespel builds his house according to a plan in his own head. The angles are crazy, the layout is odd, and, yet, when he's done, the home is beautiful. He indulges himself in music.

The back story of "Councilor Krespel" is that he had an extraordinary love, a singer named Angela, but she died, and all he has left is his beautiful daughter, Antonia. Antonia, however, is frail, and it becomes clear that if Krespel were to allow his daughter to sing at the fullness of her vigor, she would risk killing herself. Antonia falls in love with a man known as B—, with a dash after it, and Councilor Krespel knows that she, Antonia, is tempted always to make beautiful music with B—, not only metaphorically, but literally. B— plays the piano. One evening when B— is in the house, Councilor Krespel leaves the room, but he hears them singing. An appalling fear was combined with a rapture he, Krespel, had never heard and never before experienced. At the moment of hearing his daughter singing, instead of stopping her—perhaps he listens, perhaps he swoons—the next thing the narrative tells us is that he awakens from an unconscious state, goes into the parlor, and finds his daughter has died. Councilor Krespel indulges his own passion, his romance for music, to retrieve the romance for Angela that exists only in the body of Antonia, with fatal consequences for his daughter. Art is powerful in the fantasies of E. T. A. Hoffmann.

One of Hoffmann's most extraordinary stories is called "The Doubles," *Die Doppelganger*, in German. This story is full of characters who are, in fact, doubles of each other. In literary terms, a doppelganger is one of a set of characters who, together, map out a single psychological space. In Hoffmann's tale, "The Doubles," we have two young men who are doubles for each other, although they don't know it. One of the young men is in love with a woman named Natalie, but he does not know that she exists. He is a painter, and has been painting her from his imagination. The other young man actually knows Natalie, and he is in love with her. They compete for Natalie's love. It turns out that they are, themselves, the children of two men—a prince, Furst; and a count, Goethe—who, themselves, were doubles in running the princedom. They were married to women who, themselves, were doubles, and all of these were friends of each other. They had, these two couples, two sons. The sons were switched at birth and raised by one of their councilors. He kept them safe, because of political upheaval, and later they come to fall in love with Natalie, his daughter. The story has even more doubles in it. There are, for example, the innkeepers of the Silver Lamb and the Golden Ram Inns, which are on opposite sides of the same street.

What is amazing about this story is that they way in which it is told, we ourselves, as readers, find that we can not follow the story. That is, we are confused as to which character is which, not because we can't write it down and make a map of them, but because their physical characteristics, their desires, are so interchangeable in some ways that it's almost as if we see one when we think we're seeing the other. At one point, one of the characters is shot and wounded, and develops a wound that now makes him physically identical to the character he had previously been a double for, but physically different. When the painter sees the real Natalie, he realizes that this has been the woman of his dreams all along, and so they are both vying for the same woman.

In grammatical terms, technical terms, the word "ambiguity" refers to a semantic structure which is susceptible to more than one interpretation, each equally valid. So, for example, "flying planes can be dangerous." That sentence has two meanings. Piloting aircraft can be dangerous. "Watch out, there can be planes coming by"—flying planes are dangerous. If the two different meanings are from the same realm, than ambiguity simply creates indecision; but if the two different meanings come from fundamentally different realms—that is, if they are in worlds that have basically different ground rules—then ambiguity creates the fantastic. I walked down the street and turned into a drug store. In one realm, I simply made a left; in the other realm, poof! I became an aspirin dispenser. Those two realms, the ground rules of one world are like ours; in the ground rules of the other, magic applies. When ambiguity makes us shift instantly from one set of ground rules to another, we have the fantastic.

More generally, the fantastic is the affect—that is, the psychological response—created by the quick, complete reversal of the fundamental assumptions held by a reader at a given moment as the reader proceeds. Or, more technically, the fantastic is the affect generated by the diametric, diachronic reversal of the ground rules of the narrative world. Diametric means all the way across, as in the diameter of a circle. Diachronic means through time, that's as opposed to synchronic, all at one time. I'll repeat: The fantastic is the affect generated by the diametric, diachronic reversal of the ground rules of the narrative world.

In a fairy tale that reversal happens with the opening conventional formula: "Once upon a time there was a beautiful golden-haired princess." We know we're in a fantastic world, in fact, one in which animals can talk; and if we encounter them talking, we don't have that as a shock. There's no new reversal. But, if I were to say, "Once upon a time there was a beautiful golden-haired princess, and she fell deeply in love with an accountant named Harry Mendelbaum," that would be more fantastic yet. Because, in the world that begins, "Once upon a time," there are no accountants. There are only wealthy kings and poor beggars. The ground rules have made a diametric, diachronic reversal. Note that the fantastic arises not out of something that does not exist. There really are accountants in the world. It arises in the process of reading. Grimms' fairy tales are fantastic, but they are not true fantasies. But a work like "The Doubles" by Hoffmann, in fact, is a true fantasy, because it's use of ambiguity, our inability to be able to know which character is which at any given moment, makes us feel this constant off-centering that characterizes the fantastic.

In "Ritter Gluck," we see that this reversal occurs at all four levels of the narrative that can conserve—that is, hang on to—diachronic, happening through time, information. Those four levels that conserve diachronic information are style, thematic development, character development, and plot. There's a place at the beginning of "Ritter Gluck" where our viewpoint character is sitting outside in a plaza in Berlin. It is autumn. He's watching the people walk by, and he sees dandies—which represents, I guess, something about how people dress—solid citizens with their wives and adored children—I'm not sure you can tell how adored they are by the way they are dressed, all dressed in their Sunday best—clergymen, maybe or maybe not identifiable by dress; Jewesses, certainly not identifiable by dress; junior barristers—their junior status how understood?—prostitutes who are supposedly blending in with everyone else; professors; milliners; dancers; officers; et cetera. That is, the very catalog of passersby keeps asking us to redefine how we know what these people are. The ground rules at the level of style are changing. I walked down the street and turned into a drug store.

In fact, in "Ritter Gluck" the viewpoint character listens as a band starts to play, and he suddenly hears an octave interval and screams out, "Ah, an execrable octave." The man next to him understands and says, "Ah, you find that terrible as well?" It turns out this man claims to be a great composer named Ritter Gluck. Now, this particular story was published years after Gluck really died, as Hoffmann's readers would have known. As you read the story, you realize that nobody ever sees Ritter Gluck but the viewpoint character. The viewpoint character goes back to Gluck's—or whoever's it is—house, and enters his backroom through dark and parting curtains. It's almost as if it were a regression.

He is told that Ritter Gluck had a vision in which he went off to a celestial realm and heard the euphony—this ideal sound—and then came back to Earth and tried to compose music accordingly, and that was a violation. So he has been condemned to stay on Earth forever. He wants to play his own music, and he takes the books of the music off his shelf and asks the viewpoint character to turn the pages. Miraculously, the pages are blank, but Ritter Gluck is able to play the music perfectly. Since the viewpoint character knows Gluck's work, he turns the pages at the appropriate point. It is only at the end, when they had finished a composition that the ghost, or whoever he is, says to the viewpoint character "I am Ritter Gluck."

The way the story is told, we don't know whether that character who speaks is an inspired madman who just turns out to be a terrific pianist and has memorized the works of Gluck, or is a ghost, or is a projection of the insanity of our own viewpoint character, who is driven crazy by the sound of an octave interval. The fact that the story does not resolve itself, that through it's structural ambiguities it goes on with us never knowing what the fundamental ground rules ultimately shall be helps us understand why this work, unlike fairy tales, is not merely fantastic, but a true Fantasy.

Hoffmann said that his own favorite among his tales was "The Golden Pot," and he subtitled it "A Modern Fairy Tale." What makes it modern, of course, is that it goes well beyond regular fairy tales. It gives us, for instance, a character who drops ink on the very pages that he is supposedly copying and, hence, changes their meanings. He falls in love with a creature who may be one of three green snakes or may be the denizen of Atlantis. He works for an archivist who probably is a librarian, but may be a wizard from Atlantis sent to Earth. He is thwarted by an old woman who sells apples, good old apples from the Garden of Eden, who may be a witch or may be the old enemy from Atlantis of the archivist who may not, in fact, be a librarian, et cetera, et cetera. The way the story is narrated, we see through that viewpoint character, through that young man who is the copyist, and we can't tell sometimes what we're seeing or not. And, so, we feel the very fantasy that Hoffmann is explaining happens. At the end, that viewpoint character is said to be in the inkwell, and we can't tell whether he has simply decided to live out his life wanting that girl, that snake, that figure from myth, and psychologically he will spend his time writing it out, or he is really trapped as a homunculus inside a crystal inkwell, or he has now gone back to Atlantis with her and exists in our world only in the story that Hoffmann has written? The story is a true Fantasy.

One of Hoffmann's most important Fantasies, one that gives us very important insight into the general field, is one called "The Sandman." "The Sandman" is the story of a boy whose father dabbled in alchemy. One day, one of his father's fellow dabblers comes along and is vile at dinner. He touches the boy's food, making it unclean from the boy's viewpoint. The boy hides in a cupboard in the father's workroom where, after dinner, the father and the visitor repair to do alchemical experiments. And, as it happens, there is an explosion. With that explosion, the father is killed.

Years later, the boy meets an eyeglass salesman, and that eyeglass salesman causes him to swoon into some magic vision of wanting the eyes. "I need the eyes," the eyeglass salesman says in the boy's dream, now the young man's dream. All of this is set within the story of the relationship of the viewpoint character to a woman named "Clara"—clarity, clear vision. And he, the viewpoint character, is complaining of the difficulty of his relations with the eyeglass salesman in a letter he sends to his friend Lothar, but, in fact, he sends it to Clara by mistake. Clara explains that this was, perhaps, an error that he really wanted her to see it, what we would now call a "Freudian slip." But, of course, Freud had not begun writing then. Freud was not alive then.

Freud, however, takes this story in which the man becomes ever more invested in his fantasy and uses it as the main example for his own most important work of Fantasy. In the story, the man falls in love with a robot named "Olympia," but no one else understands Olympia to be real, only this fellow. Eventually, however, having projected life into it, he is driven crazy and whirls around on the top of a bell tower and plunges to his death. Freud sees this story as exemplifying first, that art—the creation of Olympia, the writing of poems to Olympia by the viewpoint character—art is created by trauma. In other words, we have something go wrong with us and we need to compensate. Art arises from the unconscious; we don't know we're doing it. Art is compensatory and art is repetitive. Art is repetitive. These four points—traumatic, unconscious, compensatory, repetitive—form the basis of Freud's theory, which he puts forth in a 1919 essay called "The Uncanny."

Hoffmann believed in depth psychology. That is, he believed in the notion that we have an underlying unconscious or subconscious mind that is more powerful than the mind that we are conscious, but he didn't particularly believe in Freudian theory. "The Sandman" does support a tripartite notion of the psyche, a super ego, the father figure in "The Sandman" say, who wants us to behave certain ways; the id, or the libido more specifically, that is, the id, the underlying energies to act and consume and have desire or, specifically, libidinous energy, sexual activity and desire, which need to come together and be conjoined coordinated for there to be a healthy ego. This tripartite view of the psyche—the super ego, ego, libido—fits perfectly with "The Sandman." But in "The Doubles," we have the ego in a quadripartite map, the map that Freud's erstwhile student, Carl Gustav Jung, had, where the ego can have a double who is a better version of the self and a dark double who perverts the possibilities of the self. If the ego is male, then the female toward which he strives is the anima—like Natalie in "The Doubles," and there is a dark woman who can be the perversion of those ideals, which you can never be—a male can't be a female—as is the witch who keeps him away from Natalie. If the ego is female, then the striving is for a male animus and a dark man.

In fact, the union of these pieces, in the tripartite manner or the quadripartite manner of Freud or Jung, is what gives psychological strength. Art is what allows that in Hoffmann. Art is a matter of inspiration. We are taken over by it, as in "Ritter Gluck," as in "Councilor Krespel." When you write a poem, you can survive it; but, if need be, as in "The Doubles," you must renounce, and neither character ends up with Natalie. They are better off. Art could help us from fantasy but could not overcome the dangers of sex. For Hoffmann, and for many of the world's great imaginative artists, the achievement of art depends upon both embracing and disciplining the fantastic.

Lecture Four
Poe—Genres and Degrees of the Fantastic

Scope:

Edgar Allan Poe sought explicitly to have each of his stories culminate in an overpowering emotional effect for the reader. In such works as "The Oval Portrait," "The Black Cat," and "William Wilson," he taps into some of humanity's deepest fantasies: fear of dying, fear of loneliness, fear of oneself. By examining these works, as well as other supposed horror stories, including "The Tell-Tale Heart" and "The Cask of Amontillado," we see how a writer can use the fantastic less or more in representing similar materials. Poe's formal variations on a theme allow us to sketch a continuum of the fantastic that provides a framework for relating all fantastic literature. In addition, what Poe called "tales of ratiocination" (which we would place under detective fiction or science fiction) provide a starting point for showing how the fantastic is crucial in the whole process of genre development.

Outline

I. The writing of Edgar Allan Poe (1809–1849) has too often been dismissed for reasons that do not hold up under scrutiny.

   A. Biographical complaints include the notion that he was an alcoholic and a pervert.

      1. Poe may have been allergic to alcohol, not alcoholic. In any event, alcoholism obviously does not itself confer artistic talent.

      2. His 1836 marriage to his first cousin, Virginia Clemm (born 1822), was public, legal, devoted, and ended only with her death (1847) from tuberculosis (diagnosed in 1842).

   B. People complain that his writing is simply too slick.

      1. "The Raven" (1845), read in light of Virginia's illness, seems to be an almost Hoffmann-like attempt to use the writing of poetry to calm the poet against the calamity of his wife's foreseen death.

2. "Annabel Lee" (1849), so easily parodied by a sing-song reading, is, like "The Raven," an emotional fairy tale of devotion.

C. On the basis of his own review of Nathaniel Hawthorne's *Twice-Told Tales* (1842), an essay now often called "The Short Story," people complain that Poe's work is too mechanical.

   1. Poe calls for an author to construct his story in order to generate in the reader a "single...preconceived effect."

   2. A work that some would say supports this complaint against mechanical construction is "The Cask of Amontillado" (1846). However, a close reading of the story reveals that it gives not a "single effect," in the sense of "only one superficial effect," but rather, "a richly layered yet thoroughly unified effect."

II. Much of Poe's most famous work engages common human fears.

A. "The Cask of Amontillado," read through an identification with the victim, Fortunato, addresses fear of chance and death unforeseen. Read through an identification with the narrator, it addresses a fear many of us feel about our own potential for violence.

B. "William Wilson" (1839), like Hoffmann's "The Doubles," asks if we really control ourselves or if we are the pawns of dark urges.

C. "The Tell-Tale Heart" (1843) shows the disorder of a mind too fixated on a sense of being slighted.

III. Poe's works can be arrayed along a continuum of the fantastic.

A. "The Tell-Tale Heart" and "The Black Cat" (1843) use the fantastic to differing degrees.

B. Any genre can go from its basic pattern toward the more fantastic.

   1. In Poe, this works with deranged narrators.

   2. In Hoffmann, this works with unambiguous and ambiguous tales.

   3. Fairy tales can also become more fantastic, as Hoffmann suggests in the subtitle of "The Golden Pot, or A Modern Fairy Tale."

IV. Poe's so called "tales of ratiocination" are, according to "The Short Story," able to convey "truth" in their single effect.

A. "The Pit and the Pendulum" (1843) is what we would now call science fiction. It suggests that our salvation may be beyond our own intellectual powers.

B. "The Purloined Letter" (1845), the first fully achieved *Tale of the Great Detective*, offers, as W. H. Auden has written, "the fantasy that hidden guilt will be revealed."

V. Poe's masterful combination of conscious artistry and deep resonance with common human fears becomes clear when we consider the relations between Poe's fantastic poetry and fantastic fiction.

A. "The Oval Portrait" (1842), which speaks of love lost to art, echoes "Annabel Lee."

B. "The Bells" (1849) is famously derided for offering more sound than sense. However, a careful reading of its four stanzas, and a comparison of them to "The Black Cat," shows that these works move the reader through a common psychological trajectory.

1. "The Black Cat" is hypotactic, meaning that the connections among its parts are made explicit.

2. "The Bells" is a paratactic version of the same story, *parataxis* being the presentation of a tale with key connections omitted. This economical presentation, if it works for a reader, induces the reader to construct imaginatively the missing connections and, thus, to feel them personally.

3. Poe's achievement in many genres is to induce us to feel fear, yet to know that we are in a fantastic world created by a precise and skillful artist, a world we need not flee but can admire.

Essential Reading:

Poe, Edgar Allan. *The Portable Poe.*

Supplementary Reading:

Auerbach, Erich. *Mimesis: The Representation of Reality in Western Literature*. See especially chapters 5–6.

Booth, Wayne C. *The Rhetoric of Fiction*.

Questions to Consider:

1. Are there particular kinds of viewpoint characters who, though they are very different from you, attract your attention most strongly? If so, what makes them attractive to you?

2. What are the moral and political effects of identifying with a character whose mind is very different from our own?

Lecture Four—Transcript
Poe—Genres and Degrees of the Fantastic

Edgar Allen Poe, an American who was one of the most imaginative writers in the history of the world, has also been among the most controversial, critically. He sought explicitly to have each of his stories culminate in an over-powering emotional effect for the reader. In works such as "The Oval Portrait," "The Black Cat," and "William Wilson," he taps into some of humanities deepest fantasies—fear of dying, fear of loneliness, fear of one's self. By examining these works, as well as other supposed horror stories, such as "The Tell-Tale Heart" and "The Cask of Amontillado," we see how a writer can use the Fantastic less or more in representing similar materials. Poe's formal variations on a theme allow us to sketch a continuum of the Fantastic that provides a framework for relating all fantastic literature. In addition, what Poe called "tales of ratiocination,"—which we would place under detective fiction or science fiction—provide a starting point for showing how the fantastic is crucial in the whole process of genre development.

The writing of Edgar Allen Poe has too often been dismissed for reasons that do not hold up under scrutiny. Biographical complaints include the notions that he was an alcoholic and a pervert. The idea that he was an alcoholic is supported by the fact that he was found lying unconscious in an alley by a bar in his relatively young adulthood, in his 40's, and ultimately, a few days later, died. In fact, modern evidence that Richard Thompson at Purdue University has uncovered, suggests that it is quite possible that Poe was allergic to alcohol rather than an alcoholic. We have no evidence that he actually drank a lot. But even if he were an alcoholic, claiming that his writing is nothing but the outpourings, as it were, of an alcoholic is clearly foolish because if drinking alcohol made one a great and lasting writer, the world would be full of them.

The idea that he was a pervert is based on the fact that he married his first cousin who was only 13 at the time and that he never married again after her early death. It's important to know that this first cousin, Virginia Clemm, was of legal age when he married her, that marrying first cousins was not only legal but somewhat common at the time. His marriage was public, it was blessed by her mother; it was legal, it was devoted, and it ended only with her death in 1847. They married in 1836, but in 1842, that is six years into the marriage but five before her death, she was diagnosed with tuberculosis. So, for half of his marriage, he lived in fear in the knowledge that his bride would come to an early demise. This does not sound to me like a pervert; it sounds to me like a deeply saddened man.

People also complain that Poe's writing is simply too slick. "The Raven," for example, is a poem that is very, very well known. It begins:

> Once upon a midnight dreary, while I pondered, weak and weary,
> Over many a quaint and curious volume of forgotten lore—
> While I nodded, nearly napping, suddenly there came a tapping,
> As if someone gently rapping, rapping at my chamber door.
> "'Tis some visitor," I muttered, "tapping at my chamber door—
> Only this, and nothing more."

The poem is so compelling in its rhythm, the language flows so liquidly, that one can honestly believe that all Poe is trying to do is show off. In fact, this fellow "nearly napping" has been trying to get surcease of his sorrow from books because his beloved Lenore has died. In the whole of this lengthy poem, the stanzas end in the first half always with the words "nameless forevermore," and then "nothing more," "nothing more." When the Raven lands on the bust of Palace Athena, the goddess of wisdom finally speaks, he hears it as saying "nevermore," and then every stanza ends with "nevermore."

To read "The Raven" as a poem about showing off one's verbal skill is to ignore that this poem, written in 1845, more than halfway through Virginia's illness, is itself an effort in which Poe, like Hoffman's characters, writes poetry in order to try to accommodate symbolically the fears that he has. In this way, using art to accommodate symbolically our own fears, we see that Poe's poem does, for him, the author, much that fairy tales have done for people for generations.

Nonetheless, it's easy to make fun of Poe's poetry because it reads so easily. "Annabel Lee" begins like this, and I apologize to Poe for giving it this sing-songy reading:

It was many and many a year ago,
In a kingdom by the sea,
That a maiden there lived whom you may know
By the name of Annabel Lee;
And this maiden she lived with no other thought
Than to love and be loved by me.

I was a child....

Now I'd like to switch to a more normal reading, because the compulsion of the rhythm does not have to be borne foolishly:

I was a child and she was a child,
In this kingdom by the sea,
But we loved with a love that was more than love—
I and my Annabel Lee;
With a love that the winged seraphs of heaven
Coveted her and me.

And this was the reason that, long ago,
In this kingdom by the sea,
A wind blew out of a cloud, chilling
My beautiful Annabel Lee;
So that her highborn kinsman came
And bore her away from me,
To shut her up in a sepulchre
In this kingdom by the sea.

The very gods conspire to keep this love from being consummated, and so, finally, this beautiful- sounding poem ends:

And so, all the night-tide, I lie down by the side
Of my darling—my darling—my life and my bride,
In the sepulchre there by the sea,
In her tomb by the sounding sea.

If we can step back from the captivating beauty of the language, we realize that Annabel Lee is a poem about necrophilia; it is a poem about not wanting to let go of the lost young love.

Poe writes gorgeous, captivating poems. These complaints that he was, in fact, just an alcoholic or merely trying to write slick stuff is, I think, wrong, but it is supported by an essay he wrote now called, "The Short Story," but originally published as a review of Nathaniel Hawthorne's *Twice-Told Tales*. In this, he claims that what people should do, what authors should do, is to construct their stories so as to create a single preconceived effect, a single preconceived effect. He wants people to see work as mechanically produced clear sightedly. Aristotle defines art as the organized habit of production.

A work that some would say supports this complaint against the mechanical construction is Poe's short story, "The Cask of Amontillado." In "The Cask of Amontillado," we begin by having a character say—this is the very first line—"The thousand injuries of Fortunato I had borne as best I could, but when he ventured upon insult, I vowed revenge." You—we don't know who this is, it's the reader, but whom are we to be—"you who so well know the nature of my soul will not suppose, however, that I gave utterance to a threat." At length I would be avenged. But, if you let the victim know, then they can defend against it, and vengeance is no vengeance if the victim does not know."

And so, what this character does is to tempt his cousin Fortunato, for this unnamed insult, down into a wine cellar to try this famous cask of Amontillado, a kind of wine. When he has him in the wine cellar, he begins to bind him, and then bricks up the wall. The last words we hear from Fortunato are a plea to be released, and he calls the narrator by his name, Montresor, or, in French, *Mon Trésor*. Fortunato means fortune; *Mon Trésor*, my treasure, is a French term of endearment used often by parents of children. What we have here is some young man who resents the authority of some older man and walls him up, puts him back in the tomb, puts him back in the womb, promising him wine and intoxication, but in fact giving him death.

Now, this looks like, you know, "For the love of God, *Mon Trésor*," and the last line, "*Requiescat in pace*," rest in peace. It sounds as if it's just supposed to give us the thrill of the horrible. But not when we understand that the names make references, not when we understand that this is a mingling of French, *Mon Trésor;* Spanish, *Amontillado;* and Italian, *Fortunato*, culture. This is a story in the Gothic tradition about that Romantic world of the Romance languages and curses and family feuds and a sense of wanting to have more power than authority will let you have. This is a very rich story, if we read it carefully.

Most of Poe's works, including this one with a fear of premature burial, can be read through an identification with the victim as dealing with common fears. In this case, however, we can also read through identification with the narrator and see this as a fear that many of us may feel about our own potential for violence. That potential is explored in "William Wilson," a story much like Hoffmann's "The Doubles," in which one character, named William Wilson, happens to be a reprobate—a gambler, a cheat—and he is at college where there is another young man named, as it happens, William Wilson, and he cheats William Wilson. As the story is narrated, it turns out that no one actually ever is reported as talking to this William Wilson, and, yet, at the end when the cheating William Wilson is so furious at having been disparaged by his college mates because he is such a cheat, he kills the good William Wilson, feeling that that William Wilson is the one that had turned him in, and then realized that he has killed himself.

The whole idea of "Doubles," which Hoffmann gives us, which Poe gives us, goes back to a fantasy many of us have as youngsters, somewhere else in the world there is another me, and when I raise my hand, he has to raise his. When you first have that idea about the second self, it's really tempting until you realize that it may be he who raises his hand and you who have no free will, and that sense of loss of control makes the entire question of doubling, problematic.

In "The Tell-Tale Heart," the loss of control is something that the narrator feels, but we have no reason to believe exists. He sees the old man, and the old man gives him an evil eye, and he comes to resent the old man. So he eventually, cleverly, he says—letting us know how insane his own mind is—decides that he should kill him, and he does by throwing the man off the bed and turning the mattress over him and smothering him. Not a convenient way to kill somebody. Now, this killing that he performs is successful, and he buries the body under the floorboards. Eventually, the police come by because the old man is not heard of, and the killer sits there and tries to have an interview with the police. But he hears the tell-tale heart, thumping—the dead heart thumping. Eventually he can't stand it anymore and he exclaims to the police, "Yes, yes, just get me away from this tell-tale heart." They rip open the floorboards and he is found and brought to justice.

The thing is, as you read this story, you recognize that is entirely possible to naturalize it fully. That is, we could suppose that the narrator of "The Tell-Tale Heart" is simply hallucinating this sound;

he is simply insane. His complaint against the knowledge of the old man and his evil eye being seen into he doesn't want to be known, that complaint may simply be manufactured by the young man. There may be no evil or ill intent at all on the part of the old man, and, yet, he dies. And in his guilt for that, the narrator hears the heart and turns himself over to the police for the justice that he knows is his due. In a sense, then, "The Tell-Tale Heart" isn't a horror story at all. It's a perfectly realistic story told from the viewpoint of a mad man.

Now, "The Black Cat" is also a story about somebody who sees some other evil attacking him. In fact, he sees the black cat as a maligned spirit in his house and he kills a black cat that he has, that his wife had given him as a present. He is angry that he has killed the cat, but he has done it nonetheless. He's hanged it from a tree and let it be strangled to death; then he goes off drinking. He comes home and finds that the house has burned down. The crowd gathered outside the house looks at the remains of the house and says things like, "amazing," "how strange." Only then does the narrator look at the wall plastered above the bed and see that the image of a black cat hanging from a rope is presented in bas relief. But, he says, ah, well, probably what happened is that the neighbors came by, saw the fire, thought that I was asleep, and they cut the cat down in order to have something convenient to throw in through the window to wake me up, and thus having justified this to myself, I went on. Well, that's a pretty hard justification.

He acquires a second cat. That cat has a white blaze on him, and that white blaze, over the course of time, changes until it looks like an image of the gallows. He comes truly to truly hate that cat. Now, that white blaze might be changing its shape as a projection on the part of the narrator, the way the tell-tale heart thumps, but there is nothing projected about the bas relief because we hear the crowd speaking about it.

He's going downstairs into the basement of his house, his wife is coming with him, but the cat is between his feet and it begins to trip him up. The wife is asking him to be calm. He wants to kill the second cat. As he raises an ax to do so, his wife tries to restrain him, and so he turns, and in fury, buries the ax in his wife's head. He then walls her up in the basement, and when, eventually, the police come by, he doesn't speak himself. What happens is they hear a sound.

They open the wet bricks, and there is her corpse standing, and on her head, the screeching black cat.

Now, this story shows us that we can take the very same tale, an unexplained insult, an antipathy, a fear of relationship, and we can present it naturally or we can present it somewhat more fantastically, as "The Black Cat" is more fantastic than "The Tell-Tale Heart." In fact, Poe gives us a whole set of stories with a range of deranged narrators, and these fall along what you could call a continuum of the fantastic—from the most realistic to the most fantastic.

Hoffmann shows us that works can be more or less fantastic by giving us relatively unambiguous works such as "Councilor Krespel." Yes, it's fantastic, but we know that the daughter truly died. Or, ambiguous works, such as "Ritter Gluck," where, at the end, we don't know whether that character was Ritter Gluck, or a ghost, or an hallucination that's permanently de-centered. The affect of the changing ground rules never goes away.

At the realistic end of the continuum of the fantastic we have works that are always, to some extent fantastic, because in fiction everything counts and in real life that's not true. At the fantastic end, when we use the fantastic exhaustively and have true Fantasy, we still have, to some extent, realism because if all we have is the breaking of the rules—up seven eleven through gray—that is, I've just uttered a sentence where the grammar breaks down so thoroughly, the rules change so quickly, that meaning is lost. We must have some meaning; we must have some fantasy. So, from the realistic end to the fantastic end, any given genre can begin at whatever is its level of the fantastic, fairy tales come right in the middle, and then become more fantastic by using that affect at the level of style, character development, plot, and thematic development. Hoffmann understood that. That's why the subtitle of "The Golden Pot" is "A Modern Fairy Tale."

Poe also created what he called "tales of ratiocination." That is to say, tales in which we look for reason; we are engaged in these by our reason. Truth will be the single effect of tales of ratiocination, according to Poe in his essay, "The Short Story." We would divide those tales into two camps, I think, these days. One, say, is science fiction. "The Pit and the Pendulum," which is often thought of as a horror story, is, in fact, also easily understood as a science fiction story. The narrator is caught in the grip of the Inquisition. He's thrown into a dark pit. In that dark pit, he is about to be cut by a lowering pendulum that has a swinging scimitar, sharpened at the end. However, he maneuvers so that the mice come by and eat the cincture, the monk's rope—belt—that ties him to a crib, like a cradle, and lets him be released just before he is to be cut. He walks around blindly inside this pit, feeling the walls as they become hotter and hotter and as this circular pit goes more and more to oval. As in many of Poe's stories, we find a female figure in a symbolic form that looks to be fearful and deadly.

But this is science fiction. The calculation is made, ah, yes, the pendulum must be descending because its period—it must be going faster because it's getting lower—and he understands that the period stays the same. Ah, yes, I know how far around it is because I've counted steps and can multiply.

"The Purloined Letter" is a detective story—it's one of the first great detective stories—in which the prefect of police explains that it is impossible to retrieve the letter that was stolen by this person, who has it, from the mistress of the king, and if that letter does not come back, the king will be subject to blackmail, at least his mistress will. There are matters of state here. Dupin, the detective, says, "How do you know that it's missing?" Then the prefect of police explains all of the activities that have been performed in order to find this letter. They have waylaid the supposed thief. They have put knitting needles through the spinning of his furniture. They have gone through his effects at home when he's been out. It can't be found.

Dupin says, "If I retrieve the letter, what will you give me?" and the prefect of police says he will give him an enormous sum of money. The next thing we see is Dupin calling the prefect back and saying "You might as well fill out your check, I have the letter here." The prefect is aghast, speaks not a word. He looks. There's the letter, and he runs off with it gladly. Dupin then explains to his sidekick what he did, and he explains that people don't look where they expect things to be; the look where they expect them to be hidden. Knowing that it was in none of the places where it might be hidden, Dupin inferred that the letter must be in plain sight. He visited the rooms of the supposed thief, and saw that there was a letter case that held letters separately, one after the other, to be dealt with, and so he made a letter that looked the same on the outside as the letter that the mistress had written. But, on the inside, it said, "I now have the letter." He, then, when he visited a second time, substituted one for the other, leaving. That meant that the thief now knew that he did not have the letter and could not use it for blackmail, but could be blackmailed in turn, and so Dupin saves the day.

This lengthy explanation about having the imagination to do the unexpected, which is to look where something is expected—this new kind of reversal—creates the modern detective story. But the story is about half leading up to the moment when the prefect runs out speechless and half explaining what was done. Over the course of time, as detective stories developed, that crux shifts toward the end and we can see the fantastic being used to make the genre of the Tale of the Great Detective ever more enjoyable for people as tastes change. Together, though, science fictions like "The Pit and the Pendulum" and detective fictions like "The Purloined Letter" are tails of ratiocination; they are, in effect, fundamentally realistic stories applauding the use of the imagination.

Not all of Poe's stories applaud the use of the imagination. "The Oval Portrait," for example, is a story in which the main character has an unexplained wound, like the unexplained insult of the main character in "The Cask of Amontillado." Pedro, his servant, needs to shelter him against the night, and so they break into a tower, into a castle, and Pedro leads him up to the bedroom at the very top of the tower. The first half of the story talks about this invasion of some other person's space in which the main character lies down and looks around and sees portraits all around the room. On the night table is a book which he opens and discovers in it descriptions of each of the portraits. The subject of the portrait, the occasion of its being made, and so on. The second half of the story is the reading of this book. It is about an artist who paints his beloved, and at the very last moment, when he puts the last touch of paint on the painting—"this is, indeed, life itself," the artist is reported to have said, and he turns suddenly to regard his beloved. She was dead. It's a horror story, I suppose. It speaks about love being lost to art.

This story, it seems to me, is actually much like "Annabel Lee." It's about someone who tries, through art, to capture love, but the love eludes him. I don't believe Poe understood quite how deeply he was responding to his own artistry. I'll remind you of how "Annabel Lee" begins. "It was many, many a year ago, in a kingdom by the sea, that a maiden there lived whom you may know by the name of

Annabel Lee. And this maiden she lived with no other thought than to love and be loved by me." "The Oval Portrait" begins that book within the story thus—it's written as prose, but I'm going to break it up: "She was a maiden of rarest beauty, and not more lovely than full of glee, and evil was the hour when she saw and loved and wedded the painter, he. Passionate, studious, austere, and having, already a bride in his art, she was a maiden of rarest beauty, and not more lovely than full of glee." Poe has written the poem and the story with the same rhythm to deal with the same issue of lost love.

The poem that perhaps is most frequently used to show that Poe is an amazing craftsman—but really only a craftsman—is "The Bells:"

> Hear the sledges with the bells—
> Silver bells!
> What a world of merriment their melody foretells!
> How they tinkle, tinkle, tinkle,
> In the icy air of night!
> While the stars that oversprinkle
> All the heavens seem to twinkle
> With a crystalline delight;
> Keeping time, time, time,
> In a sort of Runic rhyme,
> To the tintinnabulation that so musically wells
> From the bells, bells, bells, bells,
> Bells, bells, bells—
> From the jingling and the tingling of the bells.

And then follow three more stanzas of similarly musical language.

Now, what I would like to point out to you is that these four stanzas follow a deformed version of Hesiod's "The Ancient Greek's Notion of the Ages of Civilization." Not gold, silver, bronze, iron, but silver, gold, bronze, iron. And each stanza deals with that and a kind of sound and death. We have melody, a single line of music, giving a runic rhyme; it jingles.

In the second stanza we have golden bells, harmony—these are called wedding bells. Immediately in the third stanza we have alarm bells—brazen bells—as fire breaks out. And the last stanza is iron bells, a monody, that is not harmony to but, again, a single line; this, a requiem for death.

What we have in "The Bells" is the same story that we had in "The Black Cat." First we have someone who loved animals as a boy, then his wife gives him a cat; then, in what should be marital harmony the house bursts into flame, and then he is alone dealing with death. What we have in "The Black Cat" is what's called a hypotactic story. Hypotaxis—you connect all the pieces underneath, so that we see how one goes with the other. "The Bells" is a paratactic story, one part jammed right against the other. There is no explanation how we go from one stanza to the next. And yet—"The Bells" and "The Black Cat,"—the stories being acknowledged as some of the great stories of American literature—follow the same psychological trajectory. Poe's achievement in genre after genre is to induce us to feel fear, and yet to know that we are in a fantastic world created by a precise and skillful artist, a world we need not flee, but can admire.

Lecture Five
Lewis Carroll—Puzzles, Language, & Audience

Scope:

Lewis Carroll was an adequate mathematician, an extraordinary photographer, and the author of what many consider to be the greatest children's book of all time, *Alice in Wonderland*. Yet only adult analysis of *Alice* reveals its powerful, dark, underground side, a side that some have argued comes from the author's own supposed psychoses. *Alice* is a work that strikes us very differently depending upon the time in life when we read it. Comparing it to Carroll's *Sylvie and Bruno*, meant only for children, or to his books of mathematical puzzles, we can see that taken together, *Alice* and *Through the Looking-Glass* constitute a classic composite fantasy that delights children by its sympathetic indulgence of their desires for novelty, play, and power and captures adults by motivating us to rethink the roles of language, convention, and art in our lives.

Outline

I. Charles Lutwidge Dodgson (1832–1898) wrote the *Alice* books under the name of Lewis Carroll. He was, like Hoffmann, a polymath and, like Poe, often thought to be a pervert; however, he needs to be understood in his own context.

    A. Quite expectedly, as a mathematics don in residence at Oxford University, Carroll was an Anglican clergyman and a bachelor.

    B. Unexpectedly, he was the second greatest English photographer of the Victorian period (after Margaret Julia Cameron).

        1. He had a thriving business selling photographs in several genres.

        2. When the first objection was raised to his posed children's nudes, works created only with maternal permission and never sold, Carroll destroyed all his originals and plates. All Carroll originals we have of this type have been carefully preserved by the families of their subjects.

C. Carroll adored intellectual play with children.

    1. His logic texts contain amusing examples, such as the 24-pig puzzle.

    2. He wrote the first draft of *Alice's Adventures under Ground* for Alice Pleasance Liddell, the youngest daughter of his dean.

    3. Only after Greville MacDonald, son of clergyman-author George MacDonald, applauded it did Carroll redraft and publish.

II. The *Alice* books form a composite novel.

    A. *Alice in Wonderland* (1865) is a sunny, summer novel, written to stand alone.

        1. The opening chapter shows how art and the fantastic can offer an escape from boredom for children.

        2. The prefatory verses, however, while full of wordplay for children, show an attentive adult the book's abiding concern with the approach of death.

    B. *Through the Looking-Glass* (1872) is a dark, winter novel, meant to complete in a new way the freestanding earlier publication.

        1. The prefatory verses, despite announcing "the love-gift of a fairy-tale," serve as a nostalgic lament for the real Alice growing up.

        2. The opening chapter exploits reversal to create the fantastic. Carroll's own misunderstanding of the functioning of mirrors, however, once understood, highlights the source of fantasy's power.

    C. The later half of the composite novel, by using the game of chess rather than the mere personification of cards, is intellectually denser than the first half.

    D. Overall, the composite novel is a true fantasy, using the fantastic exhaustively at the levels of style, character development, thematic development, and plot.

III. Read by a child, *Alice* offers jokes, puzzles, and power fantasy.

    A. Many of the jokes depend on nonsense and wordplay.

1. Famous examples include "The Walrus and the Carpenter," "Jabberwocky," and "the wood…where things have no names."
2. For adults, however, these examples each reveal a concern with death.
   B. Such puzzles as "Why is a raven like a writing desk?" also reach a dual audience.
   C. Alice, despite her insignificance as a Victorian child, is a fairy tale protagonist living in a world of puzzles that are, by definition, soluble.
   1. In seeking the Garden, she is thwarted but ultimately arrives there.
   2. In the Garden of Talking Flowers, she is made mute but finds joy there.
   3. Alice acknowledges being reduced to the status of a character, but as a fairy tale protagonist, she ends each volume happy.

IV. Read by an adult, *Alice* offers a wealth of significant, serious, sobering subjects.
   A. The opening chapter offers the first of the myriad subtle death jokes foreshadowed by the prefatory verses.
   B. Carroll, a master poet, comments on language and logic in the pronoun poem the White Rabbit reads as evidence at Alice's trial.
   C. Some of his poems, such as "An Aged, Aged Man," are also clever poetry criticism, although Carroll also criticizes criticism with Humpty Dumpty.
   D. The most fundamental problems offered by the book are of two kinds.
   1. What are the limits of language and logic for understanding our world?
   2. How can we accommodate ourselves to the limitations of our lives? The valedictory verses offer overt and covert answers to this question.

V. With *Alice*, Lewis Carroll became the first towering figure in the new publishing category called children's literature.

A. Other writers, such as MacDonald, helped populate this field. It arose out of a new idea of children as a special class of intellect rather than simply adults-in-training.

B. Some of Carroll's other children's works, such as *Sylvie and Bruno*, failed because of their didactic sobriety and comparative lack of the fantastic.

C. *Alice*, however, sets the standard for broadly effective children's literature. It ranks third, only behind Shakespeare and the King James Bible, in the number of words and phrases it has contributed to our culture.

Essential Reading:

Carroll, Lewis. *Alice's Adventures in Wonderland and Through the Looking Glass*.

Supplementary Reading:

Carroll, Lewis. *Mathematical Recreations of Lewis Carroll: Pillow Problems and a Tangled Tale*.

Taylor, Roger, Edward Wakeling, and Peter C. Bunnell. *Lewis Carroll, Photographer*.

Questions to Consider:

1. In what ways—good, bad, and neutral—do you identify the fantastic with childhood?

2. In what ways does the fantastic help deal with intellectual problems?

Lecture Five—Transcript
Lewis Carroll—Puzzles, Language, & Audience

Lewis Carroll was an adequate mathematician, an extraordinary photographer, and the author of what many consider to be the greatest children's book of all time, *Alice in Wonderland*. Yet, only adult analysis of *Alice* reveals its powerful dark underground side, a side that some have argued comes from the author's own supposed psychosis. *Alice* is a work that strikes us very differently, depending upon the time in life when we read it. Comparing it, for example, to his *Sylvie and Bruno*, meant only for children, or his books of mathematical puzzles, we can see that taken together, *Alice* and *Through the Looking Glass* constitute a classic composite Fantasy that delights children by its sympathetic indulgence and their desires for novelty, play, and power, and captures adults by motivating us to rethink the roles of language, convention, and art in our lives.

Charles Lutwidge Dodgson wrote the *Alice* books under the name Lewis Carroll—Lutwidge, Lewis; Charles, Carroll. He was, like Hoffmann, a polymath, and like Poe, often thought to be a pervert. However, he needs to be understood in his own context. Quite expectedly, as a mathematics don in residence at Oxford University, Carroll was an Anglican clergyman and a bachelor. Unexpectedly, he was the second greatest English photographer of the Victorian period, after a woman photographer, Margaret Julia Cameron. In fact, he had a strong entrepreneurial urge and among his other achievements was a photography business. He kept an agent in London who sold his photographs composed in many genres. Indeed, some of the most important and famous portraits of the well known Victorians are Carroll's own.

For families with little children, he often posed them in costume, and sometimes—because at this time photography was thought of as modeling itself on painting—he photographed them nude. He never did this without permission of their parents, and did so only with the mothers present. However, when, once, a mother showed a picture of which she was proud, to her friend, and the friend expressed shock that the mother had allowed her child to be seen naked, the mother complained to Lewis Carroll. This sensitive man was so aghast that his artistic urges had impinged on the happiness of people he loved the most—typically little children—that he destroyed all of his plates and all the originals he had. To this day, the nude child photographs that we have from this second-greatest of all Victorian photographers, come to us only because they have been treasured and preserved by the families of those who are lucky enough to have them. Of course, one could argue that the extremity of Carroll's reaction comes from an unacknowledged recognition that he was, perhaps, too interested in children. In our context, that would probably be the right inference. But, as I say, in those days, every single Oxford don who lived in house was both a clergyman and a bachelor, and to lead an asexual life was not, in some sense, an oddity, but a desired norm.

Carroll adored children. When he traveled, he kept a trunk full of amusements with which he could play with strangers he might meet on the train. He made up logic puzzles to try to delight them. For example, one that he actually published in one of his books of mathematical puzzles is the 24-pig puzzle, which I offer to you to think about while I'm talking, in case you find what I say is not sufficiently compelling. Carroll's puzzle goes like this: Imagine a square corral. Within this corral, at its four corners, we find four smaller corals, one in each corner. We have 24 pigs, and we need to distribute them into those sub-corrals, in any combination—one, two, three, and the remainder in the fourth—any combination one likes of the 24 pigs. The problem, however, or I should say, the puzzle, is to distribute them in such a way that as one goes clockwise from one sub-corral to the next, one always is nearer 10. The difficulty is that one needs to be able to continue to do this indefinitely—moving around the corral without ever stopping. That's a puzzle.

To amuse the daughter, the youngest daughter, of his dean, Lewis Carroll wrote *Alice's Adventures in Wonderland*. The girl was named Alice Pleasance Liddell, and she was, by all accounts, a delightful child who grew up to be a delightful woman and remained a friend of Carroll's until his dying day. He handwrote this tale and illustrated it himself. After she expressed delight in it, he gave it to his friend George MacDonald, who showed it to his son Greville, who read it and replied, "Why, this is so wonderful, fifty thousand copies should be made." Lewis Carroll the entrepreneur went into action, lengthened the story, engaged John Tenniel to create illustrations, and produced what became one of the most famous books in all of history.

The *Alice* books form what could be called a composite novel. *Alice in Wonderland*, published in 1865, is a sunny, summer novel written originally to stand alone. The opening chapter shows how art and the fantastic can offer an escape from boredom for children. Here are the first words. "Alice was beginning to grow very tired of sitting by her sister on the bank of a river, and of having nothing to do. Once or twice she had peeked into the book her sister was reading, but it had no pictures or conversation in it; and what is the use of a book, thought Alice, without pictures or conversations?" It's wonderful to see at this moment that Alice is not only trying to find something to occupy her mind, an imaginative little girl, but she's also talking about the world of books as a possible escape.

In effect, what happens in the famous opening scene is that a white rabbit runs by and she concocts her escape by following him down the rabbit hole. It's often said that *Alice in Wonderland* has two worlds, the above world and the underworld—the above world being realistic, the underworld being fantastic. But that's not so. As soon as Alice, motivated by her boredom, sees the white rabbit, who says, "I'm late! I'm late!" she has already created the fantastic in that above ground world. The realm that is realistic in *Alice and Wonderland* is the realm of adults. It is, perhaps, the realm of her sister sitting by the bank reading the book without pictures and conversations. The world of the fantastic is the world of Alice's imagination, which begins in Victorian England and continues right down into all of the adventures underground. The world that we explore is Alice's psyche.

Now, this beautiful, sunny afternoon with Alice's boredom comes introduced to us after some prefatory verses. Lewis Carroll did not write much poetry, but that which he wrote was superb. This is how the book actually begins, these rich prefatory verses:

> All in the golden afternoon
> Full leisurely we glide;
> For both our oars, with little skill,
> By little arms are plied,
> While little hands make vain pretense
> Our wanderings to guide.

Lewis Carroll was in a boat with the three Little sisters, and they are having a very casual meander on the river:

Ah, cruel Three! In such an hour,
Beneath such dreamy weather,
To beg a tale of breath too weak
To stir the tiniest feather!

This is an afternoon of midsummer, all in the golden afternoon, a moment of time-out-of-time. It's the time of fairy tale; it's the time of myth; it's the time of summer vacation, when August lasts forever and school of the next year seems impossibly far away.

But notice, as an adult, "Ah, cruel three," we know who those are; those are the fates of ancient mythology. These fates control the length of our lives. "In such an hour,"—we're talking about time— "beneath such dreamy weather, a breath too weak to stir the tiniest feather." The children play with the speaker of the poem, demanding a tale of wonders, and he complies, but tires. "And faintly strove that weary one,"—the speaker—"to put the subject by the rest next time. It is next time, the happy voices cried." Already in the prefatory verses we see the wordplay that makes us look at language itself and how it communicates. "It is the next time," because it is the moment after someone has said, "the rest next time."

It ends, these verses:

Alice! A childish story take,
And, with a gentle hand,
Lay it where Childhood's dreams are twined
In Memory's mystic band,
Like pilgrim's wither'd wreath of flowers
Pluck'd in a far-off land.

In the Middle Ages people would take pilgrimage to sites, holy sites, where they could become restored, where they could regain their health, and in order to mark the fact that they had been in a strange locale, they would take flowers that grew locally there but not in their homes, and would weave them into a garland which they put on their heads. By the time they returned home, the flowers would be withered. Flowers, which as we mentioned in discussing "Little Red Cap" are the sexual organs of plants—flowers, which represent procreation—these would wither by the time one came away from those holy places. The pilgrimage, in fact, cannot ultimately prevent us from dying. But, that crown that the pilgrims wore is like the crown of Jesus, and this clergyman-poet is letting us know that he hopes that the story, though he will die, will live on because he has made a pilgrimage to the land of children in order to create something to delight them. That far-off land may be death, and if hope works for us, it will be resurrection.

Alice in Wonderland is a book very much about death. This is complemented by *Through the Looking Glass*, although *Alice in Wonderland* was written to be free standing. *Through the Looking Glass* was written with the clear understanding that it would be read after *Alice in Wonderland*. In 1872 it was published; seven years later Alice Little herself was now a teenager. This is a dark story. It's set in the winter. It begins indoors. It begins in front of a fireplace, and above that fireplace is a mirror. Alice looks into that famous mirror and sees that everything is reversed, and merges by going into that reversed world. The prefatory verses here are equally nostalgic about Alice growing up:

> Child of the pure unclouded brow
> And dreaming eyes of wonder!
> Though time be fleet, and I and thou
> Are half a life asunder,

We know that word—"what God hath put together, let no man put asunder"—this means death.

> Thy loving smile shall surely hail
> The love-gift of a fairy-tale.

And in many ways *Alice in Wonderland* and *Through the Looking Glass* are fairy tales. The word fairy tale occurs in the next stanza as well. And then, as the verses end and the book itself is about to begin, we see:

> Come, hearken then, ere voice of dread,
> With bitter tidings laden,
> Shall summon to unwelcome bed
> A melancholy maiden!
> We are but older children, dear,
> Who fret to find our bedtime near.

Lewis Carroll was letting us know that what we see here stands for larger, deeper, more fatal human concerns.

In that opening chapter, though, Alice tries to leave that world by going into a world of reversals, and it's interesting to see how Lewis Carroll, a very good mathematician but a brilliant writer, who has so much right, has the mirrors wrong. Lewis Carroll depends, for his imagistic effects, on our belief that mirrors reverse things, and indeed, that is the common belief. But, in fact, mirrors do not reverse. You can prove this to yourself rather easily. Stand in front of a mirror and hold out your right hand, and what you'll see is your right hand being held out. Well, you know we reverse right and left. After all, it takes a while to learn as a child to shake hands by extending your right hand over across your body to someone else's right hand. Little children stick their right hand straight forward and reach for someone else's left. We learn that when we face someone, their right is opposite our left; hence, the notion of reversal. If, when you look in a mirror, you were to stick one arm up in the air and the other arm down, what you'd see is that the person in the mirror has the up arm up and the down arm down. Up and down don't change in a mirror, right and left do.

The difference between up and down and right and left is this. We all have semicircular canals in our ears that understand where we are in relation to the center of gravity in the earth. It doesn't matter if we're turned upside down, sideways, insight out—we know which way is up and down; it's dependent upon the earth as its frame of reference. Right and left are dependant upon us as a frame of reference. The fantasy that comes from reversal in *Alice in Wonderland* comes from reversals that are deep within us. We see the world a certain way. The change of that is what creates the fantastic, and Lewis Carroll is in perfect control of that.

The latter half of this composite novel has as its presiding metaphor the playing out of a chess game. The former half has the use of playing cards as characters, but no particular game. Because the rules of chess themselves are an overlay on the plot, on the fantastic changes that occur as Alice goes from chapter to chapter, the information density is actually stronger in *Through the Looking Glass*. Considered alone, in that regard, I would suggest that *Through the Looking Glass* is the greater work, but it should not be considered alone because one does not have the feel and power of that work without reading it as the second half of that composite novel. The move from the sunny summer to the dark winter reinforces the approach of death, which is what the books really have as a subtext throughout.

Read by a child, of course, the *Alice* books are quite delightful. They offer jokes, puzzles, and power fantasies. Many of the jokes depend on nonsense and wordplay. For example, we have "The Walrus and the Carpenter":

> "The time has come," the Walrus said,
> "To speak of many things:
> Of shoes—and ships—and sealing-wax—...
> And why the sea is boiling hot—
> And whether pigs have wings."

"Jabberwocky:"

> 'Twas brillig, and the slithy toves,
> Did gyre and gimble in the wabe:
> All mimsy were the borogoves,
> And the mome raths outgrabe.

What is that? What does that mean? I think that when we play with these, we see that there is a delight in language. Children love language—in fact, adults love language, hence the importance of poetry in all of human history—but we see this kind of wonder being played out in language that, for adults, will have a second meaning. The walrus and the carpenter are telling their lovely little story full of nonsense to amuse a group of oysters that are following them along the strand. The oysters look like little children behind them, and as they go, they eat one after another. At the end they say, "What do you think of our song, little oysters?" But no one answered because there were none left.

"Jabberwocky" is a poem about a boy who goes into the woods and meets the Jabberwocky, but manages to dispatch him with his vorpal blade. Tenniel's illustration for the Jabberwocky itself was so horrifying that they decided that they could not use it at the intended place in the book because it would scare children too much.

Language is powerful. We understand our world through language. There is a wood in *Through the Looking Glass* that Alice walks through. She emerges from the wood with her arm around a fawn. This is a wood in which things have no names. As they walk out beautifully together—as in "the lion shall lie down with the lamb,"—

they look at each other, and Alice says, "Ah, now I realize, you're a fawn," and the fawn realizes Alice is a little girl, and takes off with a bound. Language enforces our realities. We can see Lewis Carroll recognizing this in a way that creates true Fantasy.

In the very first chapter, after Alice has fallen down the rabbit hole, she seeks to go into the garden she can see through a keyhole. She's too big, so she eats something, and she shrinks. But now she's too small to reach the key of the keyhole, which is back on the table, so she eats something else and she becomes too big; and, to fit through the door, she can't be the size right. But she sees something else to eat, and she does, and she ate a little bit, and said anxiously to herself, "Which way, which way," holding her hand on top of her head to feel which way it was growing—which, of course, is nonsense because you can't feel how you're growing if you're only touching yourself. And she was quite surprised to find that she remained the same size. To be sure, this is generally what happens when one eats cake. But Alice was so much into the way of expecting nothing but out-of-the-way things to happen, that it seemed quite dull and stupid for life to go on in the common way. So she set to work and very soon finished off the cake.

Now, what we see here in this little delightful passage is a number of things that help us understand the functioning of the fantastic in general. Here we have this reversal, into-the-way and out-of-the-way things and so on, in the style itself. Second of all, we have reversal in character development. She thinks that she has control over the world because she understands its rules, that this is, in fact, her world, but what it turns out to be is a world that responds to her own inner insecurities as well and thwarts her again and again. Thematically we see that this story, which looks to be about how the imagination can give us wherever we want, in fact is something different. It's about how the imagination may or may not give us where we want. And the plot, of course, which shows us at this point that we have a forward run suddenly hits, if not a brick wall, the locked door into the garden. In other words, I'll remind you, the fantastic is that affect which we have from the diametric, diachronic reversal of the ground rules of the narrative world. We have that here in style, character development, thematic development and plot. In fact, we have that reversal, the fantastic, at all four of the levels of narrative that conserve diachronic information, and we have it exhaustively. *Alice in Wonderland* is all the way over on the continuum of the fantastic. It's a true Fantasy.

All of these things, of course, deal with death, as we said. When adults look at these puzzles, we realize that not being able to go into the garden means not being able to return to Eden, not being able to find resurrection, and throughout we have other puzzles. "Why a raven is like a writing desk?" is in the book. In fact, the answer doesn't appear in the book. People wrote into Lewis Carroll and asked what is the answer, and he later wrote a little article in which he said he, himself, had come up with several, and hundreds others had been written to him, but he's decided that the best of them all is: Why is a raven like a writing desk? Because Poe wrote on both. But, remember, Poe's "Raven" is about loss and death; nevermore will Lenore come to the speaker.

Alice is insignificant as a Victorian child, and she understands that, but as the protagonist of a fairy tale or a fairy tale pushed all the way to true Fantasy, she is, in fact, someone who is going to be successful. She ends each book happily. She goes running off into the Victorian world at the end of the first half, and she sits happily at the end of the second half, that is *Through the Looking Glass.*

What, exactly, are puzzles? Puzzles, I think we need to understand, bear a relationship to our lives that are different from either situations or problems. Most of us think of human mortality as a situation; that's just the name of the game—we are going to die. In fact, we're known as mortals; we're defined by the fact that we must die. But some people—for instance, scientists who believe they may be able to stop the aging process—see aging not as a situation, but as a problem. A problem is a situation that you would like to change, but you don't know if you can. A puzzle, on the other hand, is a problem for which you are promised, and believe, there to be a solution. When you buy a jigsaw puzzle, and it says 12,000 parts, you don't think oh my God, I don't even know if they fit together. You begin with the assumption that ultimately the puzzle can be solved.

In the world of Lewis Carroll's art we have puzzles. Some of them Alice solves, some of them we solve, such as, "Why a Raven is like a writing desk?" In seeking the garden, she is thwarted, but ultimately she arrives. In the second part, in *Through the Looking Glass*, she comes into a garden of live flowers, and those flowers seem to her quite lovely:

> "Oh, Tiger Lily," said Alice, addressing herself to one that was waving gracefully about in the wind, "I wish you could talk." "We can talk," said Tiger Lily, "when there's anybody worth talking to." Alice was so astonished that she couldn't speak for a minute. It quite seemed to take her breath away.

The ground rules said flowers can't talk. We had imported them from our world. Suddenly they talked, and girls who could talk suddenly can not. We've seen this before, when the prefect was unable to utter a word, after Dupin in "The Purloined Letter" said well, here is the letter you want. This reversal of ground rules creates the fantastic.

Alice acknowledges her status as a character, but in so doing, she still wants to be happy, and she is, as I said, at the end of each volume. But, when an adult reads this book, we see some sobering realities. The opening chapter offers the first of these with a subtle death joke. As Alice is falling down the rabbit hole, "But quite gracefully," she says, "But why, after such a fall as this? No, I would think nothing of it if I fell of the roof of a house." And the narrator immediately says parenthetically, "Which his quite likely true," meaning that she would die if she fell off the roof of the house. There are death jokes throughout the *Alice* books, and they are foreshadowed by the prefatory verses.

Alice, at her trial, has a letter held in evidence against her:

> They told me you had been to her
> And mentioned me to him;
> She gave me a good character,
> But said I could not swim.
>
> He sent them word I had not gone;
> (We know it to be true);
> If she should push the matter on,
> What would become of you?

And so on. We understand language, even when we don't understand language. The poem makes sense, because we follow the pronouns, but we know nothing about what it actually means.

The status of language is an important issue for Lewis Carroll, the writer. In his poem, "An Aged, Aged Man,"—which is about someone who finds an old fellow and asks him what he's doing there and so on and just bats him around, asking him for answers that he never really receives—what we really find is a critique of Wordsworth's "Resolution and Independence," a famous poem sometimes know as "The Leach Gatherer," where the poetic voice listens to the old man who has this rough living he makes by gathering leaches, by letting them attach to his own body, and at one point loses track of what the old man is saying because he, himself, is just thinking, "Oh, I can make much of this story." Did Wordsworth intend for that poem to be a critique of the speaker or not? Lewis Carroll seems to suggest that he should have. And, yet, criticism itself comes in for criticism when Humpty Dumpty says, when explaining what Jabberwocky means, "Why, I make words mean whatever I want, and if I make them work doubly hard, I pay them double on Fridays."

The fundamental problems that this book offers are of two kinds. First of all, what are the limits of language and logic for understanding our world? And how can we accommodate ourselves to the limitations of our lives? The first we have a hint of by looking at the answer of the 24-pig puzzle. The answer is this: The pigs are distributed thusly—zero, six, eight, 10—wait, how can that work? Why, six is nearer 10 than zero; eight is nearer ten than six; 10 is nearer 10 than eight; nothing is nearer 10 than 10; six is nearer 10 than zero, et cetera. What Lewis Carroll does is to switch codes of representation and make words mean more than one thing, which, in fact, they do. That's how we manage to go beyond the limits of language and logic.

But the closing verses tell us that we will die.

> A boat beneath the sunny sky,
> Lingering onward dreamily

It ends:

> Ever drifting down the stream—
> Lingering in the golden gleam—
> Life, what is it but a dream?

But if you read the first letter of each of the lines in the final verse of *Through the Looking Glass*, you'll see they spell the name Alice

Pleasance Liddell. We will die, but we can make our mark and live on in others.

Once upon a time children were thought of just as adults in training, but Lewis Carroll understood them as having playful minds that needed to be addressed in special ways. When he tried to address them didactically, as in *Sylvie and Bruno*, he wound up with a story that in its small form was a delight, but when he expanded it as a clergyman it was dishwater dull and sold not a bit. But Alice sets the standard for highly effective children's literature. It ranks third only behind Shakespeare and the King James Bible in the number of words and phrases it has contributed to our culture. And, it has enriched all of our minds forever.

Lecture Six
H. G. Wells—We Are All Talking Animals

Scope:

In the first decade of the 20th century, before the extended triumph of realism in the marketplace of literary criticism, H. G. Wells was considered by many to be the preeminent novelist working in English. His debate with Henry James illuminates the history of how we view the fantastic. In such works as "The Strange Orchid," Wells touches lightly on the psychosexual drives that social structures of class and gender often repress. In such works as *The Invisible Man*, Wells shows how science offers a fantasy of revenge against such repression. And in such works as *The Island of Doctor Moreau*, the scientist unrestrained by society fulfills ancient fairy tale fantasies while simultaneously adulterating all that is natural. In what Wells called his "scientific romances," the fantastic highlights the eternal tension between society's need for stability and the disruptive desires of individuals.

Outline

I. Herbert George Wells (1866–1946) wrote superb fiction and nonfiction.

   A. At the turn of the 20th century, Wells and Henry James were considered the two foremost living writers of English prose.

   1. James publicly asserted that the novel must explore individual psychology, as in *The Portrait of a Lady* (1881 and 1909).

   2. Wells publicly asserted that the novel must explore the powerful social forces that shape us, as in *The Food of the Gods* (1903).

   B. Wells's *The Outline of History—Being a Plain History of Life and Mankind* (1920) was the first attempt to trace the interconnected history of all of humanity. Wells focused on social forces, including changing material conditions (such as new weapons), rather than on the lives and deeds of remarkable individuals.

II. In his fiction, Wells built his analyses of the modern world on fairy tale foundations.

    A. "The Plattner Story" (1897) shows a desire to belong to a larger group.

        1. The protagonist's fantastic adventure is told in appealing fairy tale terms.

        2. The narrator's credibility, however, depends on scientific confirmation.

    B. "The Strange Orchid" (1897) seems to be the story of the one extreme experience in the quiet life of an eccentric gentleman.

        1. The backstory, however, suggests that the protagonist represents the Victorian middle class.

        2. The living situation suggests repressed sexuality.

        3. The setting suggests the modern need for romance.

        4. The description suggests ancient erotic myth, like "Rapunzel."

        5. The plot suggests both a critique and a ratification of Victorian fantasies.

III. *The Invisible Man* (1897) tells a fantastic tale of the relation of the individual to society.

    A. Griffin, the title character, like many of Poe's characters, feels great personal bitterness.

    B. The novel reflects and critiques Victorian attitudes.

        1. Repressed sexuality arises in the treatment of nudity and invisibility.

        2. Religion resonates in such names as Thomas Marvel and Griffin and in Griffin's desire to be a god.

        3. Imperialism drives Griffin.

    C. The ending, however, implies that society must maintain stability against unique individuals, just as it was tragically successful in shaping Griffin.

    D. Wells's conscious use of the fantastic to offer a specific critique here is clarified by comparing the rules of invisibility in *The Invisible Man* with those in "The Plattner Story."

IV. *The Island of Doctor Moreau* (1896) is a deceptively simple novel.

    A. The novel functions on two levels.

        1. The story Prendick tells concerns a series of monstrous experiments that imply criticisms of misused science and of European colonialism.

        2. The story we can infer about Prendick implies a critique of the way personal guilt can be hidden by class and language.

    B. Language is crucial in the novel.

        1. Both Moreau and Prendick use language as a colonial tool.

        2. Both Moreau and Prendick unwittingly imply more than they say about themselves.

        3. Just as in "The Frog Prince," speech supposedly marks the human.

    C. Prendick's narration reflects a recurring confusion about what is and is not human. Our vocabulary acknowledges that confusion in the common meanings of such words as *brutal* and *beastly* and such phrases as *dumb creature*.

        1. Prendick first sees M'ling as a man. Prendick's later recognition of the truth accords with Freud's analysis in "The Uncanny."

        2. Prendick's supposed misunderstanding of Moreau's experiments shows a culpable human- (Euro-) centrism.

        3. The novel ends with a supposedly changed Prendick reminiscent of Jonathan Swift's Gulliver returned from living with the utopian horse-creatures called Houyhnhms.

    D. Walking across the island toward the Beast People, "Moreau, Montgomery, myself [Prendick], and M'ling" exemplify the Hobbesian great chain of being.

        1. Among those links, M'ling presides over transition.

        2. M'ling is associated with the beach, which throughout art is typically the zone of conflict for elementally contending forces.

    E. The question Wells here and often leaves with us is this:

Which way shall we go, toward the colonial or toward the respectful, toward the egotistical or toward the social, toward the isolated or toward the integrated? It is no surprise that he is the first writer to popularize the use of the word *ecology*. No progress can be made without the imagination of humans, but all humans must recognize that they, too, are subject to great forces beyond them, that indeed, we are all talking animals.

Essential Reading:

Wells, H. G. "The Invisible Man," in *Best Science Fiction Stories of H. G. Wells*.

Wells, H. G. *The Island of Dr. Moreau*.

Supplementary Reading:

Huntington, John. *The Logic of Fantasy: H. G. Wells and Science Fiction*.

Questions to Consider:

1. In what ways do the messages of Wells's novels add or detract from his artistry?

2. In what ways is it appropriate or inappropriate to mix the issues of religion and the techniques of the literary fantastic?

Lecture Six—Transcript
H. G. Wells—We Are All Talking Animals

In the first decade of the 20th century, before the extended triumph of realism in the market place of literary criticism, H. G. Wells was considered by many to be the preeminent novelist working in English. His debate with Henry James illuminates the history of how we view the fantastic. In works like "The Strange Orchid," Wells touches lightly on the psychosexual drives that social structures of class and gender often repress. In works like *The Invisible Man*, Wells shows how science offers a fantasy of revenge against such repression. And in works like *The Island of Doctor Moreau*, the scientist unrestrained by society fulfills ancient fairy tale fantasies while simultaneously adulterating all that is natural. In what Wells called his "scientific romances," the fantastic highlights the eternal tension between society's need for stability and the disruptive desires of individuals.

Herbert George Wells wrote suburb fiction and nonfiction. At the turn of the 20th century, he and James were considered the two foremost living writers of English prose. James publicly asserted in a debate that they carried on in print that the novel must explore individual psychology as, for example, in his famous work *The Portrait of a Lady*. In that novel, the protagonist walks into a room and sees the man she thinks of as someone who is her lover, sitting while another woman stands. In the flash of a moment, she understands that there must have been a prior relationship between these two, or even a continuing one, for him to be so relaxed, seated in the presence of a standing woman. That little detail, that little nuance, that inference from the smallest little interaction between individuals brings the entire emotional structure of the novel crashing down on the protagonist. It's that psychological exploration, that realism of response, that James argued the novel was for.

But Wells asserted that the novel needs to explore the great social forces that shape all of us, regardless of our individual differences. For example, in *The Food of the Gods*, one of his late, great scientific romances, a group of scientists manage to produce artificially a food that greatly increases the size and the intelligence of people. They are becoming supermen, and they want to share this with everyone. In fact, what happens is the little people, meaning all ordinary folk like us, begin to resent the fact that these big folk think that the world is better and that they can tell us how we should behave, and they go to war against them. The big folk, wanting to bring the little folk along, begin to lob shells full of this food into the cities where the little folk live, and the little folk sue the big folk in the international courts of law under the Geneva Convention, claiming that the food of the gods is poison, and poison gas is prohibited under the Geneva Convention. In other words, what Wells is trying to show us is that even the most obvious technological improvement, when we see how it works its way through social structures, may turn out to be good or bad, positive or disruptive, depending upon the ways in which people understand these inventions to function in their own worlds.

The pursuit of pattern is something that Wells did for his entire writing career. In order to earn his way through college, at one point for two years he was the lab assistant to T. H. Huxley, Darwin's great disciple and publicist, and Wells was probably the very first writer who truly understood evolution and the theory of patterns of forces shaping the world. He wrote single handedly, *The Outline of History—Being a Plain History of Life and Mankind,* published in four hard-back volumes in 1920. In the days when a hard-back volume cost about a day's worth of labor for an average working man that series sold a quarter of a million copies in its first American printing alone. *The Outline of History* was an attempt to see how all of human history, particularly that driven by geography, technology, climate, and so on, was an evolution, as opposed to the traditional way of looking at history as the stories of the deeds of great men and rulers and conflicts and wars.

In his fiction, Wells analyzed the modern world, but in his early great scientific romances, he did this built on a foundation of fairy tales. For example, in "The Plattner Story," he has a man discover some green powder in his laboratory. It blows up, and suddenly he finds himself at the top of a ramp looking down into a world covered by a green miasma in which folks are wandering back and forth in some stately interchange. He walks down into the miasma. He joins them, and as he goes toward them, he passes through them. It turns out that he wanders, trying to find out what's going on, unsuccessfully, for about nine days. That's a pregnant number that Wells has chosen. When he returns, he walks up the ramp and is discovered by his headmaster—he's a chemistry teacher at a high school—lying on his floor, and he explains that he didn't know what was going on there, but he felt that there were these "watchers," perhaps even the souls of his parents, who were keeping concern over him as he wandered.

No time has passed at the school, and so his story is completely disbelieved until, on physical examination, it's discovered that his internal organs have been reversed. What to make of "The Plattner Story?" Is it, in fact, a visceral reversal of our lives to come to believe that we can be back in the presence of our departed loved ones? Is this a critique of religion?

"The Strange Orchid" is a fascinating story about a man who lives a completely pedestrian Victorian life. He owns a home, and he has installed in his home his distant female cousin as an act of charity to serve as his housekeeper. He has independent means, and spends his time reading and, in particular, in the greenhouse he has in his garden, growing orchids. He gathers orchids from around the world, but never, of course, goes around the world himself. He orders them from orchid collectors. He has come upon one orchid which brings with it the extraordinary story that it was found on the body of an orchid gatherer in the Amazon. The bulb was collected, put in a glass jar, and is now sold.

He takes the bulb and he plants it in his greenhouse. To make this story even shorter, he goes out one day to look at this wonderful, flowering, developing orchid, and is overcome by the scent of this lush purple blossom. It has filled the entire greenhouse, and he swoons—that's the word, swoons—and falls down on the ground. The next thing he knows, his eyes are opened and there is a cold wind blowing on him. His cousin, his asexual housekeeper, has come down, seen what was going on, gone into the greenhouse, and discovered that the orchid had it's tendrils no longer flying around in the air, these aerial tendrils, but they had descended onto his cheek, face, and hands, and there was a little trickle of blood coming off his cheek, so she broke the glass of the greenhouse. The Victorian, northern, English air came in, and the orchid shriveled to a black putrescence, a lot like the putrescence at the end of Poe's "The Facts in the Case of M. Valdemar."

What we have here is clearly, at a repressed level, a sexual competition between the vampire orchid and the Victorian housekeeper. They are both vying for the economic support of the

Victorian gentleman. What do you think he thinks of this? In fact, what he things is this, in the last lines of the story:

> The next morning the orchid still lay there, black now and putrescent. The door banged intermittently (of the greenhouse) in the morning breeze, and all the array of Wedderburn's orchids were shriveled and prostate, but Wedderburn himself was bright and garrulous upstairs in the glory of his strange adventure.

This is an adventure, of course, that he did not take himself, but was only infected by. The story, in other words, suggests the protagonist, represents Victorian middle class; the living situation suggests repressed sexuality; the setting itself, with the attachment of the greenhouse to keep these exotics alive, suggests a modern need for romance; and the description suggests an erotic vegetation myth, much like that of "Rapunzel." The plot suggests a critique of Victorian fantasies, and yet at the same time, a ratification of them, because we need to be more than just living on our investments.

The Invisible Man has created an image that goes throughout all of modern literature. We all know about this man who can just go around the world completely unseen. In Wells's story, Griffin—his name, after all, is that of a mythical beast—Griffin, the title character, is a chemist. He fools with things and finds a way to make himself invisible. What happens, of course, is that his invisibility works only if he is unclothed, and so he needs to go naked in the world. Going naked in the world, he is cold, like the orchid in the previous story, and what can you do with invisibility besides indulge your own prurience? Well, it turns out that you can steal and you can murder; at least, that's what Griffin does. He is, in effect, someone who wants to turn against society. He doesn't, for instance, think he can use his invisibility in the service of the intelligence corps to keep His Majesty's—or in this period, Her Majesty's—government safe. He is a man of great personal bitterness.

The novel reflects and critiques Victorian attitudes. Again, we have repressed sexuality; again we have reference to other things that are not explicit. For instance, in order to extend his dominion over an English county, he wants to enlist the help of an ordinary Englishman, and he finds a dissolute who can be convinced to serve him by being punched by an invisible hand, until he is sure that, indeed, he is in the hands of an angry god. The man's name is

Thomas Marvel. Like Doubting Thomas, he won't have faith in Griffin until he can feel him. But unlike Jesus, who says to Thomas, "Put your hands inside my wound," this deity, or would-be deity, punches the Thomas. His name is Marvel because he needs to see marvels in order to function. Griffin desires to be a god. His aim is imperialistic, just like England's. But at the end, in fact, he fails. Of course he could murder anyone, but he'd have to live naked and alone.

The people realize that they are being marauded, and eventually when it is recognized that he is in a public place, a pub, they surround him. They can't see him, but they can feel him as he tries to break out of their circle. When they surround him, they punch him, and eventually they beat him to death. As he dies, he becomes visible again, in a marvelous description first of his bones, then of his inner organs and circulatory system, and, finally, of his skin. It is at that moment that the crowd around him goes, "Oh, horrible, horrible." And we are told that three little children who tried to push through the crowd were turned away by their parents to keep from seeing him because Griffin is an albino. Griffin, we have learned already from one of the characters earlier in the novel, was always shunned by his fellows at University because he was physically different. It's not simply that he has aboriginal viciousness and bitterness, the way some of Poe's characters do, he has been rejected by society, and then having been rejected, he attacks society in turn.

Yet, society did have to defend itself against the aberrant individual who had claimed so much power as to be able to change it. The ending lets us know that there is a critique here, and this critique is one that is intended to balance, quite carefully, the relationship between the individual and society. We can understand that quite well, I think, by comparing the use of invisibility in *The Invisible Man* with the use of invisibility in "The Plattner Story."

You see, in *The Invisible Man*, Griffin would not have been caught by the villagers, would not need to worry about the cold, if Wells had simply decided that in Griffin's case, invisibility goes along with insubstantiality. If, as in "The Plattner Story," Griffin could walk through people, they never could have killed him; and clearly Wells was capable of creating an invisibility that allowed insubstantiality because he did it in "The Plattner Story." In other words, we can infer that Griffin's invisibility is a conscious, rhetorical device created specifically to show us that even when we think that we are invisible to society, and even when we think that we can behave regardless of the desires of society, we must, in fact, recognize that we can only thrive by making some accommodation with society. But that is not to say that society needs to dominate the individual because the fundamental problem, conflict in this novel, arises because first society was not able to see past the visible to the brilliant man within. Parables like this, taking fairy tale ideas—ah, the invisible—putting them in a scientific context, have made Wells one of the great writers of all times.

Another of his works that gives us an image that comes down throughout modern literature and our culture is that from *The Island of Doctor Moreau,* the making of beasts into people. Now, we all know that because we've heard of the story *The Island of Doctor Moreau*, but when the story was first published, of course, people had not yet heard of the story and, as we read the story, we find that there are no beast-people initially. In fact, the first of the beast-people we see, someone named M'ling, is not described as a beast-person at all, but rather metaphorically; his eyes had a certain kind of animal fire. "He turns with an animal swiftness," the narrator says. Only later do we find out that M'ling had begun as an animal and that Moreau had manipulated him surgically and chemically to make him into something that passes for a rather coarse, but nonetheless real, human being.

This is a novel about a series of monstrous experiments. These experiments critique science, because we see that science can be misused. It brings unhappiness on the animals that are changed by it. There is something natural about an animal, even a predatory animal, and to stop them from being their natural selves is to impose on them. But this is also a critique on European colonialism, because Moreau has taken over an island and he has populated it with these beast-people of his own creation, and he seeks to rule over them as if he were a god.

Now, in fact, this is what the English did. I'm going to read to you from the birthday speech—that is, the queen's birthday in 1938— given by the governor of Australia to a collection of aboriginals, black men. "We wish to make you happy, but you cannot be happy unless you imitate good white men, build huts, wear clothes, work and be useful. Above all, you cannot be happy unless you love God, who made Heaven and Earth and man and all things. Love white men; love other tribes of black man; do not quarrel together; tell other tribes to love white men and to build good huts and wear clothes. Learn to speak English. If any man injures you, tell the protector and he will do you justice." Quite famously, in *The Island of Doctor Moreau*, Moreau has created what he calls "The Law" and the beast-people are told to chant this, and they do it as if it were a religious litany that they must go through again and again. "Not to go on all fours, that is the law; are we not men? Not to suck up drink, that is the law; are we not men? Not to drink flesh nor fish, that is the law; are we not men? Not to chase other men, that is the law; are we not men?" This is an amalgamation of the queen's birthday speech and the rhetoric of religion.

The answers to all of these questions are no, you are not men. And even if you were, men eat meat and fish and fight with each other and suck up water if that is the only way they can take a drink. This is a critique of colonialism, as well as a critique of misuse of science. But it's also more subtle because the story is told by Prendick, a man who strategically leaves things out, and it's told of a Doctor Moreau, a man who strategically leaves things out.

The story begins with an introduction by Prendick's nephew:

> On February the 1st, 1887, the *Lady Vain* was lost by collision with a derelict when about the latitude one degree south and longitude 107 degrees west. On January the 5th, 1888—that is eleven months and four days later—my uncle, Edward Prendick, a private gentleman, who certainly went aboard the *Lady Vain* in Callao, and who had been considered drowned, was picked up in latitude....

Et cetera, et cetera, et cetera. The language is the language of science; there's no emotion here. And, yet, his uncle is a private gentleman, like Wedderburn in "The Strange Orchid," he lives on someone else's labor. He owns—that's all he need do.

He goes to the island of Doctor Moreau, and on the island of Doctor Moreau he comes under the sway of the doctor. Language on this island is crucial. Moreau and Prendick both use it as a colonial tool. The way that Prendick gets to the idea is disembarking with M'ling, as M'ling is bringing cages of new animals in—it turns out, to be experimented upon. However, there's no way to leave the island, and

Prendick becomes an unwilling, at first, and then quite willing, guest of Moreau. He asks Moreau about his prior experiments, and he says, well, he was trying to create in the image of man. Of course, God created man in his image; Moreau is the god. "Did you always create men?" "Well, once I had a snake and I tried, but failed, with that." And we realize that this is a fallen world, not a paradise at all. "And then there was another time when I tried to model it not on a man, but—ah, yes," and then he breaks his concentration and changes the subject. In other words, Moreau, unwilling to say it, tried to create a woman for himself, but had decided that it didn't quite work out. They're unwilling to speak of themselves; we need to read more closely.

In the very first chapter of Prendick's narration, the manuscript his nephew has put before us, he talks about how he was originally picked up by this vessel that was making a special trip to Moreau's island, after the vessel on which he was, had been destroyed in collision. As you heard, he and two sailors were shipwrecked on a particular lifeboat. They were under the sun; it became pitiless:

> The water ended (that is, the fresh water they had with them) on the fourth day, and we were all ready thinking strange things and saying them with our eyes, but it was, I think, the sixth before Helmer gave voice to the thing we all had in mind. I remember our voices, dry and thin, so that we bent toward one another and spared our words. I stood out against it with all my might; was rather for scuttling the boat and perishing together among the sharks that followed us, but when Helmer said that, if his proposal was accepted, that we should have a drink, the sailor came around to him.

Now, we're not told what this thing that he won't say is, but we know what it is—it's cannibalism. They're going to kill one of them by lot and drink his blood to survive, but our narrator says, without ever saying what it is, that he won't participate. Now, the lot falls to the sailor, but the sailor decides he won't accept being slaughtered for the sake of the other two, or so Prendick says, and he and Helmer grapple with each other. Then we're told they fell upon the gun well and rolled overboard together. They sank like stones. And that's the last we hear of them, but fortunately enough, Prendick manages to go to the island or is picked up by another boat. Or does he?

Maybe, in fact, he's the last survivor of cannibalism. Why should we believe him? We know, for example, that he actually lies. We know that he lies because he, himself, tells us that after Moreau is killed, he goes to the beast-people and says, "Moreau is still watching us from above. He can still inflict pain upon you from above. You still must follow the law." He turns Moreau into a god so that he can use god as a religious institution that will, in fact, control the beast-people for his own safety. That's why the law says do not eat flesh or fish, are we not men? Because Moreau realizes that these beasts, leopards, for example, and bears and hyenas, which could easily kill him, would, if they were not convinced to behave differently.

These characters say more about themselves then they intend. Language, here, is the mark of being human; and that is, indeed, as it should be. Because, as it says, an animal may be ferocious and cunning enough, but it takes a real man to tell a lie, and that's what Prendick and Moreau do all the time. We need to come to understand them better. Here, I think, is one of the great lies and beautiful pieces of writing in the book. Moreau is dead. Montgomery has scuttled the boats so that Prendick cannot leave the island:

> A sudden convulsion of rage shook me. I was almost moved to batter his foolish head in as he lay there helpless at my feet. [He's been wounded, Montgomery has.] Then suddenly his hand moved so feebly, so pitifully, that my wrath vanished. He groaned and opened his eyes for a minute. I knelt beside him and raised his head. He opened his eyes again, staring silently at the dawn. And then they met mine; the lids fell. "Sorry," he said presently, with an effort. He seemed trying to think. "The last," he said, "the last of this silly universe, what a mess." I listened. His head fell helplessly to one side.

Now, you notice, of course, he had been holding—Prendick had been holding this head—Prendick is probably from the Latin *prehendere*, "to hold." If his head fell helplessly to one side, it's because Prendick let it go, but Prendick doesn't say that. "I thought some drink might revive him, but there was neither drink nor vessel in which to bring drink at hand." Notice the word "hand" coming up yet again. "He seemed suddenly heavier. My heart went cold. I bent down to his face, put my hand through the rent in his blouse. He was dead." I don't know about you, but when I'm in a strange place and there's a faucet running and I want a drink and there's no vessel at hand, I use my hand to drink. There was something at hand to help Montgomery, but Prendick wouldn't do it. I think, in fact, Prendick killed Montgomery and just doesn't want to say it.

What we see in the beast-people is the confusion of what is truly beastly and what is truly human. Is a dumb creature, in fact, stupider than we, or only silent in expressing his nature? Prendick first sees M'ling as a man, but then he comes to realize that M'ling is a primate that has been modified into a man. This accords perfectly with Freud's idea of what creates the fantastic in the uncanny. We see the familiar in an unfamiliar place; we take a metaphor and we make it literal. He threw his eye—he cast his eye—about the room. Prendick's misunderstanding shows a culpable European centrism.

When the novel ends, Prendick has been changed. He can no longer stand the company of humans, just as Gulliver could not, after having been with the Utopian Houyhnhms at the end of *Gulliver's Travels.* Earlier we see a march of people from the house of pain to the house of the beast-people, and the line says, "Moreau, Montgomery, myself, and M'ling went across the island." Um, um, um, um—Moreau, the god; Montgomery, the protector of the hill, his viceroy; myself, Prendick; and M'ling. Suddenly we know that M'ling is a manling. He is the transitional character between the animal and the human. M'ling is associated always with the beach, the place where the boats were burned, the place where they disembarked. The beach is always in literature—when it's a crucial setting—the zone of conflict between elementally contending forces. In *The Island of Doctor Moreau*, those forces are civilization and true empathetic civilization.

The question Wells here—and often—leaves us with is this: Shall we go toward the colonial or toward the respectful? Toward the egotistical or toward the social? Toward the isolated or toward the integrated? It is no surprise that it is he who is the first writer to popularize the use of the word "ecology." No progress can be made without the imagination of humans, but all humans must recognize that they, too, are subject to great forces beyond them; that, indeed, we are all talking animals.

Lecture Seven
Franz Kafka—Dashed Fantasies

Scope:

Franz Kafka, a frail Jew writing in German in Christian, Czech-speaking Prague, was triply alienated by a failure to achieve an intimate adult relationship, by being the deprecated Other, and by associating himself with a foreign culture. Yet in many ways, this precisely mirrors the widespread modern condition we have come to call *Kafkaesque*, struggling vainly against every sort of indifference to find a connection with a person, belief, or social institution that will support us. In such parables as "A Common Confusion," "An Old Manuscript," and "Before the Law," Kafka makes these failures poignantly clear. Nonetheless, in his masterpieces, including *The Metamorphosis* and "The Judgment," we see that his knowledge of existential failure led to artistic success. Still, reading "The Truth about Sancho Panza" and "A Hunger Artist," we can understand why Kafka (fortunately, unsuccessfully) ordered his unpublished manuscripts destroyed.

Outline

I. Franz Kafka (1883–1924) lived a triply alienated life.

   A. He was a frail, German-speaking Jew born in Christian Prague.

      1. Although German was often the language of Prague's intellectuals, they were all aware of being different from the Czech-speaking majority. For the Christian intellectuals, this difference often felt like a mark of superiority; for the non-Christian intellectuals, this difference often felt like a mark of Cain, privileged though shunned.

      2. Judaism originally mattered little to Kafka—except as a mark for others to use against him.

      3. In his later 20s, he was moved by Yiddish theater, became close friends with one of the actors, and began his serious study of Judaism. In other words, he came to his heritage through art, but that heritage, like his art, gave Kafka neither social justice nor personal happiness.

B. The term *Kafkaesque* has entered modern languages to indicate the implacable futility felt so commonly today amid the inhumanity of institutions in our industrialized world. The global currency of the term acknowledges that Kafka's writing epitomizes this alienated condition.

II. Kafka's shortest works, typically called parables, re-present his felt life transformed through the fantastic.

A. "A Common Confusion" is one of the greatest but most enigmatic short stories of the 20th century.

   1. Its structural truths emerge from subtle ambiguities of language, which we can see from the title itself and the very first sentence.

   2. Its psychological truths about individuality and perception emerge from the almost algebraic generality of its plot.

   3. Its social truths emerge from its ultimate allegorical critique of religion.

B. "An Old Manuscript" focuses on the psychological and the religious, suggesting the antiquity of the failure of social institutions to serve the needs of individuals.

C. "Before the Law" focuses on the psychological and the legal, suggesting the failure of modern social institutions to serve us any better in modern times.

III. In many of his masterpieces, Kafka, like Hoffmann, seems to use the fact of creating written art to imply the possibility of some salvation, even though Kafka's art is about the inevitability of loss.

A. *The Metamorphosis* (1915), which so famously begins with Gregor Samsa awakening to find he has become a gigantic insect, is a fairy tale set in the gritty modern world.

   1. Gregor's transformation, like the unwarranted success of Hansel and Gretel, supports the infantile fantasy known as the *illusion of central position*.

   2. Gregor needs to escape his condition as a traveling salesman. Even his name suggests his need to escape.

3. Gregor's own metamorphosis leads to metamorphoses for each member of his family.

4. Gregor becomes a pitiable Christ figure who, surprisingly, potentiates the resurrection of his sister.

B. "The Judgment," too, allegorizes Christianity to remind us of key moral issues.

1. The father's references to St. Petersburg suggest the old man's superiority to the young man.

2. The charwoman here, as in *The Metamorphosis*, serves to put the Christ figure in his failing place.

3. The compulsive plot suggests the implacability of destiny in the modern world.

IV. With such a worldview, it is not surprising that, despite creating works of enduring art, Kafka remained a man in despair.

A. "The Truth about Sancho Panza" is a Kafka parable suggesting that only those without aspirations can be made happy by literature.

B. "A Hunger Artist" is a Kafka parable suggesting that even a willingness to suffer cannot achieve permanently useful art.

1. It was sent to a publisher in 1923.

2. It appeared only after Kafka's death in 1924. Kafka's tuberculosis had made him, like Gregor, too difficult to feed, and like the Hunger Artist, he apparently died of starvation.

C. It is no wonder that Kafka asked that his unpublished manuscripts be burned at his death. It is also no wonder that his executor and friend, Max Brod—fortunately—defied him. Was this Kafka's ultimate ambiguous failure or the triumph of his imagination?

Essential Reading:

Kafka, Franz. *The Metamorphosis*, in *Collected Stories*.

Supplementary Reading:

Kafka, Franz. *Amerika*.

Kafka, Franz. *The Trial*.

Questions to Consider:

1. In what ways would you think Kafka's writing shows that he is or is not a religious person?

2. Was Max Brod right to disobey Kafka's will and have his manuscripts published?

Lecture Seven—Transcript
Franz Kafka—Dashed Fantasies

Franz Kafka, a frail Jew writing in German in Christian, Czech-speaking Prague, was triply alienated by a failure to achieve an intimate adult relationship, by being the deprecated other, and by associating himself with a foreign culture. Yet, in many ways, this precisely mirrors the wide-spread modern condition we have come to call Kafkaesque, struggling vainly against every sort of indifference to find a connection with a person, belief, or social institution that will support us. In parables such as "A Common Confusion," "An Old Manuscript," and "Before the Law," Kafka makes these failures poignantly clear. Nonetheless, in masterpieces such as *The Metamorphosis* and "The Judgment," we see that his knowledge of existential failure led to artistic success. Still, reading "The Truth about Sancho Panza" and "A Hunger Artist," we can understand why Kafka—fortunately unsuccessfully—ordered his unpublished manuscripts destroyed.

Franz Kafka, as I say, lived a triply alienated life. He was a frail German-speaking Jew born in Christian Prague. Although German was often the language of Prague's intellectuals, they were all aware of being different from the Czech-speaking majority. For the Christian intellectuals, this difference often felt like a mark of superiority, but for the non-Christian intellectuals, this difference often felt like a mark of Cain, privileged, though shunned.

Judaism originally mattered little to Kafka, except as a mark for others to use against him. In his later twenties, he was moved by Yiddish theater, became close friends with one of the actors, and began his serious study of Judaism. In other words, he came to his heritage through art, but that heritage, like his art, gave Kafka neither social justice nor personal happiness.

The term *Kafkaesque* has entered modern languages to indicate the implacable futility felt so commonly today, the inhumanity of institutions in our industrialized world. The global currency of the term acknowledges that Kafka's writing epitomizes this alienated condition.

Kafka's shortest works, typically called parables, re-present his felt-life, transformed through the fantastic. "A Common Confusion" is one of the greatest but most enigmatic short stories of the 20th

century. It begins, "A common experience resulting in a common confusion." Its structural truths, I think, emerge from subtle ambiguities of language, which we can see from the title itself and the very first sentence. In English, the word "a" really has two meanings. "A" can mean something drawn from a sample, "I have a book here in my hands;" or it can mean one, "I have a wife who is without peer." Common has, itself, a couple of meanings. It can mean something we see all over the place, as common as dirt; or it can mean something that is *déclassé*, he had a very common manner about him. Confusion has two meanings as well. The prime meaning is some sort of befuddlement, but etymologically it means to melt—fusion—together, confusion. When things melt together, you can't distinguish one from the other.

So, "A Common Confusion" actually is composed of words which are each ambiguous, that is, technically speaking, we can't decide which of the meanings they have. In fact, in the original German, the title is "Eine alltägliche Verwirrung." *Eine* has exactly the same two meanings in German that "a" has in English. *Alltägliche*, which is translated as "common," actually has three meanings in German. It means "every day;" it means "common" in the sense of every place; and it also means "trite." And *Verwirrung* means "befuddlement," but just as it comes to mean that, just as confusion comes to mean that in English by meaning to melt together, *Verwirrung* means thoroughly mixed together. So, in German, the title actually has 12 possible meanings, two times three times two.

The title itself is a common confusion, something shared between us. The story begins, "A common experience resulting in a common confusion." The word "experience" is, in German, *Vorfall*. That's not the only German word for "experience," but that's the one Kafka uses, and it does mean an occurrence. It means "that which befell us," but it also can mean "that which fell in front of us." That is, an impediment, something that kept us from moving forward. And, in rare instances, *Vorfall* has another meaning in German; it is what we call in English "an escapement". An escapement is a pivoted set of teeth that engage the teeth on a gear to prevent the gear from simply rotating. When you wind the spring of a clock, if you released the spring, the clock would simply unwind and we could not tell time. The *Vorfall* rocks back and forth to engage the teeth and release them, engage them and release them, marking off the time; in the case of this story, the time of our lives.

Kafka uses ambiguous language, technically ambiguous language, in order to let us see that the most common things stand for the most mythically, idealistically, important things. This story says, in its second sentence, "A has to transact important business with B in H." And he goes to H. He makes it there in ten minutes. Because he has to finish the business the next day, he travels again, this time he says, "feeling that all the surrounding circumstances,"—surrounding, going around one; circumstances, standing around one—again, multiplying the possible meanings. "All the surrounding circumstances seem to be the same, and yet it took ten hours to get to H." It took ten hours to get to H. In fact, when he arrives there, the housekeeper tells him that he must have passed B on the road on the way, because B was tired of waiting for him. Then A decides to return home to see B, and he says, without thinking of it all, without paying any particular attention to the fact, he returns home "practically in an instant."

What Kafka doesn't say explicitly, but what I think is quite clear here, is that when we think of time, when we think how hard it will be to go where we want to go, the time lengthens, and in this fantastic tale, the world's time lengthens around him. He leaves in the morning and doesn't arrive at H until evening. But when you don't think of it at all, time flashes in an instant, for all practically purposes, practically in an instant. Time, in other words, which seems to be one of the great externalities, in fact, is one of the great internalities. When A arrives home, he finds that B has been waiting for him upstairs in his own room. He goes up the stairs hoping to reach B and finish his business, but, we are told that he twists a sinew, he stumbles, and almost fainting with pain, incapable even of uttering a cry, only able to moan faintly in the darkness, he hears B—impossible to tell whether at a great distance or quite near him— stamping down the stairs in a violent rage and vanishing for good. And that's the end of the parable; A fails in his errand.

Yet that last phrase, "for good," has two meanings. "For good" can mean that he leaves forever and will no longer be in our lives. But there is in Christianity the so-called Doctrine of the Fortunate Fall. Why did God create us so that we would be tempted in the garden and we could be disobedient and we could incur original sin? And the answer to that is, in the Doctrine of the Fortunate Fall, by becoming sinners we now have the power, though we don't all seize it, to overcome our sins and to rise to be saints, even higher than the angels. In other words, God let us fall for our good. B comes down and goes past A "for good." Is this story of "A Common Confusion" about, perhaps, the confusion that we misunderstand the spiritual world with? Kafka sees a world in which spirit is often very, very badly served.

"An Old Manuscript" is another of his parables. This is a story in which the emperor withdraws when barbarians come down into the city. The barbarians even eat their own; they sleep with their own horses in the street. In order to keep the barbarians from depredating them, one of the shopkeepers brings out an ox, leaving it to the barbarians to slaughter. In fact, they eat it live, bearing their teeth into the ox alongside their carnivorous horses. The ox bellows pitifully, and the shopkeepers hide under their counters.

If you take a look at a Roman Catholic Church, or certainly a cathedral in Europe, you will often see a design that shows the 12 months of the year, and figured among them you will see four symbols—an angel, a lion, an ox, and an eagle. These four familiars stand in order for the Gospels according to Matthew, Mark, Luke, and John. The ox is the symbol of the Gospel according to Saint Luke, and it is, in fact, in Christian iconography, the symbol of great patience. The ox suffers because the tradesmen don't know how to deal with the emperor.

But the narrator says he thought he saw the emperor for a moment at a window, but he withdrew from it to look at the interior courtyard. God has kept the garden for himself; we are on our own. We live in a Kafkaesque world.

There is no old manuscript in the story called "The Old Manuscript." The story is the old manuscript. It's the human condition. We believe that someone will protect us. It's up to us; we are inadequate to the task. It's a grim, grim world.

In "Before the Law," a man presents himself for justice, but he gatekeeper will not allow him to enter unless certain things happen first. The man accomplishes each of these things, but when he finally reappears, he's told it's too late, now, to go before the law, and this door will never be opened again because it was meant only for you. The law is constructed to keep us from having justice.

Consistently in Kafka, what we have is the use of references to social institutions, be they law, be they language, be they religion. To show us that we think that we should be satisfied, supported, and made happy by them; but, in fact, we are not. In many of his masterpieces, Kafka, like Hoffmann, tries to use the fact of creating a written art, to imply the possibility of there being some salvation; although, in fact, Kafka's art is about the inevitability of loss.

In his, perhaps, most famous work, *The Metamorphosis*, Kafka begins with Gregor Samsa awakening with this line. "As Gregor Samsa awoke one morning from uneasy dreams, he found himself transformed in his bed into a gigantic insect." This is a fairy tale set in a gritty modern world. Why does he become an insect? He becomes an insect because, if we read between the lines, he wants to withdraw from human responsibility. We come to understand that he has been what's called a commercial traveler. That is, a salesman, scurrying here and there in order to create an income that can support his family. He wants to support his sister's music lessons. He wants to contribute to the rent. He's been told that the family needs the money.

Freud talks about infantile fantasies—infantile, meaning that they arise at the time when one is an infant; infant, meaning without speech. Freud's notion is that each of us comes to learn, as an infant, that when we bellow, the world will respond to us. We cry out and someone cleans our bottom; if that's not what we want, we cry more and they feed us. Eventually, we have what we would like, and we stop bellowing. This experience, which is our earliest interaction with the world, Freud suggests, leads to two psychological fantasies. One of these is called the "illusion of central position". For all I can tell, the world entirely is around me. The other is called the omnipotence of thought. If I want it, so it shall be.

Although these both grow out of infantile experience, they are, in fact, separate. Children reading fairy tales often see the omnipotence of thought carried out. Because the protagonist wants to succeed, the protagonist succeeds. For adults, we haven't quite given up these fantasies, but we view them perversely. If I were to say to you, "Tomorrow is supposed to be beautiful and I haven't had a chance to chat with you in ages; let's have a picnic," and you agreed that would be lovely. If the next day I called you and said, "I'm sorry. I woke up this morning and guess what? It's raining." You might say,

"Wouldn't you know it." But if I called you and said, "Guess what? It is a beautiful day, as predicted," you wouldn't say, "Wouldn't you know it?" You'd say, "Oh, good. Thank goodness." In other words, as adults, we still believe that the world responds to us, except we believe that it does the opposite of what we want. We don't have omnipotent thoughts, but we still may feel the illusion of central position. Of course, we may not. We may believe that the weather is bad or good for some other reason entirely. Well, the weather is beautiful because it is Easter Sunday, and God always makes it beautiful on Easter Sunday.

These illusions, in fact, are taken up by all fairy tales and modified in adult fairy tales. So, Gregor, wanting unconsciously—I'm sure, like Gretel who wanted to displace her mother in "Hansel and Gretel"—Gregor not wanting to be a commercial traveler anymore, thinking of himself as some mere insect in the absolutely unending and trivial world of retail economy, wishes that he could be out of it, and he does. You notice he does not wake up horrified; he just wakes up.

The transformation is unwarranted, but it supports this fantasy. He needs to escape his condition as a traveling salesman. Even his name suggests this need. Gregor comes from Gregory; it's just like the English Gregory, and it may mean "watchman", the person who watches the flock. Gregor comes from the Latin *grex*, meaning flock, and it leads to words such as egregious—something that is outside of the flock. Gregor is a watchman. He should be taking care of the family. Samsa, though, that's a strange word. Now, you need to know that beginning with the Grimm brothers, the Germans had a strong interest in pursuing research in antique religions and cultures, and this included studying Indian religion.

Nirvana is that famous crossing over from the unending cycle of birth and death and rebirth to a place of peace and quiet. Every English speaker knows the word nirvana. The alternative to nirvana, that cycle of birth, death, and rebirth, is *samsara*. Gregor Samsa is caught in this cycle and wants out, although he does not admit it to himself. His psychology brings about this metamorphosis, and his metamorphosis brings bout metamorphoses for every other member of his family. His sister, who had just been practicing her violin, becomes a milliner's clerk; his mother begins to become a seamstress, making other people's undergarments; and the father, in a demonstration of how the Samsa family relates to the economy, takes a job as a bank guard, in uniform guarding other people's money, but bringing home some money for himself. In other words, these people have all been changed in response to Gregor's change, and only then do we discover that the father actually had the money all along. He didn't need to have Gregor support the family.

There is a crucial moment when Gregor as insect—who's fed only by his sister who brings food into his room—begins to come out of the room because he hears music. The father becomes angry and tries to push him back and heaves an apple at him, which catches in his back—like original sin—and festers there. If you read the details carefully, you discover that his transformation occurred on Christmas Day, and he finally died on what we realize is Easter.

As Gregor dies, his sister rises. The viewpoint of the story changes, and Gregor's sister Greta—G and G—Gregor has gone down, Greta has gone up. Greta is taken out to the park for a picnic with her parents. In the last line says that in the spring, "she stood up in the burgeoning spring time and stretched her young legs." Gregor becomes a self-sacrificing character to bring happiness to the world, not by empowering someone, but simply by moving out of the way, and they, then, can become better on their own. Good for them, not good for Gregor.

To make money, in fact, the family has brought in three boarders and these three boarders—maybe they are wisemen—demand the use of the kitchen. They see Gregor and decide they can't stay anymore, and they storm out. When Gregor finally dies, a charwoman, we are told, is the only one who will deal with the body. Later, when the family comes back from services, they ask about the body, and she says, "Oh, don't worry. I've taken care of that." There's no explanation of how she took care of it. However, just before the family comes back, we're told that the butcher boy goes up the stairs as the three boarders go down the stairs. He passes them, and on his head he is carrying a tray full of fresh sausages to deliver, clearly, to the people that live in the apartment building. Obviously, what the charwoman has done is given this body to the butcher's delivery boy so that the body of Gregor, like the body of Christ, will be made into sausage—that's what the modern economic world does—and is fed to the masses.

Now, this perverse kind of Christ imagery is not meant to suggest that Christianity is good or bad. It's meant to suggest that we are pitifully on our own, and the institutions that would support us, in fact, consume us. This runs through much of Kafka's work.

In "The Judgment," another one of his great works, we have a character who claims to be having correspondence with a friend of his in St. Petersburg. This character, as far as we can see, mostly takes care of his frail, old father; so frail that he has to pick him up in his own arms and put him into bed and carry him away to the chamber pot, and so on. But, strangely, the father begins to criticize, and then insult the son. "You have a friend in St. Petersburg? I have a friend in St. Petersburg." Saint Peter's burg, the city of Saint Peter—Peter, the rock on which I will build my Church, Rome, The Vatican—what old man has a friend in St. Petersburg? This old man in "The Judgment" becomes a god-like figure. He stands up and virtually touches his head against the ceiling of the room, and he condemns his son to death. The son goes out of the house. He walks across a bridge, and he jumps over into the stream of traffic. Again, what we see is that the old gods do not support us. The belief that we can find some connection to them through institutions fails us, and the failure is not of the old parabolic, out-in-the-desert-with-the-burning-bush failure, but a failure brought about by being engaged implacably in modern, industrial, technological society. A traveling salesman, a stream of traffic—these are images of why we are all fundamentally alienated—why we live in a Kafkaesque world. Is there no way out of this?

Well, in another one of his shorter parables called "The Truth about Sancho Panza," Kafka gives us an interesting possibility. Sancho Panza, you will remember, is the fat—in fact, Sancho Panza in Spanish dialect means wide belly—Sancho Panza is a fat, happy lower-class character who tags along with Don Quixote as Don Quixote, a great fantasist himself—he sees giants where we know there are only windmills—sets out to right the wrongs. Although the wrongs he sees are often imagined in their details, the world of Don Quixote, indeed, has many wrongs that need righting.

Sancho Panza follows him through *Don Quixote*, one of the great novels of western culture. "The Truth about Sancho Panza" begins thus:

Without making any boast of it, Sancho Panza succeeded in the course of years, by feeding him a great number of romances of chivalry and adventure, in the evening and the night hours, and so diverting from himself his demon, whom he later called Don Quixote, that this demon set out....

And Sancho Panza follows his own demon that is to say, his own spirit, which he has creating by diverting his own spirit with Romance, with excitement, with imagination. Then, a free man, no longer having his demon within him, Sancho Panza philosophically followed Don Quixote on his crusades—perhaps out of a sense of responsibility—and had of them a great and edifying entertainment to the end of his days. That has a much happier sound than most of Kafka's writing. But we need to think more deeply. The only reason Sancho Panza finds the contemplation of Don Quixote great and edifying is because Sancho Panza demands nothing back from the world but to be able to watch someone else having an adventure. Sancho Panza is disengaged. Art can only save us if we don't care to be in the world.

Once upon a time there was actually, in reality, something called a "hunger artist." These were people who made livings by being in side shows for example, by being on public display, and simply not eating. Sometimes they were allowed to drink, sometimes they weren't, but people would watch see how long they could survive without eating.

Kafka has a story called "A Hunger Artist," and in Kafka's story the man at first thinks, "I'm a great artist," then, as he persists in not eating and not dying, but becoming thinner and thinner, the public interest in him wanes. Eventually, the exhibitor removes him and puts in his place a panther who stalks angrily back and forth—that the public enjoys—but the hunger artist withers away and dies without anyone even noticing that he is gone.

Kafka died of tuberculosis, which he suffered from most of his relatively short life. He never tried to publish most of his stories. He submitted "The Hunger Artist" for publication in 1923, then he died, and it was published in 1924. Kafka's tuberculosis had made him, like Gregor Samsa, too difficult to feed, and probably, then, like the hunger artist, he died of starvation. It is no wonder that Kafka asked that his unpublished manuscripts be burned at his death, because art did not offer consolation and did not, for him, represent triumph. Yet the power of these parables is so great that it is no wonder that his friend and executor, Max Brod, fortunately, defied him. Was this Kafka's ultimate ambiguous failure, the publication of these manuscripts he did not want published? Or was it the triumph of his imagination?

Lecture Eight
Woolf—Fantastic Feminism & Periods of Art

Scope:

Although Virginia Woolf's *Orlando* has been slighted as lightweight in comparison to such works as *To the Lighthouse*, which critics use to rank her among the founding giants of Modernism, this brave fantasy is a subversive, satiric masterpiece. Emily Dickinson's poems, often unacknowledged fantasies, such as "I heard a fly buzz when I died," reflect the socially imposed crippling of volition in women. Charlotte Perkins Gilman's classic story "The Yellow Wall-Paper" explores the origins of some madness in gender-based repression. Woolf, who died a suicide, addressed these conditions in famous essays, including *A Room of One's Own*, and in *Orlando*, in which the title character shifts sex and lives his/her young adulthood over four centuries. In its focus on the role of writing to free a woman's—or person's—thoughts and in its progressive modulation of style, *Orlando* also demonstrates how literary periods themselves reflect humanity's fantastically shifting understanding of Nature.

Outline

I. Virginia Stephen Woolf (1882–1941) is famous as a founder of literary Modernism and as a powerful voice for feminism.

    A. Virginia Woolf was one of the Bloomsbury group of London-based intellectuals that included Vanessa Stephen Bell (artist), Clive Bell (critic), John Maynard Keynes (economist), E. M. Forster (novelist and critic), Roger Fry (critic who assembled the First Postimpressionist Exhibition, 1910), and Lytton Strachey (biographer of *The Eminent Victorians*, 1918).

    B. With Leonard Woolf, Virginia established the Hogarth Press, which issued *The Standard Edition of the Works of Sigmund Freud*, edited by James Strachey, and brought modern psychoanalytic theory to the English-speaking world, including its avant-garde artists and writers.

    C. Woolf's serious, superb, psychologically subtle realistic novels include *To the Lighthouse* and *Mrs. Dalloway.*

D. Woolf's powerful feminist essay, *A Room of One's Own* (1929), argues for the necessity of security and independence for anyone's self-realization.

E. Many great women writers have struggled with the challenge of social repression of themselves and their imaginations, a condition that can split the self.

    1. Emily Dickinson (1830–1886), living a spinster's life in Amherst, Massachusetts, exploited the cadences of hymns to explore the conditions of her life in fantastic poems, such as "Because I could not stop for death" and "I heard a fly buzz when I died."

    2. In the classic short story called "The Yellow Wall-Paper" (1892) by Charlotte Perkins Gilman (1860–1935), a sexist, loving husband fatally attempts to repress his wife's imagination.

    3. Virginia Woolf—who always suffered a crisis of sapped imagination whenever she finished writing a major work, despite a supportive social group—finally died a suicide.

II. *Orlando* (1928) was well received by the public but thought lightweight by the critics.

A. The title character of this comic, fictional biography begins at 16 in the reign of Elizabeth I, later metamorphoses from male to female with almost no comment, and is in her early 30s at the book's end in the 20th century.

B. The book has been called a love letter from Woolf to its dedicatee, Vita Sackville-West, an object of Woolf's erotic attraction in life.

C. The book includes a delightful love story but offers much more than that.

    1. From the first pages, the book explores issues of gender in social expectations about violence, clothing, property, and independence.

    2. Stylistically superb satires address many targets, for example, doctors.

    3. Woolf's critique of biographies, such as her own father's famous *Dictionary of National Biography*, reflects her Kafkaesque understanding of time.

III. Literary periodization silently underlies *Orlando*'s progress in style and plot.

    A. Writing is an essential element within the novel.

        1. The novel has many self-reflexive moments, in which the work forces us to recognize it as art. Ironically, self-reflexivity always makes a reality claim for the work of art, no matter how fantastic that work may be.

        2. Orlando meets many writers and struggles herself to write successfully.

        3. Only after passing through much experience and many periods does Orlando succeed.

    B. A literary period is a set of shared, culturally dominant beliefs and values.

    C. Each literary period includes a characteristic understanding of Nature.

        1. In the Classical period, Nature defines us.

        2. In the Middle Ages, Nature is God's harsh book.

        3. In the Renaissance, Nature is to be exploited.

        4. In the Enlightenment, Nature is to be understood and manipulated.

        5. In the Romantic period, Nature is a source of virtue.

        6. In the Victorian period, Nature is an economic resource.

        7. In the Modernist period, Nature is alien from humanity.

        8. In the Postmodern period, Nature is a phenomenological construct, that is, an intensional act of consciousness.

    D. *Orlando* unfolds historically and stylistically from the Renaissance to the Modern period, although the continuing bass line to this melodic modulation is the Enlightenment style of Laurence Sterne in *Tristram Shandy* (1759–1767).

IV. In *Orlando*, vacillation finally subsumes the Enlightenment's balanced antitheses. The heroine thus achieves an integrity that allows her to embrace Nature on an equal footing.

    A. Vacillation characterizes the book's style.

B. Vacillation is reflected in the plot, with its silent acceptance of violations of the rules of gender and chronology.

C. Vacillation supports the productive androgyny needed for Orlando's marriage.

D. Having achieved integration, *Orlando* culminates in three parallel ways.

  1. The fiction ends on the day of the book's real publication, thus merging fiction and fact.

  2. Orlando's writing is honored, and she bears a son. Her earned integrity allows her biological and imaginative offspring freedom in a man's world.

  3. The final ambiguity of a "wild goose," as with all true fantasies, is never resolved. It persists, urging us to consider the nature of reality.

Essential Reading:

Woolf, Virginia. *Orlando*.

Supplementary Reading:

Woolf, Virginia. *A Room of One's Own*.

Woolf, Virginia. "Mr. Bennett and Mrs. Brown," in *The Virginia Woolf Reader*.

Questions to Consider:

1. Woolf, like Kafka, has a main character react dispassionately to a fantastic metamorphosis. How do those reactions influence your sense of connection with each of those characters?

2. In what ways does the device of allowing Orlando an extended life enrich or impoverish your ability to take this story seriously?

Lecture Eight—Transcript
Woolf—Fantastic Feminism & Periods of Art

Although Virginia Woolf's *Orlando* has been slighted as lightweight in comparison to works such as *To the Lighthouse*, which critics use to rank her among the founding giants of Modernism, this brave fantasy, *Orlando,* is a subversive, satiric masterpiece. Emily Dickinson's poems, often unacknowledged fantasies such as "I heard a fly buzz when I died," reflect the socially imposed crippling of volition in women. Charlotte Perkins Gilman's classic story "The Yellow Wall-Paper" explores the origins of some madness in gender-based repression. Woolf, who died a suicide, addressed these conditions in famous essays such as "A Room of One's Own" and in *Orlando* in which the title character shifts sex and lives his/her young adulthood over four centuries. In its focus on the role of writing to free a woman—or person—mentally, and in its progressive modulation of style, *Orlando* also demonstrates how literary periods themselves reflect humanity's fantastically shifting understanding of nature.

Virginia Stephen Woolf is famous as a founder of literary Modernism, and is a powerful voice for feminism. Virginia Woolf was one of the Bloomsbury Group of London-based intellectuals who lived in the Bloomsbury area. They included Vanessa Stephen Bell, Virginia's sister, a famous artist; Clive Bell, Vanessa's husband, a famous critic; John Maynard Keynes, one of the most influential economists of the 20th century; E. M. Forster, a towering novelist and a significant critic; Roger Fry, the art critic who assembled the first post-Impressionist exhibition in 1910; and Lytton Strachey, the biography of the eminent Victorians, for example; and Leonard Woolf, Virginia's husband, with whom she established the Hogarth Press, which, in turn—among its other pioneering publications—issued what is now called "The Standard Edition of the Works of Sigmund Freud," edited by James Strachey, Lytton's brother, and thus brought modern psychoanalytic theory to the English-speaking world, including its *avant-guard* arts and writers, a whole group of whom were, in fact, the Bloomsbury folk of whom Virginia was a leading member.

Woolf's serious, superb, psychologically subtle, realistic novels include *To the Lighthouse* and *Mrs. Dalloway.* Both works explore, from the woman's viewpoint, what it means to be, in a sense, privileged by being in the middle class, and yet constrained by not having the freedom that the middle class allows clearly to its men. Woolf's powerful feminist essay, *A Room of One's Own* argues for the necessity of security and independence for anyone's self-realization. Many great women writers have struggled with the challenge of social repression of themselves and of their imaginations, a condition that can split the self. Emily Dickenson, an American living a spinster's life near Amherst, Massachusetts, exploited the cadences of hymns to explore the conditions of her life in fantastic poems such as "Because I could not stop for death" and "I heard a fly buzz when I died." Let's take a look at the first:

> Because I could not stop for death, he kindly stopped for me.
> The carriage held but just ourselves and immortality.

That word, immortality, is, I think, quite telling. We are mortals; we must die. For us to become immortals, this poem suggests, we must die:

> We slowly drove, he knew no haste, and I had put away
> my labor and my leisure too, for his civility.
> We passed the school where children strove at recess, in the ring;
> we passed the fields of gazing grain, we passed the setting sun.

These are images of growth and time passing; but, in the carriage with death, the speaker passes, passing.

> Or, rather, he (the sun) passed us. The dews grew quivering and chill,
> and only gossamer my gown, my tippet only tulle.
> We paused before a house that seemed a swelling of the ground.
> The roof was scarcely visible, the cornice but a mound.

Is this the hill of Calvary on which Jesus died? Or was this simply anyone's grave?

> Since then 'tis centuries, and yet each feels shorter than the day
> I first surmised the horses' heads were toward eternity.

This is a Fantasy. It's being narrated centuries after the death of the viewpoint character; a woman, we know, from her gown and her tippet, who is being taken away by death alone, only thus to achieve immortality.

Woolf understood that for a woman to have true power, she needed economic power; she needed security. When this didn't happen, we see as in a work such as "The Yellow Wall-Paper" that a woman's self can be divided. In this classic short story by the American, Charlotte Perkins Gilman, the viewpoint is that of the woman who is put up in a nursery, locked away for a rest cure, because her husband, a physician, has decided she's become too nervous—they word "hysteria" comes from the Greek word for womb. The belief was that women, subject to their hormonal changes, were somehow less sane, less grounded, less trustworthy than men. He infantilizes her by forcing her to rest in a locked nursery. As her narration goes on, she begins to see things moving in the wallpaper. We understand, of course, that nothing is really moving in the wallpaper; what we understand is that she is projecting the movement into the wallpaper, and she finally projects a rope that's hanging there, and she projects the shadow of a head being placed inside the noose. The last lines of the story show the noose swinging in the nursery. Not to have one's self is fatal; to imagine one's self trapped is terrible; but to imagine one's self released is glorious. That brings us to *Orlando*.

Virginia Woolf, herself, suffered a crisis of imagination at the completion of every one of her works. We know that she attempted suicide at least two times before the ultimately successful suicide that ended her life, each time shortly after the completion of a work of fiction. She felt herself, it seems, satisfied, taken up, controlled, able to make a world of her own while she wrote, but when that world was done and put aside, she had nothing to live for. In that sense, she's like Poe's and Hoffmann's characters who use writing itself as a way of exercising their imaginations and controlling their positions in the world.

In *Orlando*, the title character, in fact, writes and writes and writes, and all of the elaborate writings that the character produces come to nothing, save for one brief, elegant work called, "The Oak Tree." Many writers are encountered in *Orlando*, and Orlando himself—or I should say herself—or I should say both because Orlando begins male and turns into a female and finished the book female—many writers come into Orlando's life, famous writers from different periods of literary history, including Stern and Pope and so on, yet writing has saved none of them.

Orlando was well received by the public, but they thought it lightweight. I think they're mistaken. The title character begins at the age of 16, during the reign of Queen Elizabeth I, and when he metamorphoses into a female, he simply awakens one morning, looks in the mirror, and notices that he's female, and carries on with as little comment about the significance of the change as Gregor Samsa makes when he awakens one morning to discover that he's become a gigantic insect. The book ends in the 1920's of the 20th century, Orlando having reached the age of the mid-30s—in other words, 16 years over nearly 4 centuries.

The book has been called a love letter from Woolf to its dedicatee, Vita Sackville-West, who was an object of Woolf's erotic attraction throughout her life. It's clear that she—that is, Virginia—and Leonard had a powerful, strong, mutually supportive marriage. When there were times of trouble for either, each came to the other. But it seems to have been one without Eros, and it seems that Virginia's attraction to women was, if ever attempted, not successfully or satisfactorily consummated. Nonetheless, in *Orlando*, love finds a way. It is, in fact, a delightful story, but it is much more than that.

From its very first pages, the book explores issues of gender and social expectations about violence, clothing, property, and personal independence:

> He—for there could be no doubt of his sex, though the fashion of the time did something to disguise it—was in the act of slicing at the head of a Moor which swung from the rafters. It was the color of an odd football, and more or less the shape of one, save for the shrunken cheeks….

The very beginning of this novel shows Orlando a high-born young man practicing his military maneuvers using, horribly, as his target, the head of a darker-skinned enemy, a non-Christian enemy, removed in battle, we're told, either by his father or his grandfather. Later on, when Orlando changes, we realize that he has always been unfit to be this kind of active individual; and, in a sense, the metamorphosis to female Orlando may simply be a carrying out of the psychological state that existed previously, as Gregor the traveling salesman becomes the cockroach in the economic world.

Orlando is full of self-reflexivity—moments when the book talks about itself. We see this when the book begins to make its own style obtrusive. For example, here is a satire, quite typical, of doctors. Orlando has been under the weather:

> But the doctors were hardly wiser then than they are now. And after prescribing rest and exercise, starvation and nourishment, society and solitude, that he should lie in bed all day and ride 40 miles between lunch and dinner, together with the usual sedatives and irritants, diversified, as the fancy took them, with possets of newts' slobber on rising, and drafts of peacock's gall on going to bed, they left him to himself and gave it as their opinion that he had been asleep for a week.

In other words, nothing is gained, but the language goes back and forth, back and forth, vacillating between opposites—sleep and rest, starvation and nourishment—and we come to realize that the language itself is obtrusive. It makes us ask, "Well, isn't his nothing but a story?" Indeed, the doctors could have had him ride any distance, but they had him ride 40 miles—40 days in the wilderness, 40 years in the desert, 40 days of rain—in the Bible the classic number of death and rebirth. The doctors have him ride 40 miles, which maybe will bring him back to life. And, indeed, after seven days of sleep, a week later, he's brought back to life.

When a work calls attention to itself as a work of art, when it is self-reflexive, it says, "Look at me. I'm a work of art." In one sense it says, "I'm nothing but a work of art." But, in another sense, it claims a kind of reality for itself. It says, "I _am_ the work of art," and that has a reality and it needs to be listened to.

Woolf critiques other kinds of works of art and other ways of imagining the world. For example, she points out that the way in which human beings measure time is quite formally subject to our own imaginations. The true length of a person's life, whatever the _Dictionary of National Biography_ might say, is always a matter of dispute. "Indeed, it is a difficult business this timekeeping. Nothing more quickly disorders it than contact with any of the arts." Now, this idea that the length of time that seems to pass comes from the arts really tells us that it's the imagination, and this we've seen, of course, back in Kafka's story, "A Common Confusion." "When I didn't think about traveling, I made the journey practically in a second." What makes this particular passage a little bit more enjoyable for those in the know is that the *Dictionary of National Biography*, that great monument to the importance of English people, was founded by an editor named Leslie Stephen, Virginia Stephen Woolf's father. This book is a way of saying to her father, there are other kinds of biographies, perhaps truer kinds of biographies.

In this biography, what we have is a movement of a character from the Elizabethan period through to the 20th century. This travel encompasses many different literary periods. Since writing is an essential element within the novel, one would expect that this ironic use of self-reflexivity would make us aware of the literary periods.

What is a literary period? A literary period is a shared set of dominant beliefs and values. When I say dominant, I mean to imply that most people most of the time have these feelings. They share these beliefs; they share these values. A literary period doesn't begin—oh, hey, it's Thursday, it's the Renaissance now. That doesn't happen. What does happen is that over time people shift their understandings of things. I would like to suggest that one way to understand what is going on in this shift of dominant beliefs and values is to ask what is the modal relationship that people have at a given period to nature.

In the Classical period, nature defines us. Remember when we talked about Poe's, "The Bells," I mentioned that Hesiod had talked of the Golden, Silver, Bronze, and Iron Ages. The Golden Age was the age of gods. We, in the Iron Age, are mere fallen humans. The natural world around us defines us.

In the Middle Ages, nature was seen as God's harsh book. We live in a fallen state; we are all children with original sin. What kind of world must we make our way? In the world—post-garden—of labor, childbirth, and death.

In the Renaissance, the Age of Exploration, nature is there to be exploited, and that exploitive notion is, I think, clear on the first pages of *Orlando,* when the white, male, Christian Englishman feels that it is appropriate to hone his skills by bashing at the head of someone else.

In the Enlightenment, nature is to be understood and manipulated. We have thesis-antithesis. A famous line would be Pope's, from

"The Essay on Criticism:" "Author's are partial to their wit, it is true, but are not critics to their judgment, too." Two lines, perfect rhyme, each line divided in half, and so on.

In the Romantic period, nature is seen as a source of virtue. We think, for instance, of Rousseau's idea that contact with nature will make us nobler. In the Victorian period, nature is an economic resource.

In the Modernist period, the period of Virginia Woolf, nature is fundamentally alien from humanity. It's out there and we have to understand what it is.

In the Postmodern period, nature is a phenomenological construct. Let me explain what this means. According to Husserl, the founder of phenomenology, a phenomenon is an intensional act of consciousness; intensional, S-I-O-N-A-L, not T-I-O-N-A-L. It is intensional—opposite of extensional—an intensional act of consciousness that limits all of the possible things we can notice and says, "Ah, this constitutes a phenomenon."

When did World War II begin? On a day? In a year? In a decade? Did it being in 1939 when the Germans marched into Poland, or, for Americans, did it begin in 1941 when Pearl Harbor was bombed? A war is a phenomenon; it's constructed by our minds. In the Postmodernist period, nature is a phenomenological construct. *Orlando*, the book, unfolds historically, stylistically changing as it goes from the Renaissance to the Modern period. Although, there is—to use a musical metaphor—a continuing bass line to this modulation, to this stylistic modulation, and that baseline is the Enlightenment style—that is, the balance and antitheses—not simply of Pope, but particularly of Laurence Sterne, whose book *Tristram Shandy* was published, in parts, between 1759 and 1767, and became, perhaps, the single best-selling new fiction of a 20- or 30-year period. That novel is characterized by a very, very special style. Let me exemplify. Here is how it begins:

> I wish either my mother or my father or, indeed, both of them, as they were in duty both equally bound to it, had minded what they were about when they begot me, had they truly considered how much depended upon what they were then doing, that not only the production of a rational being was concerned in it, but that possibly the happy formation

and the temperature of his body, perhaps his genius, and the very cast of his mind—and, for ought they knew to the contrary, even the fortunes of his whole house might take their turns from the humors and dispositions, which were then uppermost, had they duly considered and weighted all this…I am verily persuaded I should have made a quite different figure in the world from that in which the reader is likely to see me.

That is one long sentence, with all of its pieces balanced and within each piece other pieces balance, but notice the glorious solecism, it's a sentence that begins with "I wish either my mother or my father" and ends with "me." It goes nowhere. It stays within the self. It's a matter of reflecting the self.

Orlando is a book about the self. It's a book that also uses this stylistic idea of vacillation. Laurence Sterne is actually a character in *Orlando*. Vacillation characterizes the style of the novel, and it also characterizes the content of the novel.

> Anyone moderately familiar with the rigours of composition [of writing, that is] will not need to be told the story in detail; how he wrote and [how] it seemed good; read it and seemed vile; corrected and tore it up; cut out; put in; was in ecstasy; in despair; had his good nights and bad mornings; snatched at ideas and lost them; saw his book claimed before him and it vanished; acted his people's parts as he ate; mouthed them as we walked; now cried, now laughed; vacillated between this style and that; now preferred the heroic and pompous; next plain and simple; now the vales of Tempe; then the fields of Kent or Cornwall; and could not decide whether he was the divinest genius or the greatest fool in the world.

That's Orlando trying to write.

Now, vacillation is what he does. Vacillation is a very interesting concept, particularly psychologically. We have two terms that refer to people who are of more than one gender—I guess I should say, since we mean to speak of biology here rather than of social construction, more than one sex. One term is "hermaphroditic." A hermaphrodite, an individual who has physical characteristics both of the male and the female, is traditionally thought of as monstrous.

There's some terrible fusion of things that should not go together. The "androgyne," however—an individual who has the characteristics both of the male and of the female, in an integrated whole—represents not the monstrous, but the fulfilled. In Plato's myth of "The Origin of Love," he speaks of the fact that once upon a time there were perfect two-faced spherical beings which the gods so envied that they cut them in half, tied them off—hence, our belly buttons—loosed them on the world, and they spent the rest of their lives looking to have union with the other half. Some halves were male of a two male half, some where female, and some were male and female. Whatever you were drawn toward, that union is perfection. While hermaphrodism is monstrosity, androgyny is perfection.

And, it seems to me what *Orlando* does—the book that is—is to create a character who moves from one sex to the other, having always the characteristics of both, writes in a way that vacillates back and forth in order finally to arrange for a fulfillment that represents a new kind of wholeness.

The book ends in a productive marriage with a character named Shel. When Shel and Orlando first meet each other, they speak rapidly, "Do you this? Do you that? Do you this? Do you that?" And after you can see that they are really coming together emotionally, suddenly Shel looks at Orlando and says, "Why, you're a woman. I thought you were a man." And Orlando looks at Shel and says, "Why, you're a man, and I thought you were a woman." They had gone beyond sex, in vacillating through the different ways of communicating, and at that point the text says, "And nothing more needed to be said." There's a blank in the page, and it says they got up; in fact, at this point they are married. Later Shel goes off following the wind to do his adventures, and ultimately Orlando gives birth. It happens magically, the way it does for Rapunzel. We just have to know that the right people have come together. The ending, in which she gives birth, I think is wonderful. She gives birth exactly on the last day on which the book is narrated. The last day on which the book is narrated is also the day in which she knows that she has won an important literary prize for "The Oak Tree." It is also the day when, in reality, *Orlando* was published.

So, the creating of a child, the creating of a marriage, the creating of a book within the book, and the creating of the book itself are all ways to function to make something that has real value—in fact, economic value—in the real world.

Now, that particular book that is published is the one we hold, but the way the book ends is, I think, something that we should hold in our minds. As Shelmerdine—that's his full name—as Shelmerdine, now grown to be a fine captain, hale, fresh colored and alert, leapt to the ground from a hot air balloon that he used to come back to Orlando at the very end, there sprang up over his head a single wild bird. "It is the goose," Orlando cried, "the wild goose," and the twelfth stroke of midnight sounded—the twelfth stroke of midnight, Thursday the 11th of October, 1928—the day of publication of the book.

Orlando looks up and sees the wild goose. What's a wild goose? I think we all know. We chase after them as Shel chases for adventure. The very phrase, "a wild goose chase" is one that connotes going after something that can never be found, yet perhaps it can be found for Orlando. Orlando began as a man, and as a woman Orlando loses property, loses power—all things devolve from Orlando because women have to depend upon men—but, over the course of centuries, over the changes through literary periods, Orlando manages to make her way, and when she finally has come to feel centered enough within herself that her own sexuality becomes merely a detail, not a defining characteristic, she is able to merge with another individual who feels the same, and at that point, she is able to give birth. The child that Orlando is able to create is a male, because still in 1928, only a male would be able, like her book, to go out into society and succeed on his own. But we, who have been blessed with contact with her imagination, can close the book and have our own wild goose chase. We can have imagination while she has silence.

Lecture Nine
Robbe-Grillet—Experimental Fiction & Myth

Scope:

The publication of Alain Robbe-Grillet's *The Erasers* motivated the creation of the term the *New Novel*. On first reading, it is a detective story pushed to the condition of true fantasy. Its radical style, Robbe-Grillet claimed, has important epistemological consequences and, in that way, is both a fantastic development of Émile Zola's idea of the *experimental novel* and the fulfillment of Roland Barthes' prediction about the evolution of writing. On closer examination, the novel also reveals itself as a reworking of the materials of the Oedipus myth as the structural anthropologist Claude Lévi-Strauss understood it and as a critical reexamination of Freudian ideas about psychological fantasy. Indeed, for a clever minority of readers or re-readers, there is a last fantastic trick that converts this apparently ambiguous detective novel into a stable work of aesthetic didacticism.

Outline

I.   For most people, on first reading, *The Erasers* (1953), by Alain Robbe-Grillet (1922–), seems to be a fantastic, compelling, but deeply confusing detective novel. Yet because of what close reading and re-reading reveal, it had huge critical and popular success and even led to the creation of a new critical term, the *New Novel*.

   A. *The Erasers* is told primarily from the viewpoint of a detective, Wallas, sent to a provincial town to solve a murder.

      1. Many of his observations are less obviously reflective of gathering clues about this murder than of inquiries into his own sense of reality. What should he make of coincidences? Can anything significant be read in the pictures he thinks he sees in random assemblages of flotsam on stagnant canal water?

      2. Much of what is reported in the novel, such as the behavior of the café manager or of the riddling drunkard, seems irrelevant to solving the crime.

     3. Astonishingly, in the penultimate regular chapter, Wallas himself suddenly seems to kill the man whose murder he had been sent to solve.

     4. At the very end, neither we nor the detective know who truly killed Dupont or how to understand reality.

  B. The story is told in a relentlessly meticulous, flat style that seems cinematic.

     1. Like a dogged detective, the text pays enormous attention to superficial detail, as in the famous description of a tomato slice.

     2. The novel's movements from one passage to another often mimic tracking, panning, and montage techniques from film.

II. *The Erasers* was received at publication not only as a novel but as a cultural experiment.

  A. The term *experimental novel* goes back to Émile Zola (1840–1902).

     1. In such works as *Germinal* (1885), Zola sought to represent society in a believable way, to set characters and social forces in motion, and then to see what they would do.

     2. This served both Zola's artistic and political ends.

  B. Roland Barthes (1915–1980), in *Writing Degree Zero* (1953), studied the evolution of French narrative prose.

     1. He was able to place Zola within an evolutionary pattern based on Zola's style.

     2. Barthes saw the evolution of style as pointed in a specific direction. Barthes' theory seemed to be confirmed by *The Erasers*. However, the theory did not account for the novel's contents.

  C. At about the same time, Claude Lévi-Strauss (1908–) was publishing some hugely influential ideas about culture.

     1. In *Structural Anthropology* (1958), he argued that culture itself has invisible, controlling structures. Like Vladimir Propp, he was extending the methodological insights of Ferdinand de Saussure (1857–1913).

     2. In chapter XI, "The Structural Study of Myth"

(originally 1955), Lévi-Strauss used analyses of several versions of the Oedipus myth to argue that the key elements of a true myth in a deep sense coexist even though they must be sequenced in any given telling. This parallels St. Jerome's notion that "Christ dies for us daily."

    3. Careful readers of *The Erasers* had already noticed that many of its details, such as the description of the patterns on a curtain, also seem drawn from the Oedipus myth.

III. On re-reading, *The Erasers* changes from a detective story to a philosophical exemplum.

    A. Once we recognize the importance of Oedipus to the novel, all its elements fall into place.

        1. Details, such as the flotsam and the drunkard and both his successful and his unsuccessful riddle, become appropriate.

        2. Details of merely overheard conversation, such as that between two bus passengers, reinforce a Lévi-Straussian reading of the power of myth.

        3. We readers discover in the exact center of the book, on an artist's eraser, the solution not to the murder but to the detective's problem with reality.

    B. This discovery, which Robbe-Grillet allows us rather than his detective, also comments on the importance of Freudian theory for our lives.

        1. In "The Uncanny," Freud's discussion of "the familiar in an unfamiliar place" seems to mirror the detective's experience. Thus, the murder the detective uncannily commits seems inevitable for him.

        2. The central key to "erasing" the power of ever-present myth, however, is available if we free ourselves from habitual ways of making images of the flotsam we see around us. This revises Freudian psychoanalysis.

    C. Robbe-Grillet's experiment is important both artistically and politically.

        1. On a first reading, *The Erasers* gives a fantastic twist to the prior evolution of detective fiction. This is central to creating a new subgenre, the New Novel. *The Erasers* on first reading is a true fantasy, sitting at the extreme opposite end of the continuum from realism.

2. On re-reading, what is left, represented in a new cinematic style, is a pattern that we can understand. To Robbe-Grillet, this understanding resolves the reader's mysteries and ambiguities, undoes a confining "humanism," retrieves the otherness of Nature, and allows us to "lay claim to…freedom."

Essential Reading:

Robbe-Grillet, Alain. *The Erasers*.

Supplementary Reading:

Freud, Sigmund. *Totem and Taboo*.

Lévi-Strauss, Claude. "The Structural Study of Myth," in *Structural Anthropology*.

Questions to Consider:

1. How might reading this book change the way you read other detective fiction?

2. In what sense do you think this book, or any book, can liberate you?

Lecture Nine—Transcript
Robbe-Grillet—Experimental Fiction & Myth

The publication of Alain Robbe-Grillet's *The Erasers* motivated the creation of the term the *New Novel*. On first reading, it is a detective story pushed to the condition of true Fantasy. Its radical style, Robbe-Grillet claimed, has important epistemological consequences, and in that way is both a fantastic development of Émile Zola's idea of the "experimental novel" and the fulfillment of Roland Barthes's prediction about the evolution of writing. On closer examination, the novel also reveals itself as a reworking of the materials of the Oedipus myth as the structural anthropologist Claude Lévi-Strauss understood it, and as a critical reexamination of Freudian ideas about psychological fantasy. Indeed, for a clever minority of readers or re-readers, there is a last fantastic trick that converts this apparently ambiguous detective novel into a stable work of aesthetic didacticism.

For most people, on first reading *The Erasers* by Robbe-Grillet, it seems to be a fantastic, compelling, but deeply confusing detective novel. Yet, because what close reading and rereading reveal, it have a huge critical and, indeed, popular success and let to the creation of the term in France, *le nouveau roman*, "the New Novel."

The Erasers is told, primarily from the viewpoint of a detective, Wallas, who is sent to a provincial town to solve a murder. Many of his observations are less obviously gathering clues about this murder than inquiries into his own sense of reality. What should he make of coincidences? For example, one witness tells that after the murder occurred, she observed someone running down the street, and that someone was wearing an overcoat with a triangular shaped wound in the cloth. While in the town, Wallas, wearing an overcoat, snags his shoulder on a piece of fence post and winds up having exactly the same clue. But is it a clue or is it something about Wallas?

Can anything significant be read into the pictures that Wallas thinks that he sees in random assemblages of flotsam on the stagnant canal water? For instance, he sees corks, bits of orange peel, and as the wind moves the surface of the dead canal water about, he thinks they form, perhaps, the image of Punch and Judy. Or, maybe a map of America, if charitably read.

Much of what is reported in the novel, such as the behavior of the café manager who does things mechanically, again and again, or the riddling drunkard, seems entirely irrelevant to solving the crime. There is a drunkard who comes up repeatedly in the novel. At this point, he's asking a riddle. He stands up on a table in the saloon, the back room of which Wallas is using as his residence and base while in the town investigating, and he says, "Tell me, what animal is a parasite in the morning?" "That's all we need was this goon here," Antoine, the manager objects. "You don't even know what an oblique line is, I'll bet." "You look pretty oblique to me." And so on, and then he continues: "What animal is parasite in the morning, incestuous at noon, and blind at night?" He thinks, "Oh, no. Now wait a minute. It's blind in the morning, incestuous at noon, and a parasite at night, what animal is it?" "No, no. Deaf at noon, blind at night, limps in the morning." "I'm just asking a riddle." In fact, this strange book full of strange details has one that threw the original readers way off.

In the next to the last chapter, Wallas goes to the murder scene and tries to recreate the passage that the murderer must have taken up the stairs to go and kill the victim. While in the victim's study, he hears someone on the stairs. He hides behind the desk, the light flashes on, and he shoots the intruder and winds up killing the man whose murder he was sent to solve.

At the very end of the book, neither we nor the detective knows who truly kills this individual, or how to understand reality. The individual who was killed is named Dupont, French for "at the bridge." There were two Duponts mentioned in *The Erasers*, Albert and Daniel—A. and D. Dupont. Maybe this is an AD kind of story— after the birth of Jesus.

The novel is told in a relentlessly meticulous, flat style, which seems almost cinematic. Indeed, much was made of this idea that this book got rid of rhetorical devices and only gave us the facts ma'am, nothing but the facts. Here is a famous example—famous because it's been written about on numerous occasions—"A quarter of a tomato that is quite faultless; cut up by the machine into a perfectly symmetrical fruit." This isn't even a sentence. It is, however, a detailed description of something for sale in a cafeteria. "The peripheral flesh compact, homogeneous, in a splendid chemical red, is of an even thickness between a strip of gleaming skin and the hollow where the yellow graduated seeds appear in a row, kept in place by a thin layer of greenish jelly, along a swelling of the heart." And this goes on for twice as much longer than I have just read.

These descriptions, I think, are not truly cinematic. We need to understand that the word "flesh" is a metaphor. The flesh of a vegetable is not flesh. "A splendid chemical red" reflects someone's attitude, in fact, an ironic attitude toward that color. There is no "hollow" inside a fruit—tomato slice—it is our view of that curve that makes it be a hollow rather than, say, a bump viewed from the other way. The seeds are not graduated, that's our idea; they are of different sizes. And there is no swelling toward the heart; tomatoes have no hearts. In fact, even at its most cinematic, language tends to give us a projection of ourselves. The novel's movements also attempt to be superficial, cinematic, detailed, and somehow get rid of the observer; although, as we can see, that does not truly happen.

For instance, the novel, as it moves from one passage to another, mimics the cinematic techniques of tracking, panning, and montage. There is one lovely passage where we see Wallas looking at an eraser. He puts the eraser down on the front left corner of a desk. The next phrase tells us about a sheaf of papers being raised from a desk and underneath the papers is another eraser. These cinematic techniques make the book feel as if it is not really a novel, but just some strange, imaginary report of some investigation. The book has been called experimental. The term "experimental" goes back to Émile Zola, a great French novelist.

In works such as *Germinal*, Zola sought to represent society in a believable way, to set characters and social forces in motion within the novel, and then to see what they would do. In that sense, Zola saw the novel as an experiment. That is, if he could create a world within the novel, which had believable characters and believable social forces, and they led to certain outcomes, in a sense he was running an experiment that would convince his readers that those forces in our lives would have these outcomes. *Germinal*, for example, tells the story of a town where the main industry is a coal mine, and we see the lives of the miners, the owners, and so on. The economic interactions among them lead to death and a Communist revolution. In other words, an experimental novel served Zola's purposes both aesthetically and politically.

Roland Barthes, a great French literary critic and cultural theorist, in one of these early books, a book called, in English, *Writing Degree Zero*, studied the evolution of French narrative prose. His idea of writing degree, in French, *écriture*, is that we understand something that is more general than style, and yet more specific than language. Now, he understood language and speech as being the synchronic and diachronic aspects of any given language. Language—*langue*, speech—*parole*—he borrows this from Ferdinand de Saussure, a Swiss-born linguist.

But we all know that between the stable, synchronic language and the ever-moving diachronic *parole*, speech, we can see regularities that are more stable than just speech. For instance, we can identify a Hemmingway style or a biblical style. What Barthes did was to suggest that yet more generally than style, but more flexibility than *langue*, we could have *écriture*, a kind of style of styles. What in English we could call a grapholect. The way an idiolect is a person's way of speaking, a grapholect is a way of writing. We could have a grapholect that would identify, for instance, a cultural moment or a literary period, such as Romantic or Modern or Postmodern, as we discussed in talking about *Orlando*. In fact, I've tried this with my students. I've asked ordinary sophomores—well, none of the sophomores at the University of Michigan are ordinary—but I've asked my students, when they happen to be in the office, to close their eyes. I take a random book off the shelf, I open it to a random page, I cover the running head so they cannot see the title, and I ask them to read a random paragraph and tell me when the page was written.

For works that were written in the last century, my students almost invariably can date it to within 10 years; to works within the last 200 years, they can almost invariably date it to the last 20; and works from the Renaissance forward, they almost always date it within 40 years, without ever having seen the work before. It's not that they're responding to the style, they're responding to the *écriture,* to the grapholect, to what Barthes's translator has called "writing degree."

What Barthes did was to study the evolution of French prose from the Renaissance to the present—his present, 1950's when he wrote this book—and he noticed that in the Renaissance we had a very ornate style—lots of metaphor, lots of periphrasis—that is, going the long way around to say something, such as "that finny tribe" instead of "fish," and so on. And that as we move from the Renaissance forward, the degree of ornamentation and decoration that we find in French fictional prose, is lower and lower. What he suggests is that what might have been once a very high writing degree, will ultimately go to writing degree zero. That was his prediction.

Wonder of wonders, without ever acknowledging to the general reading public that Roland Barthes and Robbe-Grillet were friends, out comes *The Erasers* in 1953 and out comes *Writing Degree Zero*, and people read passages such as the one about the quarter slices of tomato and they say, "My Goodness. There's no rhetorical decoration here. We've reached writing degree zero, just as Roland Barthes said we would." So we have "The New Novel," a novel dependant upon surfaces and details that, nonetheless, is involved with a completely imaginary space, a space where the detective is, in fact, the murderer. And, if we read it more deeply, we realize it's not writing degree zero at all; we still push our own feelings into those descriptions.

Now, at about the same time that we have this stylistic development, we also have Claude Lévi-Strauss, one of the great anthropologists of the 20th century, coming up with his ideas about culture. While Roland Barthes predicts—if he is, in fact, really predicting—the style that we see in *The Erasers*, we can turn to Lévi-Strauss to look at its content. In *Structural Anthropology*, a very, very important book, he also used de Saussure's ideas about structural analysis to analyze the Oedipus myth, very famously in Chapter 11, where he shows that every version of the myth, if we line up its different parts, really coheres into a quadripartite structure where one and two, and three and four, those columns of story elements, have a relationship to each other, and the conjoined one-two and three-four have another relationship to each other, and that set of relationships is, in fact, a powerful, permanent, synchronic, mythic structure that exists in our mind in Western culture. Later, [Edmund] Leach, an anthropologist, shows that that structure is exactly the same structure we find in the story of the Fall in the Garden of Eden, a famous essay called "Lévi-Strauss in the Garden of Eden."

Now, what we need to understand is that this story of Oedipus is not the story of Oedipus that Freud gives us. Freud gives us a story of Oedipus in which the child is eager to supplant the father, kills the father, and decides to marry the mother. But Sophocles's story is not that at all. Sophocles tells the story, which is worth our remembering so that we can free ourselves from Freud. As Sophocles tells the story, Laius and Jocasta, the king and queen of Thebes, are told by the oracle at Delphi—Laius is told—that he will have a child who will kill him. When Jocasta bears a child, he has that child taken out to the wilderness and staked to the ground, through the foot, so that the wild animals will come and kill him. A shepherd comes by, sees this poor, staked infant, takes him away, and crosses the peninsula to Corinth, where he presents the infant to the king and queen of Corinth, who are childless. We are back in the realm of fairy tales, of course.

The king and queen raise Oedipus. Oedipus, which means "swollen foot" or "lame foot," is that way because of the staking, but that's his name. He grows up to be an upright young man, and he goes to the oracle at Delphi and is told he will kill his father and marry his mother. Not wanting to hurt the king and queen of Corinth, who he takes to be his father and mother, he leaves.

Along the way he comes to a bridge. He is crossing the bridge, but someone comes the other direction and says, "Get out of my way!" A man with a retinue, a wealth man. Oedipus, of course, doesn't yield. He's used to being a prince himself. When they meet, the other man starts an altercation. Oedipus punches him. He falls down, hits his head on a rock and dies.

As the story continues, Oedipus goes and passes by the Sphinx. The Sphinx is a mythical beast which kills people by strangling them. The word "sphinx" comes from the Greek *sphingein*. It's the same root as the word "sphincter," having to do with opening and closing sections in the human body. The Sphinx asks of all who pass before it a riddle. If you fail to answer the riddle correctly, you are killed. If you do answer the riddle correctly, or so the story predicts, the Sphinx will allow you to become the monarch of Thebes.

The Sphinx's riddle is quite famous. She asks, "What goes on four in the morning, two in the afternoon, and three in the evening?" Oedipus answers, "Man." You crawl on fours as infants; we stand up on our own two legs as adults; and we use a cane in old age." The Sphinx throws herself from a cliff and kills herself, thus opening the road to Thebes. The people greet Oedipus joyfully, and since their king has died, they make him their king. In order to cement the legitimacy of his authority, he marries the king's widow. In order to bring justice to the land, he sends out servants to discover what really happened. Of course, we know what really happened. They come back with the message, and tell it first to Jocasta, that the person who killed the king, Laius, was now their own king, Oedipus.

When Oedipus hears this, he is aghast at what he has done. This is no Freudian child who wants to sleep with his mother. This is an upright man who rejects the idea of sleeping with his mother. He runs in to find her, to share the news with her, he goes in, and finds that she has hanged herself. He takes the fibula out of her toga and uses the pin to blind himself. At the end, he's led away by his daughter.

Now, the story of Oedipus, as Aristotle understands it, is a story of what we translate as tragic flaw, as if there were something wrong with Oedipus, a hint that Freud accepts. But Aristotle's word is *hamartia*; it is a term from archery, and it means "a missing of the mark." Oedipus didn't do something wrong, he did the right, but sometimes in this world of ours, doing right still produces wrong. That's the human condition. It's no wonder the story has attained mythic status. What does it mean to say, as Lévi-Strauss did, that all of the parts of this story coexist at one time? It means—perhaps more easily understandable for those raised in a Christian nation—what Saint Jerome meant when he said of the story of the totality of the life of Jesus, "Christ dies for us daily." It doesn't mean that Christ dies and then is resurrected and then dies, forever having to go again and again through a cycle, the way Prometheus has his liver plucked anew very day. It means that at all times suffering exists, and simultaneously, the promise that is the resurrection, that matters so much to any believing Christian, exists. It's a synchronic reality because it's in the world of myth. In the world of myth, as Lévi-Strauss showed, it doesn't matter the order in which you tell the story parts, the whole of the story coexists at one time.

In *The Erasers*, we have one time. That one time is the time when you are a parasite in the morning—you kill your father first and then are blind at night. Is this myth the only myth that could possibly tell this story? No. Robbe-Grillet lets us see the difference. The riddle man comes up again—as he is so-called—later in the book. "What animal in the morning," he tries to remember, but he can't remember. Then he gives a different riddle. He says, "What animal is black, has six legs, and flies?" "No," Wallas says, "the riddle was something else." What animal is black, has six legs, and flies? A fly.

In 1943, John Paul Sartre published a very famous drama called "The Flies." It is a version of "The Furies," the Ancient Greek myth about the harpies that drive us and make our lives terrible. It was published under the German occupation in World War II, and savvy French audiences were able to see that "The Flies" was a critique of the Nazis, that the forces that were driving the lives of the French were nothing but numerous, though powerful, insects making garbage out of everything they touched. This subversive play, "The Flies," plugs into the myth of the Oresteia, the only complete myth cycle that we have from Greek drama. What Grillet is saying to us is there are other myths we could have used, but in this book the myth is the Oedipus myth.

Once we recognize this myth, we discover that all, all the details in this book that look to be random and irrelevant, actually cohere. They are parts of that larger story. For example, Wallas is given instructions to take a bus to a particular place where he is going to do some investigation. The bus line in Route 6, which he is told he should use until it comes to the place where it crosses Route 4. So, remember to go where six crosses four—6 x 4, 24. When Wallas begins investigating, his watch stops at a certain moment. When he accidentally kills the man who may be the man whose murder he was intending to solve, his watch starts up again, exactly 24 hours later. The one day, the 24 is, as we are told of that bullet, something that comes out of myth.

As Wallas is walks up the stairs in Dupont's house, he notices that there are draperies over the windows. The draperies are net, and they have a pattern in them, a pattern that shows an Ancient Greek column blasted by lightening, at the base of which is an infant and a shepherd, and next to that is another column and another infant and another shepherd. In other words, now that we realize that the story of Oedipus is crucial here, what Robbe-Grillet is showing us is that Wallas is seeing a clear sign that the story of Oedipus, the staked-out child whose royal heritage has been destroyed by the gods, is going to be doubled. What happened in the ancient world still happens here.

Freud, in "The Uncanny," said that the uncanny is produced by seeing the familiar in an unfamiliar place. If you're on a trip to a different country, walk into a store, and suddenly see someone from back home, it feels uncanny. If we take the metaphoric and make it literal, we have the uncanny. For instance, I'm so hungry, I could eat a horse. If I then sat down and began to eat a horse, your eyes would bulge. That's uncanny. This is an example of Freud's way of looking at the fantastic. In this book, Wallas keeps trying to get away from where he is, from his residence in the saloon, in order to explore the city, and keeps coming back to the same piece of dead canal. He asks, "Don't I know this city?" And realizes that yes, he does. In fact, he'd been there once before; in fact, perhaps as a child with his mother; in fact, perhaps as an infant. The canny reader then realizes that this dead canal is a version of the birth canal—that Wallas is here in his own birth city, the one he has never seen because he has been away from it since his infancy.

The owner of the stationary store that keeps attracting him is a woman named "Evelyn," with a carnal, throaty laugh we're told, repeatedly. But he finds himself drawn to her. Uncannily, he keeps going back to this stationary store asking for an eraser, the kind that artists use.

Outside the stationary store, there's a picture of Thebes. The store itself is on the corner of *The Rue of Corinth*—the rue, the street of Corinth. This picture of Thebes has before it an artist's model, a little wire and wood model in a little toy smock, painting the picture of Thebes. But the picture of Thebes is actually oil, and the painting—supposed painting—is a photograph. Everything here is mirrors and reversals. The canny reader finds this.

Wallas wants a special eraser. "What kind of eraser," Evelyn—maybe his mother—says. The manufacturer's brand was printed on one side, but it was too worn to be legible anymore. Only two of the middle letters were still there, D and I. There must have been at least two letters before and perhaps two or three letters after—in Greek, OE, DI, PUS, Oedipus; in French, OE, DI, PE, *Oedipe*. It has two letters before, and two or three after.

If we read this book the way we read it at first, it is a fantastic inversion of the detective story and it drives genre development forward. But if we read it again and find at the very center of the novel—that passage I just read is exactly halfway through the book—we realize what Wallas never did, the thing that controls him is the inexorable power of myth in our lives. And the only way to be rid of myth is to give it its true name, to find that it is Oedipal, that it is someone else's story—not inevitably Oedipus's, we could have had Oresteia's story—that will allow us to erase it, not the erasure of simply recognition of trauma that Freud suggests, it is, in fact, a way of overcoming the language that has posed a reality on us.

In a book called, *For a New Novel*, Robbe-Grillet explains why he uses this bizarre, cinematic style. He says, "If we can go for the surface, and get rid of the language imposed upon us, this use of our imagination to counter others' imagination is nothing less," he says, "than to lay claim to freedom." For the canny reader, this is imagination leading to infinite possibilities.

Lecture Ten
Tolkien & Mass Production of the Fantastic

Scope:

English has a unique fantasy heritage in the Arthurian materials, used by authors medieval to modern, such as Thomas Malory and T. H. White. The modern Arthurian musical *Camelot* lent its name to John F. Kennedy's truncated presidency. William Morris, pioneering Victorian manufacturer and polymath artist, rejected an offer to be England's Poet Laureate, honoring in part his Arthurian poems. J. R. R. Tolkien, a brilliant philologist, revised the spirit of these ultimately nostalgic materials to create a reassuring fantastic medievalism, what he himself called "a fairy story." In "Farmer Giles of Ham" and "Leaf by Niggle," Tolkien's comforting politics and religion, respectively, emerge. Examination of the work of Tolkien's friend C. S. Lewis, particularly the children's series about Narnia and the science fictions, including *Perelandra*, clarify Tolkien's democratic consolation. The epic success of his *Lord of the Rings* trilogy launched the true mass production of the literary fantastic.

Outline

I. John Ronald Reuel Tolkien (1892–1973), an Oxford professor of Anglo-Saxon and of English language and literature, transformed fantasy publishing around the world.

    A. Middle-earth, Tolkien's most famous fictional setting, draws on Old English literature, such as *Beowulf*, with its monsters; Norse saga, with gods and heroes; Welsh legend, with sorcerers; Teutonic mythology, with world-shattering battles; and on Christianity and the Arthurian materials.

    B. English literature has a unique heritage in the Arthurian materials.

        1. "The wise man of the wood," like the Grimms' Rumplestiltskin who spins straw into gold, exists in many cultures. "The undiscovered king," like Moses found floating among the bulrushes, exists in many cultures. But historically, only English literature has integrated these archetypal stories, weaving Merlin and Arthur into a single fantastic tapestry.

2. The Arthurian materials have yielded myriad popular works, including *Sir Gawain and the Green Knight* (c. 1375), in which Arthur's boastful nephew foolishly beheads a vegetation demi-god, and *Le Morte d'Arthur* (1485) by Sir Thomas Malory (1405–1471).

3. Modern uses of Arthurian materials include *The Defence of Guinevere* (1858) by William Morris (1834–1896). T. H. White, writing contemporaneously with Tolkien, produced a fine novel series, *The Once and Future King*, that inspired the Broadway musical *Camelot* (1960), which in turn, supplied the nostalgic nickname for John F. Kennedy's abbreviated presidency.

C. Tolkien's personal background bore on his artistic creation.

1. A superb philologist, he knew a diversity of time-tested narratives and the words that resonated through them. His linguistic inventions ring true.

2. His love of poetry and work as a translator inform his style.

3. His committed Roman Catholicism flavors the morality of his tales.

II. Tolkien's most famous work is *The Lord of the Rings* (1954–1955), a fantastic epic consisting of *The Fellowship of the Ring*, *The Two Towers*, and *The Return of the King*.

A. The trilogy meshes earthy, sensible "hobbits" with figures of legend.

1. Frodo, recruited by Gandalf, a Merlin figure, must help destroy an ancient, magic ring before evil sorcerer Sauron can seize it and enslave the world.

2. Frodo's "fellowship" includes humble hobbits, magic elves and dwarves, and a dashing loner, Aragorn, ultimately revealed to be a hidden king.

3. Through grit, self-sacrifice, and Gandalf's help, the ring, despite its tempting power, is destroyed; Middle-earth is saved, and the hobbits' Shire returned to domestic peace.

4. We can see Gandalf as Merlin, Aragorn as Arthur, and

Frodo and friends as solid English folk, but in Tolkien's world, unlike Malory's, the folk are our focus. In a sense, Tolkien makes us the true heroes.

B. Like the Arthurian materials, Tolkien's are extensive. *The Hobbit* (1937) and *The Silmarillion* (1977) are prequels. Other works are simply set in the same world.

C. *The Lord of the Rings* appeals for many reasons.

    1. Like a Proppian folk tale, Tolkien's distillation of traditional materials resonates immediately.

    2. Tolkien's own storytelling is often stylistically gorgeous.

    3. The works are easily allegorized. Is the questing Fellowship the Allies against Sauron's Hitler, a resurrection of Jesus' disciples, or the middle class resisting privilege? Tolkien always refused to say.

III. The ingredients of Tolkien's epic are clear in his shorter works.

A. "Farmer Giles of Ham" (1949), set in a version of Middle-earth, demonstrates Tolkien's love of language and his preference for comfortable democracy. Key moments include Giles using a tame dragon to take the abusive king's crown and the opening and closing play on the switch from Latin to English.

B. *The Adventures of Tom Bombadil* (1962) gathers poems from the marvelous woodsman of the *Ring* trilogy, such as "Errantry," which shows us the seduction of language, and "The Hoard," which shows us the good we might be seduced from.

C. "Leaf by Niggle" (1964) is a gentle and deeply moving Christian parable.

IV. Tolkien's writing both includes and invites theoretical discussion.

A. His "On Fairy-Stories," published in *Tree and Leaf* with "Leaf by Niggle," gives Tolkien's own explanation of his fantastic writings.

    1. Fairy stories, unlike the *Alice* books, must never discuss their own magic.

    2. Fairy stories offer "Fantasy" ("Imagination" and

"Unreality"), "Recovery" (of defamiliarizing vision), "Escape" (liberation), and consolation.

3. The Gospels are the epitome of fairy stories.

B. We can understand Tolkien's success by comparing his work with that of others.

1. Tolkien was one of The Inklings, a writers' group that included Charles Williams (1886–1945) and C. S. Lewis (1898–1963). Lewis's Space trilogy (1938–1945) for adults and Narnia series (1950–1956) for children reveal a doctrinal difference between adult- and youth-oriented religious fantasies that suggests the importance of writing morally forgiving narratives.

2. *The Erasers* suggests how daunting intellectual challenge can be.

3. Tolkien's trilogy offers adventure for the active, poetry for the contemplative, and simple consolation for us all. Chosen as the best book of the 20th century in many reader surveys, *The Lord of the Rings* knocked open the door to fantasy publishing in our time.

Essential Reading:

Tolkien, J. R. R. *The Lord of the Rings.*

Tolkien, J. R. R. *The Tolkien Reader.*

Supplementary Reading:

Lewis, C. S. *The Chronicles of Narnia.*

Questions to Consider:

1. In what ways does the quest of Tolkien's diverse characters in *The Lord of the Rings* trilogy speak to conditions of our contemporary lives?

2. Are fantastic works, such as "Farmer Giles of Ham" and "Leaf by Niggle," made stronger or weaker as art by their didacticism?

Lecture Ten—Transcript
Tolkien & Mass Production of the Fantastic

English has a unique fantasy heritage, the Arthurian materials, used by authors from medieval to modern such as Thomas Malory and T. H. White. The modern Arthurian musical *Camelot* lent its name to John F. Kennedy's truncated presidency. William Morris, a pioneering Victorian manufacturer and polymath artist, rejected an offer to be England's Poet Laureate honoring, in part, his Arthurian poems. He rejected the offer, because he saw himself as a Democrat. He was one of the first people to try to give profit sharing to his employees. His idea of Arthur's realm was one of great inclusiveness, like that attributed to Kennedy's. This was a shift in the Arthurian poems.

J. R. R. Tolkien, a brilliant philologist, also revised the spirit of these ultimately nostalgic materials to create a reassuring fantastic medievalism, what he himself called "a fairy story." In "Farmer Giles of Ham" and "Leaf by Niggle," Tolkien's comforting politics and religion respectively emerge. Examination of the work of Tolkien's friend, C. S. Lewis—particularly the children's series about Narnia and the science fictions including *Perelandra*—clarifies Tolkien's democratic consolation. The epic success of his *Lord of the Rings* trilogy launched the true mass production of the literary fantastic.

John Ronald Reuel Tolkien was an Oxford professor of Anglo-Saxon—that is to say, Old English—and of English language and literature. He transformed Fantasy publishing around the world. He is most widely knows for his creation of a Fantasy realm Middle-earth. This setting draws on Old English literature, like *Beowulf*, the oldest epic of English literature, where the hero fights extraordinary monsters, and even the monster's mother; Norse saga, with gods and heroes; Welsh legend with sorcerers; Teutonic mythology, with world-shattering battles, as well as Christianity and the Arthurian materials. Tolkien drew on them all.

English literature has a great heritage in these Arthurian materials. There is a character we see around the world known by folklorists as "The Wiseman of the Wood." Rumplestiltskin, for example, who spins straw into gold, is an example of "The Wiseman of the Wood." There is another character we find around the world, the undiscovered king, like Moses, found floating among the bulrushes. And this exists in many cultures, but historically, only English literature had integrated these two archetypal characters, weaving them into a single story, where Merlin becomes, in a sense, the Godfather who brings forward Arthur to take his place as the rightful king and set the world in order, a story that not only sets the world in order, but sets the world on its inevitable path to disillusion.

These Arthurian materials have yielded myriad popular works, among them for example, *Sir Gawain and the Green Knight.* This is a famous magical fairy take for adults, from the late 14th century. Sir Gawain is, by convention, one of the more foolhardy members of the Round Table, Arthur's fellowship of knights. In comes a huge green knight who asks that someone take the challenge of attacking him with a blow of a sword, that he will not try to counter, but if he should survive this blow, the man who accepts the challenge must meet him a year and a week and day later. Sir Gawain takes up the challenge. It turns out that the Green Knight is—although it is inexplicit here—a vegetation god, and lopping off part of the greenery does in no way kill the Green Knight.

Gawain needs to find him, and knows that he will die a year and a week and a day later, but a year and a week and a day after Christmas is New Year's Day in this Christianized version of the vegetation story. Ultimately, Gawain is saved. His pure heart comes into play, and all is well. The Arthurian materials, in other words, are malleable.

Le Morte d'Arthur, as it is pronounced in English, by Sir Thomas Malory in the 15th century, is the most famous complete telling of all of the materials having to do with the birth of Arthur, Merlin, Arthur's drawing the sword from the stone, the realm of Camelot, and the adventures of his many knights, including Gawain, Lancelot, and so on. In its modern uses, these materials include a mid-19th century book of poems called *The Defence of Guinevere* by William Morris. T. H. White, writing at the same time as Tolkien, produced a series of quite fine novels using these same materials, known collectively as *The Once and Future King,* and those novels are the source that mostly directly inspired the Broadway musical *Camelot* in 1960, which, in turn, supplied the nostalgic nickname for John F. Kennedy's truncated presidency.

Tolkien's personal background bore on his artistic creation. He was a superb philologist who knew a diversity of time-tested narratives and he knew the words that resonated through them. His linguistic inventions ring true. His love of poetry and work as a translator inform his style, and his committed Roman Catholicism flavors the morality of his tales.

Tolkien's most famous work, of course, is *The Lord of the Rings*, published between 1954 and 1955. It is an epic fantasy originally written as a single work, but broken up by the publisher to come out as three separate volumes, *The Fellowship of the Ring*, *The Two Towers*, and *The Return of the King*. This trilogy, as it is now thought of today, meshes earthy, sensible hobbits with figures of legend. Hobbits are Tolkien's own creation, and they become the central characters in the *Ring* trilogy. Hobbits, as we all know, are somewhat shorter than ordinary people; they have a wonderful appetite for food; they live happy, little bourgeois existences; and are known for having large, hairy feet.

Frodo, a Hobbit, is recruited by Gandalf, who is the Merlin figure in this epic, to help destroy an ancient magic ring which gives extraordinary power to anyone who wears it before the evil sorcerer Sauron can seize it and use it to enslave the world. Frodo cannot make this world-crossing journey on his own, so he accumulates a fellowship, the Fellowship of the Ring, which includes humble Hobbits, magical elves, powerful dwarves, and a dashing loner—a tall, elegant man named Aragorn, who ultimately, though he is at first seen to be a woodsman, is revealed to be a hidden king.

Now, on this journey, any one of these people could have carried the ring. The aim is to take the ring and bring it to the volcanic heart of a mountain where it can be destroyed. No ordinary fire can destroy this ring, but if it were to be destroyed, Sauron could not have it and it would be possible for the peoples of Middle-earth to continue about their lives and to avoid enslavement.

Though any character could carry it, only Frodo does carry it, on a string around his neck. He is torn. He must resist the urge to wear that ring and become invisible, to be able to do magical things, to conquer other people. As Wells's invisible man could not resist that urge and ultimately was destroyed by the society around him, Frodo would, himself, become destroyed. One of the key characters in this novel whom they encounter on their trip is Gollum, someone who once upon a time had given in and worn the ring, and had become less and less and less of himself, withered away to nothing but a pitiful, tenacious creature with no other desire but to return himself to the ring, wear it again, and live through the ring. "Things are in the saddle," as Emerson wrote, "and ride mankind." The ring is a killing ring. The power is more than humans can bear. Hobbits, perhaps, can resist. Frodo is the hero.

In fact—this is well known—Frodo and the Fellowship, through many dark adventures, finally manage to return the ring to the volcanic fire from which it was forged. Middle-earth is saved. All go back to their domains, and the shire is retuned to domestic peace.

We can see Gandalf as Merlin, Aragorn as Arthur, and Frodo and his friends, not so much as Knights of the Round Table because they are always ironized, but rather as solid English folk. These folk are our focus. In a sense, Tolkien makes us the true heroes of the *Ring* trilogy.

Like the Arthurian materials, Tolkien's are extensive. He has attracted to himself all of these many kinds of myths to comes up with a single, coherent, imaginary universe. In addition to the three *Ring* books, we have *The Hobbit,* which is a prequel, the story of how the ring first came to Frodo's uncle, and *The Silmarillion,* which gives us the legends and myths of the worlds of Middle-earth. There are other works as well, simply set in the same time.

The Lord of the Rings appeals for many reasons. Like a Proppian folk tale, Tolkien's is a distillation of traditional materials that resonates immediately because it is told throughout with a particular structure—absentation, journey, return, and so on. In addition, Tolkien's own story telling is often stylistically gorgeous. His language is beautiful, and with no disrespect intended to the movie versions of *The Lord of the Rings*, that poetry is missing when we leave Tolkien's page.

Another reason that this is so popular is that the works are easily allegorized. Is the questing Fellowship—this is, after all, a story written during the Depression and during World War II and published shortly thereafter—is the questing of Fellowship a representation of the Allies, who are off against Sauron's Hitler? Is it a resurrection of Jesus's disciples? Or is it simply the middle class resisting those of privilege? The story is easily allegorized. We can see its morals moving us, even if we don't know where its morals, in detail, are supposed to move us. Tolkien always refused to say.

The ingredients of Tolkien's epic are clear in his shorter works, and I think it helps us to look at those in detail. "Farmer Giles of Ham," published in 1949, is a version of Middle-earth. It demonstrates Tolkien's love of language and his preference for comfortable democracy. Key moments in this story include Giles using a tame dragon to take the abusive king's crown and open and close the work itself with a switch from Latin to English. Let me make this clearer.

Farmer Giles is an ordinary fellow, but the king comes to protect the realm from the dragon. In protecting the realm from the dragon, the king's retinue camps out in Farmer Giles's fields and eat so much and trample so much that, in fact, Farmer Giles would be impoverished but that he has the king's chits for repayment—except, of course, the king's treasury is bare. He'll only be able to fill the treasury if he has the hoard the dragon keeps. Well, he can't. Eventually, however, because Giles comes upon a magical sword, he is able to tame the dragon and, in a way, politely, drive off the king. At that moment of confrontation, the king, who always seems kingly, says, "Give me my sword." Of course, it's not his sword at all. "Give me my sword," shouted the king. Finding his voice, but forgetting his plural—he should have said, "Give us our sword," because he speaks for all. "Give us your crown," said Giles, a staggering remark such as had never been heard in all the days of the Middle Kingdom." In other words, faced with a tame dragon, the royal monarch loses his power. His power is only conferred by society, but the solid English farmer knows the power that he had in his hand, and not only tames the dragon but sends the king packing. He doesn't actually want to become the king, and he does not actually.

This story, "Farmer Giles of Ham," is a story set in a magical, imaginary world about the change from the old to the new. The title page begins, "Farmer Giles of Ham," and then we have in ornate type, Latin, *Aegidii Ahenobarbi Julii Agricole De Hammo*, et cetera. We have "Farmer Giles of Ham", and then it says in English, "…or in the vulgar tongue, the rise and wonderful adventures of Farmer Giles, Lord of Tame, Count of Worminghall," et cetera. Giles, of course, is the old form of "guile" or "wily." We have one smart farmer here.

When the story ends, after Giles has, in fact, sent the king packing, the original giant who brought about the dragon and brought about the king and started all of these stories is told that he was driven off, finally, by Giles with a blunderbuss full of nails and broken crockery that stung him on his nose. "Huh, a blunderbuss, was it?" and scratched his head. "I thought it was horseflies," or, to catch the illusion, horse feathers. "*Finis*," the book says, in ornate type, or in the vulgar, "The End." The shift from Latin to English at the end is the shift from Latin to English in the beginning, and it is what the plot does. It goes from the high-born king who issues proclamations in Latin to the solid British farmer who just takes care of business.

The use of the word "vulgar" to indicate the nature of that shift is crucial. The Vulgate Bible is the Latin Bible. The Bible translated into the language of the people is called "Vulgate." Our modern use of the word "vulgar," to mean disreputable, comes from an association of the common people as beneath those of high class. But in a religious sense, of course, certainly for a committed Christian like Tolkien, the people are those for whom God died. The vulgar is not beneath contempt. The vulgar expresses the finest form of the greatest book, the move from the monarchy to the democracy, from Latin to English, from the royal to the vulgar, is a politically and philosophically appropriate move for Tolkien.

The Adventures of Tom Bombadil gathers together a number of poems all associated with that woodsman character, that ancient woodsman character, from the *Ring* trilogy. Let's take a look at two of these to understand something about the power of language in Tolkien.

This one, the third of the poems in *The Adventures of Tom Bombadil*, none of which have Tom Bombadil in them, but poetry is his adventure, is called "Errantry." Errantry, of course, is what knights in armor did; they went out. Here is how it begins—by the way, if you buy the book, you must read these aloud, "There was a merry passenger, a messenger, a mariner, he built a gilded gondola to wander in and had in her a load of yellow oranges and porridge for his provender, he perfumed her with marjoram and cardamom and lavender."

We could take this passage apart and see how many ways the language forces us along. Merry passenger goes to messenger mariner—so, the M's in merry line up with the M's in messenger and mariner, while the –senger in passenger lines up with the –senger in messenger. But the messenger goes to mariner, the same rhythm of the word, so that the very first two lines impel us along by having these internal rhymes and repetitions. "There was a merry passenger, a messenger, a mariner," and that same kind of multiple connections is made in every line throughout the poem.

In fact, what happens is this merry passenger goes and has an errand, but he becomes involved in one magical adventure after another, fighting the king of the bumble bees, putting on some strange armor made out of the leather of moth wings, and so on, until, eventually, being driven by all of this, he comes back to where he began this errand, the nature of which is never specified.

> He tarried for a little while in little isles that lonely lay and found there naught but blowing grass and so at last the only way he took and turned and coming home with honeycomb to memory, his message came, and errand too, and daring do and glamory, he had forgot them journeying and tourneying a wanderer. So now he must depart again and start again his gondola forever still a messenger, a passenger, a tarrier, a roving as a feather does, a weather-driven mariner.

The beauty of the language, like the enchantments, enticements of the fairy tale worlds of imagination, keeps us from performing the real errand, the reason we're here. It only comes to us when we're sated and too late, and so we must venture forth again, always driven like a feather on the wind, subject to our desires, incapable of succeeding of the reason we have really come to earth.

What is that reason, we ask of this Christian writer? We may infer it from a poem called, "The Hoard," number 14 of *The Adventures of Tom Bombadil*. In the first stanza:

> The moon was new and the sun young, and silver and gold is what the gods sung. A great mass of worked precious metal is put away as a hoard by the elves. Then an old dwarf who sat upon them sees these, but he has aged and wanting nothing but to be in the presence of these, a young dragon comes along and wants the gold.

> An old dragon…(what must have happened, of course, is the young dragon killed the dwarf, the dragon had nothing of it

but the hoard, and sits on it until he is old) withering away, he can't hear so well, when a young warrior comes.

An old king sits on a high throne...(and we realize the same thing has happened again, that the love of money has been the root of the losing of one's self, the real notion of all evil)

And, so, the poem ends:

There is an old hoard in a dark rock, forgotten behind doors none can unlock (I think this is original sin) that grim gate, no man can pass. On the mound grows the green grass. There the sheep (an image of Jesus) feed, and the larks, (an image of the Holy Spirit) soar, and the wind blows from the sea's shore. The old hoard the night shall keep, while the earth waits and the elves sleep.

What does the Earth wait for? I think, for Tolkien, the Second Coming, but, again, he never says.

"Leaf by Niggle" is a deeply moving Christian parable. It is not so overtly Christian that everyone understands it as such immediately, but in fact, all understand it as such once it's pointed out to them. Niggle is a man who wants to paint. He wants to express himself in art. He is not very good at the big picture, but while his trees lack, the leaves—subject to that attention—are glorious. But, the law says certain things must be done. His neighbor needs help, and Niggle provides it. Eventually, the inspector comes by and says that Niggle's roof needs repair, and that is more important than art, and his canvasses need to be used to repair the roof. The time comes, we're told, when he is to take a long journey, and what is that journey? Well, we're never told, but people begin to gather and think about what they might do with Niggle's possessions, and we know what the journey is. But most of the story takes place after that journey has begun, while Tolkien [sic Niggle] is in some place where he hears an old voice and a young voice, they make him stay at a hospital where he learns to become healthier by work. Eventually, his neighbor joins him and they work together, and ultimately they achieve an understanding of this world at the end of the journey. What is the name of that place that the train brings people to, the one that Niggle and his neighbor have made? Why, the porter says to the old voice, it's called Niggle's Parrish. Parrish was the name of the neighbor. The porter settled it years ago, and the second voice tells this to the old voice, "Train for Niggle's Parrish in the bay." He has shouted that for a long while now, Niggle's Parrish. I sent a message to both of them to tell them. What did they say? They both laughed, laughed. The mountains rang with it. This is the consolation that true stories of the imagination can give us. It becomes possible, even after that journey, for us to find true fellowship. That world for Niggle not only has Niggle's leaves, but forests full of Niggle's trees, all perfectly achieved.

That story, "Leaf by Niggle," was originally published in a novel as the exemplification of Tolkien's own theory of fairy tales. First we have in that volume an essay called, "On Fairy-Stories." "On Fairy-Stories" tells us that fairy stories, unlike the *Alice* books, must never discuss their own magic. They cannot be self-reflexive. Magic, itself, must be accepted and taken as transparent. Fairy stories offer four things, according to Tolkien: Fantasy, which he defines as imagination and unreality yoked together; Recovery, by which he means a defamiliarizing vision. As the Russian formalists taught us, art comes from making the stone stony, from defamiliarizing what we see around us. Recovery makes things fresh again, as, in fact, Robbe-Grillet wanted to make the world fresh again by going on beyond the language that we had. Third, fairy stories offer us Escape—not escape in the negative sense, where we are failing to fulfill our responsibilities, but liberation; and, ultimately, Consolation. Fairy stories, Tolkien explains, offer us Fantasy, Recovery, Escape, and Consolation, and he says that the Gospels are the summation of all fairy stories.

Now, we can understand Tolkien's success by comparing his work with that of some of his contemporaries. He was a member of a group called "The Inklings." The Inklings, that very name, is a pun. They are scribbling and they hope that their writing will grow up and be something bigger than a mere inkling—duck, duckling; ink, inkling. But, also, these folks believed—these committed Christians, which included C. S. Lewis and Charles Williams—they down here in this world of ours had inklings about what the world above might be.

In C. S. Lewis's *Narnia* series, Eustace is turned into a dragon, a steel band is put about his arm, and as he grows and grows and grows—because dragons never have a natural ending to their growth—he hurts more and more until, eventually, he says, all right,

I believe in Aslan, the Christ figure in that series, and then he is freed and turned back into a boy. That ability to achieve salvation after death is what's called among orthodox Christians today the "Antinomy and Heresy." It's bad Christianity, but Lewis allows it in his books for children. In his books for adults, the so-called Space Trilogy with *Perelandra, Out of the Silent Planet,* and *That Hideous Strength*, the Christ figure, Ransom, who dies for us, in fact, dies for us. It is orthodox. Children deserve something softer, The Inklings seemed to feel. They constructed their imaginary worlds to make us draw ourselves into it at the child's level, at the emotional level, at the level that coordinates with all of myth.

The Erasers showed us how daunting intellectual challenge can be to really solve the mystery of what makes us behave as we do, but Tolkien's trilogy offers us adventure, activity, poetry for the contemplative, and, if we can follow it along, a simple consolation.

Chosen by many as the best book of the 20th century, *The Lord of the Rings* knocked open the door to fantasy publishing. That disparaged realm of fiction suddenly became common currency, and Tolkien made it possible to see a new world everywhere.

Lecture Eleven
Children's Literature and the Fantastic

Scope:

Children's literature, a publishing category that emerged in the Victorian period to exploit a specialized market, is both simpler and less conventionally realistic than adult literature, even while traditionally restricted in its materials. Looser constraints on style and invention invite the fantastic. As we examine works by Beatrix Potter, Margaret Wise Brown, Dr. Seuss, and Norton Juster, we see, though, that "simpler" has some quite specific implications for character, plot, theme, and style. In addition, children's literature has a visual component absent from our understanding of adult literature. The richest children's literature continues, like fairy tales and the *Alice* books, to offer adult readers, too, their own pleasures. Adult enjoyment of children's literature opens the way, in turn, for fantastic adult fables, such as George Orwell's *Animal Farm*.

Outline

I. Why have we come to associate the fantastic so strongly with children's literature?

    A. Commercial children's literature emerged with the idea of children as a distinct market. In the 18th century, children were still considered adults-in-training.

        1. In *The Blue Boy* (1770) by Thomas Gainsborough (1727–1788), the painted subject, although a "boy," has the haughty pose and expensive clothes of a wealthy, albeit small, man.

        2. In Charles Perrault's (1628–1703) version of "Little Red Riding Hood" (1697), Red remains eaten and the moral warns "children...especially well bred young ladies" against "various kinds of wolves."

        3. Even when the Grimm brothers collected tales that they knew were told to children, their books (1812–1822) were intended for adults.

    B. The power of the fantastic to teach adults was still accepted into the Romantic period, as we see with such cautionary novels as *Frankenstein* (1818). But as realism came to seem more fit for adults, as in *Pride and Prejudice* (1813), the fantastic was ever more relegated to supposedly uncritical children.

C. Heinrich Hoffmann (1809–1894) wrote and illustrated *Struwwelpeter* (1845) as a new kind of children's book. It was the most popular children's book after *Alice* until the 20th century. Mark Twain translated it into English for his own children.

1. Hoffmann, the admired director of a lunatic asylum, shared the growing view that children "do not think logically." Naturally, books with morals, such as "the good child must be truthful," were ineffective.

2. His gruesome, fantastic cautionary tales, including "The Story of the Thumb-Sucker," in which a bogeyman tailor shears off the child protagonist's thumbs, aimed to teach by fantastic shocking.

D. As the Victorian period advanced, children of wealth did not work but were schooled. The privileged ones were allowed fantasies with more gentle morals.

1. *Alice in Wonderland* (1865) was drafted for a real 7-year-old. Although it is playful and allows Alice ultimately to win, adult readers see its darker side, as when the Queen of Hearts shouts, "Off with her head!"

2. *The Tale of Peter Rabbit* (1901) by Beatrix Potter (1866–1943) aimed to please a 5-year-old. Unlike the published *Alice*, it did not aim at adults. Small but disobedient Peter evades the dangerous Mr. McGregor. Back home, his mother does not scold Peter; she comforts him with chamomile tea. A child needn't "think logically" to learn the moral.

II. Whether or not children think "logically," they certainly can understand literature subtly.

A. The classic *Goodnight Moon* (1947) by Margaret Wise Brown (1910–1952) shows a bunny protagonist in a room hung with pictures that make literary allusions.

1. The cow jumps over the moon in one.

    2. In another, the "three bears" sit in a room with the jumping cow picture.

    3. The picture of a rabbit fishing for a bunny, rather than suggesting cannibalism, quotes an illustration (from Brown's very popular *The Runaway Bunny* [1942]) of a mother rabbit trying to retrieve her child.

B. The beloved books of Dr. Seuss (Theodor Seuss Geisel, 1904–1991) train the imagination. In *If I Ran the Zoo* (1950), words and pictures grow ever more fantastic. The child protagonist ultimately returns to reality but with the comforting, implicit moral that his imagined time will someday come.

C. The wordplay in the much admired *Phantom Tollbooth* (1961) by Norton Juster (1929–) is so clever that even adults can enjoy it. The moral, that education is good, whispers throughout the work rather than blaring at the end.

III. Literature today aimed primarily at children (as opposed to young adults) generally demonstrates the following features.

A. Characters: Typically, the hero is a child or animal; relationships are among children and/or animals and/or with a parent figure (such as Juster's talking watchdog, Tock); and, unlike adults-only literature, children have full autonomy.

B. Plot: The plot is usually simple, often episodic, clearly goal-directed, motivated by a single emotion, and achieves a happy ending (Tolkien's "consolation").

C. Theme: The theme is simple, typically embodied in a single problem susceptible to a permanent, didactic solution. As with "Cinderella," if adult issues of sex or society are relevant, they are not likely to be discussed explicitly.

D. Style: Children's books, restricted in vocabulary, often use cute or periphrastic language. They can employ verse and nonsense thematically, as in Juster, or just for fun, as in *The King Who Rained* (1970) by Fred Gwynne (1926–1993).

E. Format: Format matters. Illustrations go where they belong and may even, as in *Goodnight Moon*, help tell the story. Dimensions (the Nutshell Library); font style, size, and color

(Dr. Seuss); and even texture (*Pat the Bunny* [1940]) count.

IV. Adults, supposed to have outgrown children's literature, still use it for four reasons.

    A. Adults may enjoy it on its own terms, either as nostalgia or as discovery.

    B. Some children's books, such as *Alice*, are also adult books.

    C. Some authors, such as Edward Gorey (1925–2000), use the forms of children's literature to comment on children, as in his grim *Gashlycrumb Tinies* (1962).

    D. Some authors use the simplicity allowed by adopting the forms of children's literature to deal simplistically with the complex problems of the adult world, as in the political fable *Animal Farm* (1945) by George Orwell (1903–1950).

    E. In short, children's literature nurtures the fantastic for readers of all ages.

Essential Reading:

Brown, Margaret Wise. *Goodnight Moon*.

Hoffmann, Heinrich. *Struwwelpeter*.

Juster, Norton. *The Phantom Tollbooth*.

Seuss, Dr. *If I Ran the Zoo*.

Supplementary Reading:

Gorey, Edward. *Amphigorey*.

Orwell, George. *Animal Farm*.

Questions to Consider:

1. What are the comparative strengths and weaknesses of books aimed primarily at children, such as *Goodnight Moon*, and those aimed at an audience of many ages, such as *Alice in Wonderland*?

2. Why should or should not adult books make the same integrated use of visuals that the best children's books do?

Lecture Eleven—Transcript
Children's Literature and the Fantastic

Children's literature, a publishing category that emerged in the Victorian period to exploit a specialized market, is both simpler and less conventionally realistic than adult literature, even while traditionally restricted in its materials. Looser constraints on style and invention invite the fantastic. As we examine works by Beatrix Potter, Margaret Wise Brown, Dr. Seuss, and Norton Juster, we see, though, that "simpler" has some quite specific implications for character, plot, theme, and style. In addition, children's literature has a visual component absent from our understanding of adult literature. The richest children's literature continues, like fairy tales and the *Alice* books, to offer adult readers, too, their own pleasures. Adult enjoyment of children's literature opens the way in turn for fantastic adult fables such as George Orwell's *Animal Farm*.

Why have we come to associate the fantastic so strongly with children's literature? Commercial children's literature emerged with the idea of children as a distinct market. In the 18th century, children were still considered adults in training. In the famous painting by Gainsborough, "The Blue Boy," the painted subject, although a boy, has the haughty pose and expensive clothes of a wealthy, albeit small, man. In Charles Perrault's version of "Little Red Riding Hood," in the end of the 17th century, Red remains eaten; she's doesn't get out of the wolf. And the moral warns, "children, especially well bred young ladies" against "various kinds of wolves." Even when the Grimm brothers collected tales that they knew were told to children, their books at the beginning of the 19th century were intended for adults.

The power of the fantastic to teach adults was still accepted into the Romantic period, as we see with cautionary novels such as *Frankenstein* from 1818; but, as Realism came to seem more suitable for adults, as in *Pride and Prejudice*, 1813, the fantastic was ever more relegated to supposedly uncritical children.

Heinrich Hoffmann, who lived for most of the 19th century, wrote and illustrated *Struwwelpeter*, 1845, as a new kind of children's book. It was, in fact, the most popular children's book, after *Alice*, until the 20th century. Mark Twain translated it into English for his own children. Hoffmann—no relation to E. T. A. Hoffman—was a doctor and the admired director of a lunatic asylum specializing in the care of troubled children. He shared in the growing view that children do not think logically. Naturally, books with morals, such as "the good child must be truthful," were ineffective. His gruesome, fantastic, cautionary tales like "The Story of the Thumb-Sucker," in which a bogyman tailor sheers off the child protagonist's thumbs, aimed to teach by fantastic shocking. This is Twain's translation:

"Konrad!" cried his mama dear,
"I'll go out, but you stay here,
Try how pretty you can be
Till I come again," said she.
"Docile be, and good and mild,
Pray don't suck your thumb, my child,
For if you do, the tailor'll come
And bring his shears and snip your thumb
From off your hand as clear and clean
As if paper it had been."

Before she'd turned to the south,
He'd got his thumbkin in his mouth!

Bang! here goes the door ker-slam!
Whoop! the tailor lands ker-blam!
Waves his shears, the heartless grub,
and calls for a Dawmen-lutscher-bub.
Claps his weapon to the thumb,
Snips its square as head of grum,
And while that lad, his tongue unfurled
And fired a yell heard 'round the world.

Who can tell the mother's sorrow
When she saw her boy the morrow!
There he stood all steeped in shame,
And not a thumbkin to his name.

My goodness! This was a man admired for his sensitive care of children.

As the Victorian period advanced, children of wealth did not work but were schooled. The privileged ones were allowed fantasies with more gentle morals. *Alice in Wonderland* was drafted for a real seven-year-old. Although it is playful and allows Alice ultimately to win, adult readers see its darker side, as when the Queen of Hearts shouts, "Off with her head!" But, of course, in Alice's book, while the adults see that happen, that is, see the queen yell, the children know that Alice doesn't lose her head.

The Tale of Peter Rabbit, at the very beginning of the 20th century, published by Beatrix Potter, aimed to please a five-year-old. Unlike the published *Alice*, it did not aim at adults. Small but disobedient Peter evades the dangerous Farmer McGregor. Back home, his mother does not scold Peter, she comforts him with chamomile tea. A child needn't think logically to learn the moral.

Whether or not children think logically, they certainly can understand literature subtly. The classic tale, *Goodnight Moon*, published by Margaret Wise Brown in 1947, has a bunny protagonist in a room hung with pictures. The old lady is trying to put the protagonist to sleep. He is a bunny; she is a rabbit; and the pictures all make literary illusions. In other words, the illustrator accepts the idea that children can think, if not logically, in some sophisticated way. One of the pictures shows a cow jumping over the moon; another picture shows three bears sitting in a room. In a later picture, in the book *Goodnight Moon*, we see a close-up of that picture of the three bears, and we notice that in the room in which the three bears sit, there is hung a picture, and that picture is the same picture of the cow jumping over the room that's in the little bunny's room. In other words, we have an interesting problem of a regress further and further into the world of fiction upon fiction. This is a sophisticated kind of storytelling, and children's books, although they may not suppose that children think logically, certainly understand that they can think critically.

When I, as an adult, first read *Goodnight Moon,* I was rather shocked by a picture it shows of a mother rabbit, or an adult rabbit at any rate, standing in a stream in waders and fly-fishing, trying to catch, it seems, a baby rabbit, a bunny, that goes leaping out to catch the bait at the end of the line, a carrot. I thought, my goodness, this is cannibalism. What kind of thing is that to put in a children's book, especially a sweet little children's book aiming to have the child go to sleep? This picture is in *Goodnight Moon*; it hangs on the wall of the bunny.

As I mentioned to my class that I couldn't understand the cannibalism involved, the next day one of my students came to me and said, "Ah, you were alive at the wrong time. Take a look at this. In 1942, five years before the publication of *Goodnight Moon*, Margaret Wise Brown had published *The Runaway Bunny*. *The Runaway Bunny* itself was a best seller, and in it a mother rabbit is trying to bring her runaway baby into the safety of her own home. In order to attract the bunny, she does all sorts of things, including using a fishing rod to lay a carrot out in front of the bunny's path. This isn't cannibalism, this is love. My student caught the literary illusion that I had missed. But in 1947, a child reading *Goodnight Moon* would have caught the 1942 reference to *Runaway Bunny*. In other words, children's literature, whether or not it's based on the notion that children think logically, can be quite sophisticated.

The beloved books of Dr. Seuss, pseudonym for Theodore Seuss Geisel, train the imagination. One that I particularly like is called *If I Ran the Zoo*. On the first page of *If I Ran the Zoo*, we see young Gerald McGrew in the lower left hand corner looking at the closed-eyed, quite complacent zoo keeper, standing in front of the corner of the cage that has a lion in it, and the lion is, himself, sleeping quite happily with a grin on his face. It says, "It's a pretty good zoo," said young Gerald McGrew, "and the fellow who runs it seems proud of it, too." And then what happens, double-spread page by double-spread page, is Gerald McGrew imagining ever more fantastic ways to make this zoo better; to have ever more fantastic creatures, to have ever more fantastic architecture. And, periodically, as the zoo becomes ever more extraordinary, imaginative, fantastic, larger and larger crowds of people pay homage to the wonder that has been created by Gerald McGrew.

In addition to that, we see that the capturing act is not merely imagination, but imagination that runs in every direction that the child can think of. "I'll capture one tiny, I'll capture one cute, I'll capture a deer that no hunter would shoot. A deer that's so nice, he could sleep in your bed, if it weren't for the horns that he has on his head." And that sudden move back to the practical, that move from one world back to the other, makes us remember just how fantastic this all is.

Another way that Dr. Seuss makes us remember how fantastic the world is, is by creating pictures that, themselves, are fantastic. My favorite among all of these wonderful illustrations is one that shows a family of elk. They have horns that are interconnected, wildly shaped horns, and when you look at the picture it looks like a tangle of horns. You can't resist taking your finger and trying to trace out how the horns connect to see, in fact, if his horns are hers, or the other way around.

But when Gerald has completely finished with his imagining, he doesn't need to change the world. He's happy now simply to know he can do it. The very last page of the book shows the identical scene with identical features on each of the three characters' faces—that is, Gerald, the zookeeper, and the lion—the only difference being that within the cage we now have a bright, vividly colored background. Now the world, even the ordinary world, looks different to Gerald, and he says, "Yes, that's what I'd do," said young Gerald McGrew. "I'd make a few changes, if I ran the zoo.'"

Now, what we know, of course, is that these books intended for children are not intended to have children go running out and changing the zoo. They are intended to have children think that the possibility of exercising their imaginations will make it possible for them to make a better world in the future.

The world of children is a world that can play as actively as can that of adults. The *Phantom Tollbooth*, by Norton Juster, published in 1961, is often considered to be the very best book in the line of *Alice in Wonderland*, published ever, anywhere, after *Alice in Wonderland*. Juster is primarily an architect, but he's written a few books, and this is by far his childs masterpiece. It is so clever, in fact, that even adults can enjoy it. The moral, however, is simply that education is good, a moral that most adults feel is, perhaps, too young for them. But it whispers throughout the work rather than blaring at the end.

It's the story of Milo, who a bored young boy, who comes home from school, and finds a package he'd never before noticed. He opens it up and it is, in fact, a model of a tollbooth, a large thing that he can construct. He drives through it with his little toy car. Suddenly, he's in a completely different world, and in that different world, things have metaphorical meanings. That is, as in Freud's "The Uncanny," the metaphorical becomes literal. He, for instance, is stuck in a swamp and his car won't go at all. The swamp is called the Doldrums. It's killing him that he can't leave there, but finally is distracted by something else. When he is distracted, he just sits glumly, and the car starts up, because it "goes without saying." His guardian, his mentor on this trip, is a watchdog named Tock, who has a large watch in his side. In fact, the book is full of puns. The kingdom in which he enters, The Land Beyond, is divided into two—one ruled by King Azaz, A-Z-A-Z, the Unabridged; and one The Mathemagician. In the land of King Azaz, the Unabridged, everything depends upon words. In the realm of The Mathemagician, everything depends on numbers. The book clearly describes for us that the world had two realms, words and numbers.

Once upon a time, when I was a much younger man, I was lecturing about this book in a class, and I pointed out to my class how wonderful was the distinction made between words and numbers. That particular day my son, who was then about four, was sitting in the front row, and he raised his hand. The fact that there were 200 university students sitting behind him made no difference whatsoever, and I called on him from the stage, and David said, "But, Daddy, numbers are words," and he was completely correct. David's insight makes us understand that the *Phantom Tollbooth* is not for illiterate children. It is for people who have already entered into the world defined by the symbol systems that we learn in school. It is a fantasy for those who are in school, but, like Milo, can't wait to be out of school, but it teaches them why they should be in school. They learn, for example, about the enormous powers of words.

In the chapter about the royal banquet, Milo presents himself before a king, who looks at him and says, "What an ordinary little boy you are," when it turns out he can do nothing but think. "Why, my cabinet ministers can do all sorts of things," the king says. "The duke here can make mountains out of molehills; the minister splits hairs; the count makes hay while the sun shines; the earl leaves no stone unturned; and the undersecretary," he finished ominously, "hangs by a thread. Can't you do anything at all?" Of course, what he does to is bring the twin princesses, Rhyme and Reason, back into the kingdom, and has the two brothers, Azaz and The Mathamagician to reconcile, and all is well in The Lands Beyond.

When Milo comes back to his apartment, he understands that he could return to The Lands Beyond, but as he looks around his room and sees all the books and all the things to play with that previously had bored him so, he realizes he may never have time to go there again, because his world is filled with possibilities.

These are truly children's books. What makes children's books, children's books? It seems to me that in this new publishing category, that begins in the middle of the 19th century, of illogically thinking but nonetheless sophisticatedly feeling and noticing children, what we seek is simplicity.

Characters: A typical hero of a child's book is a child or an animal. The relationships are among children and/or animals, and/or with a parent figure, just as Juster's talking watchdog Tock serves as the parent figure, giving guidance to Milo. Unlike adults-only literature, in children's books, the child character typically has full autonomy. It's a rare book for adults only in which children really have the power of decision, of affecting the world. Rather, they become encumbrances or someone to be saved or someone to come up with a clever idea, but the real action, the real decisions are made by adults. Not so in children's books. They're either made by children or animal protagonists. These are, though, simpler characters. They are not, for example, buffeted by political and large social concerns or the urgings of sexuality.

In plot, children's books are also simpler than typical adult books. What that means is that they are often episodic. Each piece of the story can, in a sense, be thought of as self-contained, one strung after the other like pearls on a necklace. Clearly, the plot is goal-directed—the child needs to come home again or bring rhyme and reason back together again. The desire here is usually attributed to a single motivation; and it is susceptible, this problem, to a happy ending—what Tolkien calls, in his discussion of fairy tales, consolation.

The themes of children's literature are also simple, typically embodied, as I say, in a single problem susceptible to permanent and often didactic solution. As with "Cinderella," for example, not only do we learn the theme of diligence, but we also see that if there are issues such as sex or society that are relevant to the story, they are not typically discussed explicitly.

The style is also simple in children's books—simple in the sense that it uses a restricted vocabulary. So, we find often that the language is cute, or periphrastic—the long way around saying something. This language, children's styles, can employ verse and nonsense thematically. We saw the verse in *Alice in Wonderland*; we see nonsense in Juster. Or, they can employ—that is, children's books—language just for fun, as in Fred Gwynne's series of books beginning with *The King Who Rained*, the cover illustration of which shows a king recumbent as a cloud with rain coming down from below him. There's nothing much to be made of that pun. The glory is just that there is a pun.

Now, in the world of adult literature today, most readers do not favor poetry. For better or for worse, most readers see poetry today as falling into two camps. There is the greeting card camp of poetry, in which we understand it to be simple, saccharine, and dutiful—although sometimes we need its help. And there is literary poetry, the kind typically published in journals with very small circulations, read by other people who write literary poetry. Most readers think that poetry is simply too intentionally arcane to them, or beneath their literary consideration. But, in children's literature, poetry is allowed because, with a simple vocabulary, the joy of rhyming, the joy of meter comes across. "Mirror, mirror, on the wall, who's the fairest of them all?" We don't look at this as a mistake; we look at this as beauty.

The suspension of disbelief that allows actors in the American musical to break into song seems to have disappeared from modern literature for adults. But, for children, it's there. So, we have these four levels of narrative that conserve diachronic meeting—character, plot, theme, and style—and all four of those continue to be simple in children's literature, and when they are reversed, we see that that generates the fantastic. But there's a fifth characteristic of children's literature that separates it from adult literature, and that is format.

If you ask an adult have you read *Moby Dick*, and the answer is yes, you will never follow up by asking if you read it in the large-type addition or one with an orange cover. Or with Boldini type? You'll just say, "Ah, you read *Moby Dick.*" But, can you imagine reading a Dr. Seuss book in a tiny Nutshell Library edition? It wouldn't be the same book. In children's literature, format matters; the visual matters. The clear sign of this is in children's literature, the visuals are where they belong in the text. In adult books, we often might have illustrations gathered together in a central section of color plates. You'd never see that in children's literature, because to tell the story depends upon engagement with the visuals. Run your finger across those horns of the family in Dr. Seuss's book.

Now, once we recognize that the visual really matters, suddenly we understand something that adult literature has lost. The visual is part of how we communicate. As you read through the book, a children's book will go from the visual to the textual, back and forth, telling the story diachronically. So, even though we may come to think of visuals as synchronic, as they are used in children's literature they add a fifth level of diachronic meaning to the work. And, so, the changes from one to the other create the fantastic, as with young Gerald McGrew, who goes from the ordinary Gerald to the ever-more extraordinary Gerald, so that, at the end—when he's the ordinary Gerald again—that's yet one more fantastic change. It's just like Alice saying, "Which way? Which way?", and being surprised that she doesn't grow because she's used to growing.

Adults are supposed to have outgrown children's literature, and yet they still use it for at least four reasons. First of all, adults may enjoy children's literature on its own terms, either as nostalgia or, frankly—as when I was shown *Runaway Bunny* by one of my students—as a new and delightful discovery. Secondly, some children's books, such as the *Alice* books, are also clearly adult books. The adult reader sees the defense against mortality that runs throughout in a very bitter way, in the *Alice* books, that the child misses entirely.

Thirdly, there are some authors—Edward Gorey for example—who use children's literature as a way of commenting upon children. For instance, he has a famous work called the *Gashlycrumb Tinies*. This work is just an ABC book—you know, A is for Alice, et cetera, et cetera. Well, this book shows a school teacher holding an umbrella with 26 children around her, and then we have 26 pages, each with a poem and a plate—actually, a line and a plate. A is for Amy, who fell down the stairs; B is for Basil, assaulted by bears; et cetera. Every single one of these illustrations shows a child gruesomely dying. The last one is Z is for Zillah, who drank too much gin. And the last page of all shows the skeletal figure of death holding an umbrella with 26 tombstones around him. It's a children's book, but it's a children's book for an adult who wants to say something about children. I'll leave it to you to decide what Edward Gorey is saying.

The fourth reason that adults may use children's literature is that children's literature, because it depends upon simplicity of story, plot, character, and theme, implies to its readers that it is legitimately simple. That means, if one writes in the form of children's literature, one can sneak an over-simple treatment of a subject before an adult consciousness. A clear example of this is George Orwell's *Animal Farm*, a beast fable that criticizes communism and has in it such foolish lines as "all animals are equal, but some of them are more equal." In fact, Orwell understands that adult leaders would never take the politics in *Animal Farm* as a cogent analysis of the weaknesses of communism, but to put across the fact that communism is caught in its own hypocrisies and caught in its own social situations, the beast fable of *Animal Farm* was, in fact, much more effective than all of the treatises that you can no longer name because they have fallen out of our consciousness.

In short, children's literature works for adults because they like it on its own terms—sometimes its intended for them, it may be a way to comment on children—and it allows us to say things we could not openly say to other adults. Children's literature allows people with minds still being shaped and which indulge in imagination to go to places they never would have gone were they not encouraged by this use of language and pictures. And adults use it, too. Children's literature, in other words, nurtures the fantastic for readers of all ages.

Lecture Twelve
Postmodernism and the Fantastic

Scope:

Each literary period relies on a characteristic understanding of Nature. Postmodernism takes Nature to be a phenomenological construct, which implies that Nature is a matter of perspective. In its extreme form, namely, true fantasy, the fantastic always problematizes perspective. Thus, Postmodern literature has a theoretical affinity for the fantastic. In Italo Calvino's fantastic *Cosmicomics*, we see, using the analytic ideas of Northrop Frye, how Postmodernism develops its own myths. In Marge Piercy's *Woman on the Edge of Time*, we see how Postmodernism calls into question individual perception. And in magical realism, which flows from the work of such writers as Jorge Luis Borges and includes Gabriel García Márquez's *One Hundred Years of Solitude* and Laura Esquivel's *Like Water for Chocolate*, we see how, as Calvino and Piercy had implied, Postmodernism offers a fantastic new framework for understanding ourselves in society.

Outline

I. Our aesthetic period is often called Postmodern. Postmodernism has a natural affinity for the fantastic.

   A. What is Postmodernism?

      1. One philosophical definition says that Postmodernism pursues "themes of 'self-reflexivity,' or the puzzles induced by allowing language to become the object of its own scrutiny in a kind of dizzying rhetorical regress" (*The Oxford Companion to Philosophy*). We find this in true fantasies, such as those by Lewis Carroll.

      2. Another definition (U.S. State Dept.) says that Postmodernism is "characterized by open-endedness and collage. [It] questions the foundations of cultural and artistic forms through self-referential irony...." We find this in true fantasies, such as those by E. T. A. Hoffmann.

3. "Emma Zunz" (1948) by Jorge Luis Borges (1899–1986), while not a true fantasy, makes clear the Postmodern aesthetic and its real-world implications.

4. The Postmodern period, like other artistic periods, can be characterized by the dominant relation of humanity to Nature. Postmodernism takes Nature—including the physical world, society, and even the self—as a phenomenological construct, that is, as an intensional act of consciousness.

B. Individual sentences can show the convergence of Postmodernism and the fantastic.

1. Self-reflexivity: "This is one sentence I can never say."

2. Unresolved structural ambiguity: "I walked down the street and turned into a drugstore."

3. Reversals of the ground rules of the narrative world: "I feel more like I did when I came in here than I do now."

II. Both Postmodernism and true fantasy problematize the world. Yet while the challenging play of Postmodernism may seem inherently destructive of many certainties, it can also be constructive.

A. We have seen that the fantastic is one key tool in artistic evolution. Northrop Frye (1912–1991) suggests how the evolution of literary forms can produce new myths.

B. Italo Calvino (1923–1985) exemplifies this fantastic myth-making in *Cosmicomics* (1965), a collection of his fantastic Postmodern stories.

III. Both Postmodernism and fantasy problematize individual perception. Many science fictions raise this issue because "science" is about "knowing."

A. Philip K. Dick (1928–1982) is certainly Postmodern in such works as *A Scanner Darkly* (1977) and *Ubik* (1969).

B. Understanding the splendid *Woman on the Edge of Time* (1976) by Marge Piercy (1936–) depends on disentangling one basis for perception from another. For the protagonist, that makes all the difference—literally—in the world.

IV. Both Postmodernism and true fantasy, then, naturally problematize the relations between the world and the individual who perceives it.

A. Gabriel García Márquez (1928–), best known for *One Hundred Years of Solitude* (1967), is a touchstone author for so-called *magical realism*. "My most important problem was destroying the lines of demarcation that separate what seems real from what seems fantastic."

    1. García Márquez's sprawling novel combines individual stories, cultural myths, and national and international politics.

    2. *Magical realism* refers narrowly to the work of a group of Latin American writers who treat the magical as fully and calmly expected as part of the real. Key exemplars include Isabel Allende, Alejo Carpentier, and Julio Cortázar.

    3. More broadly, magical realism, which includes a Postmodernist assault on previously stable markers of identity, such as race and nation, includes such non-Latins as Mikhail Bulgakov, Salman Rushdie, and even Günter Grass.

B. *Like Water for Chocolate* (1989) by Laura Esquivel (1950–), which has sold more than 3 million copies in 30 languages, is clearly both Postmodern and fantastic.

    1. The heroine, Tita, cannot express her love except through her cooking. Magically, people eating her food are affected by her emotions.

    2. Other magical moments include two spontaneous fires.

    3. The structure of the book, which seems to be a mixture of novel, calendar, and cookbook, assaults our notions of genre propriety.

    4. The characters' actions and setting subtly embed them in Mexican national politics and international politics.

    5. At the end, the book is also a family saga that asks us to think deeply about what makes us who we are and how we know who we are.

    6. Thus, the fantastic, which once drove such culturally foundational works as the *Odyssey*, again drives narrative that is broadly powerful, artistically honored, and personally moving. As in this imaginative novel, the fantastic is at the center of our lives.

Essential Reading:

Esquivel, Laura. *Like Water for Chocolate*.

Supplementary Reading:

Calvino, Italo. *Cosmicomics*.

Frye, Northrop. "Third Essay: Theory of Myths," in *Anatomy of Criticism: Four Essays*.

García Márquez, Gabriel. *One Hundred Years of Solitude*.

Questions to Consider:

1. In the context of a Postmodern fantastic work, what do we mean by "truth"?

2. In what ways, if at all, do you notice in your daily life that our era might well be called Postmodernist?

Lecture Twelve—Transcript
Postmodernism and the Fantastic

Each literary period relies on a characteristic understanding of nature. Postmodernism takes nature to be a phenomenological construct, which implies nature is a matter of perspective. In its extreme form, namely true Fantasy, the fantastic always problematizes perspective. Thus, Postmodern literature has a theoretical affinity for the fantastic. In Italo Calvino's fantastic *Cosmicomics*, we see—using the analytic ideas of Northrop Frye—how Postmodernism develops its own myths. In Marge Piercy's *Woman on the Edge of Time*, we see how Postmodernism calls into question individual perception. And in Magical Realism, which flows from the work of writers such as Jorge Luis Borges and includes Gabriel García Márquez's *One Hundred Years of Solitude* and Laura Esquivel's *Like Water for Chocolate*, we see how, as Calvino and Piercy had implied, Postmodernism offers a fantastic new framework for understanding ourselves in society.

Our aesthetic period is often called Postmodern. Postmodernism, as I said, has a natural affinity for the fantastic. What is Postmodernism? *The Oxford Companion to Philosophy* defines Postmodernism as pursuing "themes of self-reflexivity or the puzzles induced by allowing language to become the object of its own scrutiny in a kind of dizzying rhetorical regress." But we found this already in true Fantasies like those of Lewis Carroll. When Alice is stuck in the tree, she says, "Ah, I used to read fairy tales, and now I'm in one." The complete regress based on the shifts of language, shifting from one world to another, one ontological realm to another. Outsider reader reading about a world, being in the world, thinking about the world within the world, and so on, *ad infinitem*.

Another definition—this one from, believe it or not, the official definition of the United States State Department—says that Postmodernism is "characterized by open-endedness and collage. It questions the foundations of cultural and artistic forms through self-referential irony." Self-reference, self-referentiality—these come up again and again in definitions of Postmodernism. But we found this self-referentiality in all true Fantasies. For example, in E. T. A. Hoffmann's *The Golden Pot* where, at the end, we don't know whether the character is off in Atlantis, stuck in an ink well, or just hallucinating.

This dependence upon individual perspective is made clear in a work like "Emma Zunz" by Jorge Luis Borges, one of the great writers of the 20th century. While not a true Fantasy, this story makes clear the Postmodern aesthetic and its real-world implications. The story of "Emma Zunz" is the story of a woman whose father has been cheated out of his half of a company by his partner, while Emma, herself, was still a little girl. Years pass. The family is disgraced because the partner had made it appear that her father had committed some larceny against the company. The father has gone off in disgrace from Europe to South America. She has lost touch with him because he needs to evade the law. But, finally, years later when she is an adult, a letter arrives from a friend of her father's explaining that the father has now died and what the situation really was.

Emma decides that she must have vengeance on the factory owner for what he has done to her family, so she goes down to the port and finds a sailor from a ship that's due to leave the next day. Although a virgin, she entices him up to her room and submits to sexual relations, which utterly disgust her. Then she calls up the factory owner and tells him that there is the possibility of a strike. She, as one of the workers, has heard this. He says that she should come up and talk with him, and they meet in his office. There is, in fact, a gun in the drawer of his desk.

This is how the story ends:

> After she shoots him, she picks up the telephone and repeated what she would repeat so many times again, and with these and with other words. "Something incredible has happened. Mr. Lowenthal had me come over on the pretext of the strike. He abused me; I killed him."

Actually, the story was incredible, but it impressed everyone because substantially it was true. True was Emma Zunz's tone. True was her shame. True was her hate. True was also the outrage she had suffered. Only the circumstances were false: the time, and one or two proper names." This is fundamental Postmodernism. The things we think of as details become irrelevant; the feelings, the perceptions, the truth of the human engagement as it shapes our understanding of the world, the world as a phenomenological construct, an intentional act of our consciousness—these are what we see as important in the Postmodern period. Of course, since Fantasy is always about our understanding, there is a natural affinity between the Postmodern and fantastic.

Postmodernism takes nature, including the physical world, society, and even the self as a phenomenological construct. Individual sentences can show this convergence of Postmodernism and the fantastic. Take this self-reflexive example: "This is one sentence I can never say"—but I just said it. There are unresolved structural ambiguities. "I walked down the street and turned into a drugstore. Poof! I'm a newspaper stand" or "indeed, I made a left."

We also see in individual sentences reversals of the ground rules of the narrative world. One of my all-time favorites is, "I feel more like I did when I came in here than I do now." I feel more like I did when I came in here than I do now. As you read through that sentence, or think about it, from any given word to any given word, none of the rules of grammar are broken. But, by the time we come to the end, it makes no sense whatsoever. Everything depends on our perspective. Postmodernism and true Fantasy problematize the world.

Yet, while the challenging play of Postmodernism may seem inherently destructive of many certainties, it can also be constructive. We have seen that the fantastic is one key tool in artistic evolution. For example, we have the detective story where we have the crux come in the middle in *The Purloined Letter*. As time goes on, that crux moves further and further toward the end, so that by the time we come to Agatha Christie, we're unloading all of the mystery in the last few pages of a lengthy novel. But, eventually, something called "aesthetic fatigue" sets in, and people are tired of just that same old form, and so people begin to apply the fantastic, among other devices, to make the genre fresh again. One way to do that is to use irony. But Robbe-Grillet turns that whole form inside out by making the detective fail and the reader succeed, by putting the solution not at the end, but in the middle. The fantastic is one of the driving tools for the evolution of genres. It grows out of a certain kind of irony.

Northrop Frye, in *The Anatomy of Criticism*, suggests one of the consequences of the evolution of genres. He says that with any large, dominating kind of story—let's say, for example, the story of boy meets girl or the story of the founding of a nation—we can see that story represented, in a sense, in a series of different manners. The first manner he associates with spring; this is the comic manner, the manner in which whatever problems exist we see finally, at the end, are to be solved because society has reconstituted itself. As that form develops, it moves into the summer, and in the summer we see romance. It's not just a matter of the story ending with the children of the opposing houses promising marriage, but, in fact, the children in the opposing houses now have a love affair.

In the fall, we see the same form carried out as tragedy. In fact, the love affair turns bad. One dies, for example, or a father discovers it and forces the couple to part. Further along we see the same material handled in the winter. In the winter, when it's cold and we're distant, we ironize what's going on; we make fun of such trivial notions as romantic love. We may, in fact, have bitterness or satire.

But then, Frye suggests, the same material will continue to develop, and as it develops, although Frye does not say this, it will use the fantastic to change into, as it were in a musical analogy, a new key. And in going back to comedy in its new form, it will pass through a phrase which he calls myth.

I'd like to suggest to you that Italo Calvino, perhaps the greatest fantasist of the 20th century Italy, exemplifies this in work after work. One of my favorite books of Calvino's is one called *Cosmicomics*. In *Cosmicomics* we have a single character named "Qfwfq," Q-F-W-F-Q. Every story begins with an epigraph that says something about what really happened in science. It's accurate, from what we understand of science. Then bluh-bluh-bluh-bluh-bluh said, and then follows the rest of the story. The story is always based on some perceptual understanding of that scientific fact. One of my favorites is called, "All At One Point."

It begins with a little epigraph explaining that Hubbell made us realize that all of the stars are flying away from us at ever increasing speeds, and, therefore, we can infer that once upon a time the entire universe was all at one point, the name of the story. "In those days," Qfwfq said, and then he goes on to tell what it was like when everything lived all at one point. He makes bizarre puns like the Z'zu family that always had its laundry drying and wanted to hang lines across our point. The very use of the language is Postmodern; it's fantastic; it makes us laugh. The Z'zu family, it turns out, have many, many, many items with them—chests and clothes and old detritus that they've picked up on their travels—and they are known as the immigrants and are looked down on. Although, of course, the narrator says, Qfwfq says, "There could be no idea of immigrant when there was no place to come from, and besides which we were all living there at one point."

The great wonder of that point is a Mrs. Ph(i)NK0, which is how I can only pronounce this word, which actually has parentheses in it and subscripts and so on. Mrs. Ph(i)NK0 loves everyone. She, in fact, is having an affair with one man, but on the other hand, perhaps it's not an affair since everybody is living inside everybody else since everything is all at one point. And then Mrs. Ph(i)NK0 says, "Ah, boys, if I only had some room, what noodles I would make for you." Then begins a sentence which is about a page and a-half long in which there is the imagination of the noodles coming from the flour, which had to be grown in fields, which had to be ripened under a sun, which had to be within a galaxy, which created all of space and all of time and led to the separation of everyone from Mrs. Ph(i)NK0, and everyone regretting they were now apart. And that's the end of the story.

In other words, this Postmodern story, told in the most bizarre, imaginative, fantastic way one can imagine takes a fact of science and understands it thoroughly in human terms and leaves us with an image of the very impulse of love, of generosity, of nurturing, of giving, of sexuality, of inclusion inherently leading to a downfall, not of original sin, but of human separation.

This story, *All At One Point*, gives us an image of "I want to"—and then we're all apart that, in a way, stands for a modern, mobile society where so few of us live near our family; where the extended family is extended all over the map; where we keep in touch by electronic means and rarely hug. It seems to me that Frye is right. We've taken the notion of "I want to feed you," that unsaid implicit activity of love from fairy tales and made of it a modern myth. The fantastic drives fairy tales all the way to Fantasy and from winter to spring, creating myth along the way.

Both Postmodernism and Fantasy problematize individual perception. Many of the science fictions that we most admire these days raise this issue because, after all, science is about knowing. Philip K. Dick is certainly Postmodern in works like *A Scanner Darkly* and *Ubik*. *A Scanner Darkly* tells the story of a man who, so far as he understands, is a drug agent and he infiltrates a group of people who are dealing with drugs. To do so, he deals with drugs. To build up his credibility with them, he takes the drugs. He becomes an addict and is eventually arrested for being an addict and is sent to work on a government work farm as part of his incarceration. On that work farm he discovers that he is now made to grow the drugs that the government is supplying that create the condition for which he was supposed to be the solution. Do we know where the government stands in our lives? Do we know if we're the good guys or the bad guys?

In *Ubik*, the good guy keeps watching the very nature of the world change, and at the end, when he disappears, his comrades look in their pockets and take out the money of the new world—they can only tell it's a new world because now it has his face on the coins. How did the world change? It changed because of perception. This is Postmodernism.

Marge Piercy's *Woman on the Edge of Time* is an extraordinary novel of a poor Latina, Consuelo, who has been abused by the system. We learn at one point, for example, that she's been given an unnecessary hysterectomy by interns at a city hospital because they needed the practice. Her one child, whom she loves desperately, has been taken away from her by Social Services. She is often locked up in an insane asylum, for her own good, of course.

At one point, however, sitting in her apartment, she sees someone across the table from her, and this someone is a creature from the future, a human from a better world. And most of the novel is set in that better world, where Consuelo is learning about how the world can become, where women can have their own energy; where, in fact, men take hormones to be able to breastfeed; and women give up procreation so that men and women can be truly equals. At one other point in the novel, she goes to an alternative future in which every woman is nothing but a sex object or a baby maker, and women are radically, radically suppressed by men. She then finds out that the course of the future depends upon stopping the people who control the medical establishment and define insanity in our era.

And, so, when she is back in our era, she poisons the doctors. The result of that act is she is incarcerated for the rest of her life, and the story tells us in the end that she was sent to the insane prison, followed by a document of 113 pages. It's the language of others that controls us. When we think about this book, we don't know, however, whether Consuelo was really in the future and this is a science fiction, or it was just a projection on her part. But one way or another, whether it's science fiction or it's realistic, it's Postmodern because it tells us that everything depends on our perception. Does our perception of the dangers of a situation even go so far in determining reality as to make it legitimate to kill those who are ostensibly trying to help us? Both Postmodernism and true Fantasy, then, naturally distort relations between the world and the individual who perceives it.

Gabriel García Márquez, best known for *One Hundred Years of Solitude*, is the touchstone author for so-called Magical Realism, which is a particular variety of Postmodernism. "My most important problem," García Márquez said, "was destroying the lines of demarcation that separate what seems real from what seems fantastic. His sprawling novel combines individual stories, cultural myths, national and international politics. There's a reason he won the Nobel Prize. Magical Realism itself narrowly refers to a group of Latin American writers who treat the magical as fully and calmly expected just as if it were part of the real.

For instance, in *One Hundred Years of Solitude,* birds float up from the earth, leaves turn into birds, and ice somehow is brought as a magical object into the jungle, without itself ever having been destroyed by the Equatorial heat. The key exemplars of this are Isabel Allende, Alejo Carpentier, and Julio Cortázar. But, more broadly than this South American group, Magical Realism includes the Postmodernist assault on the previously stable markers of identity, such as race and nation; and, therefore, includes such non-Latins as Mikhail Bulgakov, Salman Rushdie, and even Gunter Grass.

A wonderful work of this variety is *Like Water for Chocolate* by Laura Esquivel, which has sold over three million copies in thirty languages. It's clearly both Postmodern and fantastic. The heroine, Tita, cannot express her love except through her cooking. So, when she is feeling bitter, her tears make for food that makes everyone sick. The book begins with a recipe for Christmas rolls, and then the novel starts to talk about Tita's birth. Tita is not allowed to marry in the normal way because her mother claims that in their family they have the tradition that the oldest daughter must care for the mother until the mother dies. There is no such tradition. But, in fact, Tita falls desperately in love with a man who, because of the mother's intervention, winds up marrying Tita's sister. He marries her not because he loves her, but because it's a way for him to stay near Tita. You can see the difficulties involved.

As the story unfolds, every chapter begins with another month of the year, and there are twelve chapters. Every chapter begins with another recipe. Every chapter goes through a story in which the recipe is made. The directions of the recipe are given, and something fantastic happens because of what that means when the recipe enters into the lives of the people.

There are other magical moments as well. For instance, one of Tita's sisters goes into an outhouse, takes a shower, and is so inflamed by the possibilities of the Mexican Revolution that though she is in water, the outhouse bursts into flame, and there she is standing out in the field naked. Along comes a captain of the rebels on his horse, sweeps her up, and off she goes. Later she comes back into the story, herself having become an officer in the revolutionary army. So we see that the family life that Tita's involved in is part of the politics. She, herself, is loved by a man named John Brown; an American who bears the name, of course, of a famous-but-failed revolutionary who tried to free the American slaves before the Civil War. For that chapter in which he falls in love with her, the recipe is one for matches. Indeed, we learn how to make matches, and we're told that Tita, herself, has that heat within her.

At the end of the novel, Tita finally decides that she will join Pedro, and the two of them, after her sister's death, go off into a shed, a shed that is magically lit by a heaven's worth of candles. He dies in their lovemaking. She eats the candles. She bursts into flame, and the entire ranch goes up in ashes.

At the end of the novel, we realize that all along we have been reading the manuscript of one of the children, the daughter of the girl, and the niece of Tita, whom Tita raised. That is, this is Tita's great niece, and she tells us that after this conflagration, a layer of ash several yards high covered the entire ranch. "When Esperanza, my mother—and that name, of course, means hope—returned from her wedding trip, all that she found under the remains of what had been the ranch was this cookbook, the cookbook that expresses all of Tita's great urges, which she bequeathed to me"—that is, Tita gave it to Esperanza, Esperanza gave it to the narrator—when she,

Esperanza, died, which tells in each of its chapters this story in a love interred—this book that has a recipe at the beginning of each chapter.

"They say that under those ashes every kind of life flourished, making this land the most fertile in the region. Throughout my childhood, I had the good fortune to savor the delicious fruits and vegetables that grew on the land. Eventually my mother had a little apartment built there; my father, Alex, still lives in one of the apartments. Everything's been paved over". And, yet, this is the narrator's birthday, and she is going to make those Christmas rolls. "Somehow," she wonders, "they never taste as good as when my mother made them," and she can only wonder at how good they tasted when her Great Aunt Tita made them. The story ends thus:

> I don't know why mine never turn out like hers, or why my tears flow so freely when I prepare them. Perhaps I am as sensitive to onions (which is not only a vegetable, but an image for meaning within meaning within meaning) as Tita, my great aunt, who will go on living as long as there is someone who cooks her recipes.

You can see what Gabriel García Márquez has meant when he said that Magical Realism really was real. It's just destroying the difference—the demarcations, the boundaries between the real and the fantastic. By the end of that book, we do believe that Tita will live as long as someone makes those recipes. And I have to say, I feel the impulse to make those recipes myself, and how can Great Aunt Tita live when she's never lived. She's always been a character of fiction. In fact, what Laura Esquivel had done was to use Postmodernism, using the fantastic, created what becomes a modern myth.

Thus, the fantastic, which once drove the culturally foundational works, such as the *Odyssey* with its gods and so on, its curses, its magical changes of men into animals. It again, the fantastic, drives narrative that is broadly powerful, artistically honored, and personally moving. As in this imaginative novel, the fantastic is at the center of our lives. But, in the 21st century, our lives are conditioned powerfully, not only by our perceptions of the world, but by a world that is made to change, by the development of science and technology. So, when I say that the fantastic is at the center of our lives, I mean that, of course, in the general sense in which we've discussed this for the last twelve lectures. But also in the specific sense, in which it's incorporated in science fiction, which will be our subject in Part II.

Timeline

800–600 B.C.E............................The *Odyssey*

c. 380 B.C.E. ....Writing of *The Republic* by Plato (c. 427–c. 347 B.C.E.)

c. 8 C.E.....................................Completion of *The Metamorphoses* by Ovid (43 B.C.E.–17 C.E.)

c. 160..Writing of *Icaromenippus* by Lucian of Samosata (c. 120–180)

1321 ....*The Divine Comedy* by Dante Alighieri (1265–1321)

c. 1375......................................Writing of *Sir Gawain and the Green Knight*

1485 ....Publication of *Le Morte d'Arthur* by Thomas Malory (1405–1471)

1516 ....Publication of *Utopia* by Thomas More (1478–1535)

c. 1593......................................First performance of *The Tragical History of Doctor Faustus* by Christopher Marlowe (1564–1593)

1611 ....First performance of *The Tempest* by William Shakespeare (1564–1616)

1627 ....Publication of *The New Atlantis* by Francis Bacon (1561–1626)

1657 ....Publication of *Other Worlds* by Cyrano de Bergerac (1619–1655)

1697 ....Publication of *Tales and Stories of the Past with Morals, or Tales of Mother Goose* by Charles Perrault (1628–1703)

1719 ....Publication of *Robinson Crusoe* by Daniel Defoe (c. 1660–1731)

1726	Publication of *Gulliver's Travels* by Jonathan Swift (1667–1745)
1752	Publication of *Micromegas* by Voltaire (1694–1778)
1764	Publication of *The Castle of Otranto* by Horace Walpole (1717–1797)
1798	Publication of *Lyrical Ballads* by William Wordsworth and Samuel Taylor Coleridge
1812, 1814, 1822	Publication of *Kinder- und Hausmärchen* by the Grimm brothers (Jakob, 1785–1863; Wilhelm, 1786–1859)
1816	Publication of "The Sandman" by E. T. A. Hoffmann (1776–1822)
1818	Publication of *Frankenstein, or The Modern Prometheus* by Mary Shelley (1797–1851)
1819	Publication of *The Vampyre* by J. W. Polidori (1795–1821)
1837–1901	Reign of England's Queen Victoria (1819–1901)
1842	Publication of *Twice-Told Tales* by Nathaniel Hawthorne (1804–1864)
1845	Publication of *Struwwelpeter* (*Straw-Headed Peter*) by Heinrich Hoffmann (1809–1894)
1851	Publication of *The House of Seven Gables* by Nathaniel Hawthorne (1804–1864)
1858	Publication of *The Defence of Guinevere* by William Morris (1834–1896)
1861–1865	U.S. Civil War

1864	Confederate *Hunley* sinks the U.S. *Housatonic* in the world's first successful submarine attack
1865	Publication of *Alice in Wonderland* by Lewis Carroll (1832–1898)
1869	Completion of the world's first transcontinental railroad, in Utah
1870	Publication of *20,000 Leagues Under the Sea* by Jules Verne (1828–1905)
1871	Proclamation of the German Empire after the defeat of France in the Franco-Prussian War (1870–1871)
1872	Publication of *Through the Looking-Glass* by Lewis Carroll Publication of *Erewhon* by Samuel Butler (1835–1902)
1878	Publication of *Frank Reade and His Steam Man of the Plains* by "Noname"
1888	Publication of *Looking Backward* by Edward Bellamy (1850–1898)
1889	Publication of *A Connecticut Yankee in King Arthur's Court* by Mark Twain (1835–1910)
1895	Publication of *The Time Machine* by H. G. Wells (1866–1946)
1897	Publication of *Dracula* by Bram Stoker (1847–1912)
1901	Publication of *The Tale of Peter Rabbit* by Beatrix Potter (1866–1943)
1912	Publication of *A Princess of Mars* by Edgar Rice Burroughs (1875–1950)

1914–1918 .... World War I

1915 .... Publication of *The Metamorphosis*
by Franz Kafka (1883–1924)
Publication of *Herland* by Charlotte
Perkins Gilman (1860–1935)

1916 .... Publication of *Course in General
Linguistics* by Ferdinand de
Saussure (1857–1913)

1919 .... Publication of "The Uncanny" by
Sigmund Freud

1920 .... Composition of *We* by Yevgeny
Zamyatin (1884–1937)

April 1926 .... Publication of *Amazing Stories*, the
first science fiction magazine, by
Hugo Gernsback (1884–1967)

1927 .... Publication of V. Propp's
Morphology of the Folktale

1928 .... Publication of *Orlando* by Virginia
Woolf (1882–1941)

1929–1939 .... The Great Depression

1932 .... Publication of *Brave New World* by
Aldous Huxley (1894–1963)

1939–1945 .... World War II

December 7, 1941 .... Japanese bombing of Pearl Harbor

August 6, 1945 .... U.S. atomic bombing of Hiroshima

1947 .... Publication of *Goodnight Moon* by
Margaret Wise Brown (1910–1952)

1949 .... Publication of *Nineteen Eighty-Four*
by George Orwell (1903–1950)

1950 .... Publication of *If I Ran the Zoo* by
Dr. Seuss (Theodore Geisel, 1904–
1991)

	Publication of *The Martian Chronicles* by Ray Bradbury (1920–)
	Publication of *I, Robot* by Isaac Asimov (1920–1992)
1952–1960	Dismantling of the American News Company by a Wall Street syndicate
1953	Publication of *The Erasers* by Alain Robbe-Grillet (1922–)
1954–1955	Publication of *The Lord of the Rings* trilogy by J. R. R. Tolkien (1892–1973)
October 4, 1957..........................	Soviet Union launches *Sputnik*
1960	Approval of first oral contraceptive
	Broadway debut of the musical *Camelot*
1961	Publication of *The Phantom Tollbooth* by Norton Juster (1929–)
July 23, 1962..............................	First live transatlantic television transmission using Telstar, first communications satellite
November 22, 1963.....................	Murder of U.S. President John F. Kennedy
1965	Publication of *Cosmicomics* by Italo Calvino (1928–1985)
1967	Publication of *One Hundred Years of Solitude* by Gabriel García Márquez (1928–)
1968	Publication of *2001: A Space Odyssey*, a novel by Arthur C. Clarke (1917–)
	Release of *2001: A Space Odyssey*, a film by Stanley Kubrick (1928–1999)

Glossary

aesthetic fatigue: The dissipation of our pleasure in a particular form of art through repeated exposure to too many similar works. "Oh, I just can't stand to read another thriller."

allegoresis: The general mental process by which we understand immediately that something in the work we are reading (or hearing or seeing) should call to mind something from another work. For example, a baby floating in a basket in a river should bring to mind the story of Moses. Allegoresis is a subset of allusion.

allegory: Allegory refers to works that use allegoresis systematically so that the work being read makes consistent allusions paralleling some other work. For example, Christian, the hero of John Bunyan's *Pilgrim's Progress* (1678 and 1684), lives out a life like that of Jesus told in the Gospels.

allusion: In general, allusion is a reference in a work to something specific outside that work; for example, "she felt like Cinderella" or "this was the best day since the fall of the Berlin Wall." If the reference is implicit and to another work of art, the allusion is more specifically an example of allegoresis.

ambiguity: As a technical term, *ambiguity* refers to a condition in which the structure of a communication supports more than one meaning; for example, "I walked down the street and turned into a drugstore."

American myth: This archetypal story has an in-group (for example, townspeople) threatened by an out-group (for example, outlaws). The in-group typically has social institutions (for example, schools and churches and lawmen) and represents America east of a frontier ever-receding westward. The out-group typically has only men, no law, but very high survival skills, representing America west of the frontier. A lone hero who shares the values of the in-group and the skills of the out-group typically arrives to settle the conflict in favor of the in-group, but then must himself either convert to the more settled ways of the in-group or ride off over the frontier.

androgyny: The amalgamation of both male and female characteristics in a single individual. In psychological terms, this is usually seen as representing a positive completion. It contrasts with hermaphroditism.

anima: In Jungian psychology, the idealized Other, a female figure with which the male ego aspires to unite. If the ego is female, the idealized Other is a male figure called the *animus*.

compensation: In psychological terms, compensation is a benefit gained from participating in a story or belief. For example, someone who is a failure in romance may compensate by seeking inordinate business success. Reading about a character who faces an issue the reader shares may help the reader compensate. For example, children fearful of taking on new responsibilities may find "Little Red Riding Hood" allows them compensation.

composite novel: This term indicates a set of stories, such as Ray Bradbury's *The Martian Chronicles*, that may each be readable independently but that together, form a larger narrative that adds extra meaning to each of the stories now viewable as chapters.

continuum of the fantastic: All works of art are, to some extent, realistic, because to make sense at all, they must call to mind something of our shared knowledge gained by living in the world. On the other hand, all works of art are, to some extent, fantastic, because even the most realistic offer the fantasy that life can be seen in limited, integrated units (like stories) and that everything we notice in the (narrative) world matters. The *continuum of the fantastic* refers to the distribution of more and less fantastic works, often from within the same genre (say, fairy tales), from the most realistic to the most fantastic.

convention: In linguistics and literary study, this term refers to a widespread agreement that something will have a certain form or function that it need not have intrinsically. For example, there is nothing about the shape of a cross that makes it symbolic of a god or religion; it has those meanings by convention.

cyberpunk: This term refers to a combination of style and stance. The style is fast and hard-edged, with the animate and the mechanical clashing; the stance is a cynical distrust of all large institutions. "Case [the protagonist in William Gibson's *Neuromancer*] fell into the prison of his own flesh."

dark double: In Jungian psychology, an aggrandized but negative version of oneself. An ordinary man, for example, might find that his dark double is a bully. This contrasts with the *double*.

defamiliarization: Viktor Shklovskii wrote that defamiliarization "makes the stone stony." The unexpected repetition makes us feel the stone in a way the word alone would not. "How are you?" "Compared to what?" The Russian Formalist critics asserted that taking the familiar and defamiliarizing it (as the fantastic necessarily does) is the heart of all art.

depth psychology: This term refers to the notion that the human psyche has a visible, conscious upper level and an invisible, unconscious lower level, in which the invisible drives the visible. There are alternative psychologies, such as B. F. Skinner's behaviorism, which sees all behavior as conditioned responses and the consciousness as a specious "epiphenomenon."

detective fiction: This general term refers to any fiction in which the protagonist or the viewpoint character (which are sometimes different) is engaged in detection, that is, solving a mystery. Police procedurals, "hard-boiled detective stories," and *Tales of the Great Detective* are all versions of detective fiction.

diachronic: This term refers to phenomena considered as extending through time. When we say that the plot of a narrative is one of journey and return, we are making a diachronic statement. This is opposed to *synchronic*.

diametric: This word, from *diameter*, the line across a circle, means "directly opposite."

doppelgänger: Literally "double goer," a doppelgänger is one of a set (usually a pair) of characters that together, represent one psychological persona in the narrative. In E. T. A. Hoffmann's "The Doubles" (*"Die Doppelgänger"*), we find many pairs of characters. The two main males, both attracted to the same female (one in person, one in dream), represent the civil and artistic side of a man seeking a certain type of woman. A doppelgänger is sometimes called a double, but that term has a different primary meaning.

double: In Jungian psychology, an aggrandized, positive version of oneself. An ordinary man, for example, might find that his double is a champion athlete. This contrasts with the *dark double*. Sometimes, the term *double* is used not in this Jungian sense but to refer to the dramatic relationship of one character to another known as a doppelgänger. Sometimes, characters that are doppelgängers are also Jungian doubles.

dystopia: A variety of utopia in which the reader is clearly intended to disparage the social system that is represented.

Eden complex: I use this term for the phenomenological complex that underlies the majority of science fiction. It has six constituent elements. (1) It uses garden, or sometimes more specifically Eden, imagery. (2) The vivid, magical aesthetics of fairy tales apply. (3) The narrative presumes that there are natural limits to human success. (4) A main character is a scientist type who wants to be god or godlike. (5) The plot follows an Oedipal dramatic structure. (6) The symbol system relies on clear, well-known dichotomies, such as light/dark, male/female, and mechanical/animate. As with any other phenomenological complex, when one element of it is present, all are potentially present. For example, in what Gaston Bachelard, in *The Psychoanalysis of Fire*, calls the Prometheus complex, when fire-as-light-and-knowledge is present, fire-as-destroyer is also implicitly present and may emerge.

ego: In modern psychological parlance, ego is the "self"; in Latin, "I."

Elektra complex: See **Oedipus complex**.

epic: An epic is a narrative of sweeping scope, traditionally but not necessarily in verse, that focuses on the great deeds of heroes and gods and, often, on the founding or reconstituting of civilizations.

epistemology: Epistemology is the branch of philosophy that concerns "knowing." Intuition and deduction, for example, are epistemologically distinct.

epistolary novel: An epistolary novel is a narrative composed mainly or exclusively of written documents, strictly speaking, of the letters written by one or more of the characters.

eutopia: A variety of utopia in which the reader is clearly intended to admire the social system that is represented.

experimental novel: The term *experimental novel* has two main meanings. Originally, it referred to works, such as those of Émile

Zola, that try to deploy a full range of characters in diverse but mutually involved social situations, then see what happens to the characters and society when they all interact. In other words, the novel performs a vicarious social experiment. Over time, the term has more generally come to mean a work in which the novelist is experimenting with the forms and possibilities of the novel.

fairy tale: The term *fairy tale* has two principle meanings. First, it is used for works that seem to come to us from a deep oral tradition of folk tales, such as "Cinderella," or for works written to emulate those, such as "Beauty and the Beast." Although there may be no fairies in a fairy tale, there will be some sort of magic. The second meaning is an unbelievable, childish story, "a mere fairy tale" that any sensible adult ought to reject.

fantastic: As a literary phenomenon, the fantastic is an affect that arises during reading from the diametric, diachronic reversal of the ground rules of the narrative world.

fantasy: As a literary phenomenon, fantasy is the mode in which the devices of the fantastic are used exhaustively. As a psychological phenomenon, fantasy is the imagination, usually persistent, of something untrue or not yet true. A literary fantasy, such as *Alice in Wonderland*, may also indulge psychological fantasy, such as the illusion of central position and the omnipotence of thought, classic "infantile" fantasies, arising from life before one learns to speak.

felt life: Life in the world as one feels it to be or to have been lived.

folk tale: In the strictest sense, a true oral composition passed through the generations. More loosely, works written to capture or resemble these. True folk tales share a universal structure elucidated by Vladimir Propp in 1927.

formula: This term refers to elements that may be repeated within or between works and that are recognized when encountered as both known and appropriate for certain works. Homer uses verbal formulae, such as "wily Odysseus" and "wine-dark sea." The story of the long-absent husband, like Odysseus, undergoing a series of adventures until he returns home to overthrow his wife's suitors, has become a formula. The cast of characters and the general plot of the Tale of the Great Detective and of Westerns employing the American myth are formulaic. Large-scale formulae (as opposed to verbal formulae) may be built of motifs.

framing: In fiction, framing is the embedding of one narrative within another. *Full framing* is, say, a story-within-a-story, as with H. G. Wells's *The Time Machine*. *Front framing* begins with one story and moves into another without ever returning to the first; *back framing* begins in one story that is then contextualized by another without that other having been previously apparent.

genre: Literally, a genre is a type. In the arts, *genre* has two main meanings. In the first, we mean any definable type of art. Science fiction is a genre. There can be genres within genres. Science fiction novels are a genre that is a subset of the genre of novel and a superset that contains other genres, such as alien contact stories and mad scientist stories. In the second meaning, *genre* refers to formulaic, popular works of specific types. The American Western story and the locked-room mystery are often thought of as genres.

Gothic romance: Romantic fiction that typically involves extraordinary powers, massive but perhaps crumbling architecture, and heightened—often sexual—emotions.

hard SF: This term denotes those science fictions that suggest that the reader could—and some fans do—check the author's calculations about key points of setting and plot.

hermaphroditism: In psychological terms, the monstrous conjunction of male and female characteristics in a single individual. This contrasts with *androgyny*.

hypotaxis: In rhetoric, making explicit the underlying connections among distinct elements of the text or utterance. For example, "I am hungry. I need to obtain food. I can buy food at the store. I will go to the store to buy food to eat." Compare that with "I am hungry. I'll go to the store." In the latter example, one presumes that the store sells food, but one could be wrong. The speaker could have changed topics. Leaving out underlying connections is *parataxis*. Excessive hypotaxis can be boring, but excessive parataxis can leave a reader confused: "I am hungry. Now I'll call Fred." Does the call have to do with the hunger?

illusion of central position: The infantile fantasy that all that happens in one's world is part of a pattern of which one's own ego is the center.

image: A concrete mental representation (whether visual or engaging any other sense) inferred from reading a text or hearing language. An image may or may not be a symbol. "She had the smile of Mona Lisa" may bring that famous painting to mind but with no necessary symbolic content. "She had the breathy voice of Marilyn Monroe singing 'Happy Birthday' to President Kennedy," by its allusive force, can symbolize complex, public, but doomed sexuality.

infantile fantasy: A psychological sense, often unconscious, that arises from one's early, preverbal experience. As infants, we perceive only the world around us and that world responds to our cries. The former fact leads to the fantasy called the *illusion of central position*; the latter, to the fantasy called the *omnipotence of thought*. Although most of us as adults know those fantasies as false, we still may feel that the phone ringing in a stranger's office is for us or use bodily movements to try to influence the trajectory of a bowling ball after it has been released.

intensional: In phenomenology, *intension* is not *intention* but the opposite of *extension*; that is, *intensional* acts are the focusing of attention that define phenomena against the backgrounds of all possible present stimuli.

literary period: A literary period is a historical era with indistinct boundaries within which one may, in a broad sense, characterize some common approaches to the production of art. In the Romantic period, for example, the focus on the individual ego and the taste for heightened emotions is reflected in Percy Bysshe Shelley's "Ozymandias" and his wife, Mary Shelley's, *Frankenstein*.

magical realism: This term refers prototypically to the works of modern Latin American authors, such as Gabriel García Márquez's *One Hundred Years of Solitude*, in which a realistic, often almost matter-of-fact, approach is used in narrating the lives of individuals in which magical events occur just as arbitrarily, unavoidably, and expectably as political upheaval. Works of magical realism attend both to the nuances of characterization and to the power of the political forces shaping the characters' world. Their plots approach the feeling of myth. The term is sometimes used for non-Latin works that share these features, such as Toni Morrison's *Beloved* and Mikhail Bulgakov's *The Master and Margarita*.

Modernism: An artistic, including literary, period characterized by formal experimentation and the sense that Nature is alien from humanity.

motif: This term refers to comparatively fixed, comparatively small elements that we find in work after work, for example, the motif of the magical gift. It always confers power and is usually problematic, as with the ring in Tolkien's *The Lord of the Rings* and the title objects in the Grimm brothers' "The Table, the Stick, and the Ass." Although the terms *formula* and *motif* overlap, in general, a formula is more fixed and may involve more than one motif.

myth: This term has many meanings, ranging from a false belief to a traditional tale of gods or heroes that explains or justifies a social condition, religious belief, or natural phenomenon. In broad literary use, a myth is a story, often fantastic, that offers a picture that stands for a crucial aspect of the world of the society that takes that story as important. For example, Mary Shelley's *Frankenstein* and Franz Kafka's *The Metamorphosis* are often viewed as mythic.

narrative: A narrative is the communication of the representation of a series of events by a person (narrator) or persons to another person or persons (audience). See also **story** and **plot**.

nature: This term has been used quite variously through the centuries, with meanings that include "human nature," the supposedly immutable qualities of human beings ("the witch's desire to eat Hansel is unnatural"); understandably inevitable ("it is only natural that we overeat on sweets"); and capitalized Nature, meaning the physical and biological world, with the exception of humans and their products. In this sense, although it is clearly part of human nature to build shelters—and houses and villages—cities are not considered natural. Thus, there is a traditional contrast between the city and the country or forest, between the human and the animal, between the amoral functioning of weather and the morally freighted decisions of people.

neologism: A neologism is a newly coined word.

nested narrative: Nested narrative uses framing to put one story inside another. In some cases, such as Mary Shelley's *Frankenstein* and Ovid's *Metamorphoses*, there may be many levels of nesting, one story within another within another.

New Novel: This English phrase translates the French *nouveau roman*, the term first made current by discussions of Alain Robbe-Grillet's *The Erasers*. New Novels are characterized by minimal use of ornate rhetorical figures, such as metaphor; by a cinematic attention to surfaces; and by uncertainty in the face of large social institutions or forces.

New Wave: In science fiction, this term refers to the explicit attempt by such writers as J. G. Ballard to bring the formal experimentation of Modernism into genre writing and to other works showing such experimentation, such as those of Samuel R. Delany.

Oedipal comedy: In the Eden complex, a dramatic structure in which the intergenerational conflict is resolved in a way that restores social order, as in William Shakespeare's *The Tempest*.

Oedipal tragedy: In the Eden complex, a dramatic structure in which the intergenerational conflict ultimately disrupts the social order, as in Mary Shelley's *Frankenstein*.

Oedipus complex: In Freudian psychology, a yearning, often unconscious, to supplant one's same-sex parent in order to join with one's opposite-sex parent. Some critics reserve this term for males wishing to supplant or even kill their fathers and refer to females wishing to supplant or even kill their mothers as manifesting an Elektra complex.

omnipotence of thought: The infantile fantasy that thinking something can make it so.

parataxis: See entry for **hypotaxis**.

periphrasis: This rhetoric term, literally "a roundabout speaking," denotes indirect circumlocutions; for example, "finny tribe" for "fish."

phenomenology: The philosophical approaches built on the notion that phenomena represent intensional acts of consciousness; that is, by separating elements from all those available and focusing on those elements as an entity, we define the phenomena that seem to exist independently of us in the world. For example, a European might think of World War II beginning with the German invasion of

Poland on September 1, 1939, and ending with the Allied victory over Germany, officially V-E Day, May 8, 1945; however, an American might think of World War II beginning with the Japanese bombing of Pearl Harbor on December 7, 1941, and ending with the Allied victory over Japan, officially V-J Day, August 15, 1945. Both Europeans and Americans, thinking of war as emerging from many tensions rather than single events, such as attacks, and ending not with a simple signing ceremony but with the establishment of new political conditions, might think of World War II as extending from 1939 (or even earlier) through 1945 (or even later).

plot: Plot is defamiliarized story, that is, the events as narrated. The defamiliarization can be accomplished by many means, including chronological reordering, but also by temporal techniques of slowing down the narrative (for example, for lengthy description) or speeding it up (for example, by summarizing a series of actions). Compare entry for **story**.

Postmodernism: An artistic, including literary, period characterized by self-reflexivity and the sense that Nature is a phenomenological construct.

psychic economy: This term refers to the saving in psychological effort needed if one has an externally supplied symbolic structure (for example, a story) to handle psychological difficulties (for example, persistent fears), rather than having to imagine an adequate structure to deal with these matters on one's own. Depth psychologists assert that one of the attractions of art is psychic economy.

pulp fiction: Technically, pulp fiction constitutes stories published on pulp paper (cheap paper, such as newsprint). More generally, the term refers to work, typically formulaic or generic, meant for a wide, popular audience and expected to have little lasting value.

ratiocination, tales of: Term coined by Edgar Allan Poe for a single genre of narratives that engage readers' processes of intellectual reasoning (ratiocination). The works Poe saw as in this genre we see as two genres today, detective fiction and science fiction.

realism: A style that appeals to us by suggesting it provides a faithful representation of reality. As Erich Auerbach argues in *Mimesis*, different eras deem different styles to be realistic; that is, "realism" is a matter of convention.

Robinsonade: In Daniel Defoe's *Robinson Crusoe*, the main character's action is to attempt to remake the alien landscape in which he finds himself so that it approximates as much as possible the European world he had previously inhabited. A Robinsonade is a tale in which the protagonist deals with the alien by trying to make it like the world the protagonist comes from.

romantic: The term *romantic* has six meanings relevant to the study of literature: (1) languages, such as French and Italian, that derive from Latin, the language of Rome; (2) emotionally heightened content, erotic or otherwise; (3) attitudes and themes that stress the importance of the ego and strong emotion; (4) the period in art valorizing (2) and (3); (5) a set of 19th-century English poets, including Wordsworth and Percy Bysshe Shelley; and (6) a diachronic structure in which the ideals implicit at the beginning of the narrative necessarily work themselves out.

science fiction: Science fiction is a fantastic genre that claims plausibility for its narrative world against a background of science.

self-reflexivity: In criticism, self-reflexivity refers to the effect of elements of a work of art that call attention to the fact that the audience is indeed dealing with a work of art. In a novel, for example, if one character says to another, "What a coincidence! If this were a novel, no one would believe it had happened!" the novel is being self-reflexive. Self-reflexivity can also be implicit. For example, Franz Kafka's story called "An Old Manuscript" never mentions an old manuscript; thus, the alert reader realizes that the story itself must be the old manuscript, but because it is clearly a modern story, this titling calls our attention to the story being a created—not found—work of art.

story: Story is the chronological sequence of events we understand to be represented in a narrative, regardless of the reading order of the plot in which they are narrated.

structuralism: The term *structuralism* denotes study in many fields using approaches that highlight various structures of the objects of inquiry. Every work of literature, for example, can be seen as having a diachronic structure (how the work unfolds over time) and a synchronic structure (the shape of the work considered as a whole). One could extract other structures as well, for example, the structure of the social relations among the characters. A structural approach always extracts some subset of information about the object of inquiry in order to highlight the workings of the extracted elements in the whole. These approaches are grounded in the linguistic analyses of Ferdinand de Saussure.

symbol: A symbol is an image that carries general meaning beyond itself. This can be distinguished from an allusion that carries specific reference. Symbolic meaning can arise from three sources: (1) Conventional symbols function through stipulation and subsequent social agreement; for example, a cross symbolizes Christianity. (2) Natural symbols arise through shared human experience in the world; for example, thunderclouds symbolize impending danger. (3) Forged symbols acquire meaning in the course of the works that employ them; for example, Frankenstein's monster comes to symbolize science that has gone beyond the control of the community.

synchronic: This term refers to phenomena considered as existing all at one time. When we say that a plot is a circle, we are making a synchronic statement. This is opposed to *diachronic*.

Tale of the Great Detective: This term refers to a highly formulaic variety of detective fiction in which we have a great detective (for example, Sherlock Holmes), a sidekick who does not know all that the detective does (Watson), and a criminal (Moriarty). The plot, too, although often ingenious, is formulaic, beginning with the report of a crime or its likelihood, an exposition of why ordinary people are baffled in the face of this mystery, the solution by the detective "matching minds" with the criminal (as Poe wrote), and the explanation of the solution.

transformed language: I use this term to denote locutions that simultaneously indicate that the narrative world is not ours and the relation between that world and ours. For example, in Ursula K. Le Guin's *The Left Hand of Darkness*, there is a common expression in the harsh world of Gethen: "The glaciers didn't freeze overnight." For Le Guin's contemporary readers, this is obviously a transformation of "Rome wasn't built in a day." That it is a transformation lets us know that we are in a different world from ours. This particular Gethenian transformation suggests that the dominant force in that world is not human empire but implacable Nature.

utopia: The term *utopia* has two meanings. In its larger meaning, *utopia* refers to the whole class of works that focus on the creation and maintenance of stable social systems. Usually, these works are science fictions claiming plausibility against the background of political science. These works fall into three subsets. The subset of utopian works in which the social system is clearly intended to be admired by the reader is called *eutopian*; the subset of utopian works in which the social system is clearly intended to be disparaged by the reader is called *dystopian*; and the subset of utopian works in which the social system is clearly intended to motivate the reader's thoughtful ambivalence is itself called simply *utopian*. In other words, *utopia* in the general sense contains *eutopia*, *dystopia*, and in a more specific sense, *utopia*.

Biographical Notes

Isaac Asimov (1920–1992). Born in Russia and brought to Brooklyn, New York, at age 3, Asimov began writing at 11. Although his father, who owned a candy store (which carried popular magazines), discouraged "junk" reading, Asimov was allowed to read *Science Wonder Stories* because of its title. He earned three chemistry degrees from Columbia University, although his doctoral studies were interrupted by four years of wartime service as a chemist for the government. Asimov was a tenured professor of biochemistry at Boston University when he committed himself to full-time writing in 1955. He ultimately became one of the world's most prolific authors, publishing more than 400 books of science fiction, detection, criticism, popular science, and more. His Foundation series won a special Hugo Award as the best science fiction series of all time. He was survived by his second wife and two children.

Ray(mond) (Douglas) Bradbury (1920–). Born in Waukegan, Illinois, Bradbury consumed pulp fiction starting at age 8 and wrote consistently from 12 onward. After he moved with his family to Los Angeles in 1934, he ended his formal education with high school graduation but always took his writing seriously, even attending a class given by Robert Heinlein. Yet Bradbury typically rejected technology, for example, never learning to drive. *The Martian Chronicles* (1950), his great composite novel, asks us to restrain technology so we can catch up morally to our practical power. His much honored, lyrical science fiction opened the way to screenwriting (for instance, on *Moby Dick*) and consulting on the development of the original Disneyland. He later turned toward clearly unscientific, highly romantic fantasies, such as the juvenile favorite *Something Wicked This Way Comes* (1962). His long marriage produced four daughters.

Edgar Rice Burroughs (1875–1950). Born in Chicago, Burroughs attended and instructed at the Michigan Military Academy before his Arizona service with the U.S. Cavalry (1896–1897), a career ended by a heart murmur. His many jobs, including office work and mining, never supported his wife and children. Always a pulp fiction reader, he sold his first story, "Under the Moons of Mars" (1912) for $400; his next, for $700; and in 1914, earned $20,000, a fortune then. He published adventure series set on Mars, on Venus, and most famously in Tarzan's Africa. Burroughs, always dismissed by his contemporary critics, founded the first personal media empire, licensing his characters for radio, film, toys, television, and so on. His ranch near Los Angeles became the town of Tarzana. His own fantasy? "If there is a hereafter, I want to travel through space to visit other planets." He died of a heart attack

Lewis Carroll (1832–1898). Carroll, pseudonym for Charles Lutwidge Dodgson, was the eldest of 11 children of a rural English rector. He made games and puppets to amuse his siblings, mostly girls, and enjoyed younger children more than his rough peers at Rugby. He attended Christ Church, Oxford, with the aim of becoming a rector himself, but his stutter inhibited that ambition. Instead, he became a don in mathematics at Oxford, taking orders but rarely preaching, living the usual bachelor life of such scholars. Unusually, Carroll developed many interests, becoming one of the most important photographers of his century, a writer of mathematical entertainments, and the creator of the most famous and influential children's books of all time, *Alice's Adventures in Wonderland* (1865) and *Through the Looking-Glass* (1872).

Arthur C. Clarke (1917–). Born in Minehead, England, and inspired by Olaf Stapledon's sweeping science fiction, Clarke, too poor to attend university, became a government auditor, worked on the pioneering radar crucial to the Battle of Britain, and finally attended King's College, London, on scholarship, earning first-class honors in mathematics and physics. His 1945 paper proposing communication satellites ultimately won the Franklin Institute Gold Medal. After editing at *Science Abstracts* (1949–1950), Clarke became a full-time fiction and nonfiction writer. Married and later divorced without children, he moved to Sri Lanka where, in addition to writing, he co-founded a company pursuing underwater filming and safaris and has served since 1979 as chancellor of the University of Moratuwa, Sri Lanka's premier technical school. The film of his *2001: A Space Odyssey* is an artistic milestone. His *Rendezvous with Rama* is the most award-winning science fiction novel of all time.

Sigmund Freud (1856–1939). Freud, a Viennese Jew, the eldest and most favored of the eight children of his father's third wife, was early recognized as a genius. The modest resources of the family flowed to this disciplined, fastidious youngster, who read Latin,

Greek, English, and French. Although unobservant, his religious heritage greatly influenced his sense of alienation and of the importance of interpretation. Initially attracted to zoology, he practiced medicine out of financial necessity. His detailed observations, both of his patients' pathologies and of works of art, uncovered hidden patterns. Such revelations, coupled with his theories about the unconscious, its drives, operations, and deformation by trauma, led to his creation of modern psychoanalysis, the so-called "talking cure" for mental disorders. In 1938, Freud fled the Nazis for London, where a year later this addicted cigar smoker ironically died of cancer of the mouth, leaving a wife and six adult children.

Hugo Gernsback (1884–1967). A Luxembourg-born engineer, Gernsback emigrated to the United States hoping to patent his new battery. He tried several unsatisfactory technical jobs and co-founded a battery company that his partner stole into bankruptcy. Although very inventive (the walkie-talkie, 1909; radar, 1912), his major, almost accidental, achievements were in publishing. He founded *Modern Electrics* (1908) to publish popular science articles. Soon, he added fiction and, responding to his readers' comments, in April 1926, launched *Amazing Stories*, the first science fiction (which he called "scientifiction") magazine. He not only crystallized a market but launched readers' columns that initiated modern fandom. Gernsback created prolifically but usually failed with his creations. He lost one magazine after another, never made money on his patents, and even married three times (producing three children). Nonetheless, honoring all that he began, the most prestigious award in science fiction, the Hugo, bears his name.

Jakob Ludwig Carl Grimm (1785–1863) and **Wilhelm Carl Grimm** (1786–1859). These eldest sons of a Hanau, Germany, municipal lawyer were among the world's most influential scholars. For intellectual and nationalistic reasons, they sought the historical origins of German culture. Grimm's law, formulated by Jakob, is the first discovered law of phonological change from one language to another. Their publication (1812–1822) of traditional German tales—nominally collected from oral sources—almost immediately legitimized folklore studies and ignited an interest in fairy tales through worldwide translation. They also published collections of German sayings, heroic tales, and mythology and initiated the monumental *Deutches Wörterbuch*, the model for all historical dictionaries, including the *Oxford English Dictionary*. Professors at various times in Kassel, Göttingen, and Berlin, the brothers lived together their whole lives, although Jakob, who remained single, took many scientific trips, while the frailer Wilhelm stayed home, married, and had three children.

Nathaniel Hawthorne (1804–1864). Hawthorne's Puritan forebears included a judge at the Salem witchcraft trials (1692) and his own sea-captain father, who died in Surinam (1808). Young Nathaniel turned early to writing. As a student at Bowdoin College, he formed lifelong friendships with the poet Henry Wadsworth Longfellow and with Franklin Pierce who, as president of the United States, ultimately gave him the lucrative post of U.S. consul in Liverpool. Hawthorne had already endured years of hack writing and editing to support himself, his wife, and three children. He even tried the supposedly more economical life in a utopian community, Brook Farm, in 1841. However, he eventually made a comfortable living from his well-received short stories (for example, *Mosses from an Old Manse*, 1846) and novels (for example, *The Scarlet Letter*, 1850), many of which explore the relations of religion and science, the past and the present.

Robert A(nson) Heinlein (1907–1988). Heinlein, a Missouri lad, studied at the University of Missouri and the U.S. Naval Academy (B.S., 1929). After tuberculosis ended his military career (1939), he studied physics and mathematics at UCLA, tried mining, selling real estate, and even running for California state office. But from his first story sale (1939), he was able to support himself by his stylistically refined science fiction, creating also a Future History that provided the setting for many other writers. Often ill, he worked as an aviation engineer for the Navy from 1942–1945 but returned to full-time writing. His consistent admiration for unprejudiced meritocracy (his idealization of the military) and libertarian enthusiasm for individual responsibility helped set the prevailing ideology of science fiction. He won more Hugo Awards for Best Novel than any other writer. His first marriage ended in divorce; his second wife outlived him.

E. T. A. Hoffmann (1776–1822). Hoffmann, a Prussian from a broken home, was raised by his uncle to the law. Although he supported himself and his wife (their daughter died at 2) early as a law officer and, later, as a government councillor, Hoffmann was also a very successful composer (legally changing his name, Ernst Theodor Wilhelm, to Ernst Theodor Amadeus to honor Mozart), an accomplished painter, and a writer of vastly influential fantasies. His use of depth psychology and emotionally resonant dream and supernatural symbols helped create literary fantasy. His opera *Undine* (1816) is a classic German fairy tale. His stories formed the basis for the opera *The Tales of Hoffmann* by Offenbach (1880), the ballet *Coppelia* by Délibes (1870), and Tchaikovsky's ballet *The Nutcracker* (1892). His story "The Sandman" is the prime object of analysis in Freud's most important discussion of the fantastic, "The Uncanny" (1919).

Franz Kafka (1883–1924). Much alienated as a German-speaking Jew in the Czech capital of Prague, Kafka lived most of his life with his mother, from elite society, and his domineering father, a self-made merchant. Fluent with others, he stuttered before his father. Franz earned a J.D. (1906), practiced the requisite year, and then took a civil service job investigating workers' insurance claims. Each of his several engagements was broken off. Through indecision and self-doubt, he published little in his lifetime, notably *The Metamorphosis* (1915). Tuberculosis caused his resignation (1922) and, ultimately, death. Max Brod, his friend and literary executor, defied his wishes to have his manuscripts destroyed, instead editing and publishing them, including many stories and such archetypal novels as *The Trial* (1925), *The Castle* (1926), and *Amerika* (1927).

Ursula K(roeber) Le Guin (1929–). Le Guin was born in Berkeley, California, and educated at Radcliffe College and Columbia University; her parents were major influences on her writing. Her father, Alfred L. Kroeber, a towering figure of American anthropology, is perhaps best known for his arguments that all of Western culture arose from a single source. Her mother, Theodora Kroeber, a writer and anthropologist, is best known for her biography of Ishi, "the last of the wild Indians." Le Guin acknowledges also the influence of Lord Dunsany, often called the inventor of the modern fantasy short story; of Leo Tolstoi and Anton Chekov, great Russian social realists; and Virginia Woolf, a feminist founder of Modernism. Le Guin, married to historian Charles Le Guin, whom she met while on a Fulbright in France, has three children.

Edgar Allan Poe (1809–1849). Born to traveling actors who died before he was 3, Poe, sheltered but never adopted, was always poor and unhappy. He was expelled from the University of Virginia for gambling debts and from the U.S. Military Academy at West Point for drunkenness. After winning a short-story contest (1833), he began a series of editorial jobs, most notably on *The Southern Literary Messenger*. His devoted marriage to his first cousin, Virginia, whom he married when she was 13, ended 12 years later after her long struggle with tuberculosis. He was both praised and mocked for the relentless, stunning musicality of his poetry. His pioneering commitment to unitary aesthetic effects led to his achievement of prototypical works of horror fiction, detective fiction, and science fiction. After the death of his wife, Poe's chronic depression deepened. He died four days after being found delirious outside a Baltimore saloon.

Mary (Wollstonecraft Godwin) Shelley (1797–1851). Mary's birth killed her mother, Mary Wollstonecraft, a famous British feminist. Her father, William Godwin, a free-thinking political theorist, married the divorced Mrs. Clairmont (a publisher of "Beauty and the Beast"). Mrs. Clairmont's daughter, Claire, Lord Byron's lover, was at the Villa Diodati in Switzerland the night in June 1816 when the assemblage set themselves a horror-story writing competition. Percy Shelley, Mary's lover and, after his wife's suicide, her husband, left his entry incomplete. Byron's work, later published, quickly provided J. W. Polidori, present as Byron's physician, material toward *The Vampyre* (1819), the first such novel in English. Mary created *Frankenstein* (1818) with her infant son William at her side. After Percy's drowning (1822), she promoted her husband's work devotedly and published much herself, for example, *The Last Man* (1826), another first in English. Of her children, only Percy survived infancy. She died of brain cancer.

J(ohn) R(onald) R(euel) Tolkien (1892–1973). After the death of his bank-manager father (1896) and mother (1904), a convert to Catholicism, Tolkien was raised near Birmingham, England, by a Roman Catholic priest. Except for service in World War I, Tolkien spent his life as a celebrated medievalist. His marriage to his childhood sweetheart produced four children. His passion for philology, myth, and storytelling led to participation in a self-help group of religious writers, The Inklings, that included C. S. Lewis, and to creation of a fanciful universe (pieces later published as *The Silmarillion*, 1977), the setting for *The Hobbit* (1937), written in part for his children. Asked by the publisher for a sequel, he finally issued *The Lord of the Rings* trilogy (originally one book) in 1954–1955, a work meant for all ages. Often voted the best book of the 20th century, it opened the door for modern fantasy publishing.

Jules Verne (1828–1905). Raised on an island in the port city of Nantes, Verne always fantasized about travel. Sent by his father to Paris, he studied law indifferently while writing some adequate dramas and librettos and mainly inadequate narratives. He married (1857), had a son and two stepdaughters, and wrote while barely surviving as a law tutor, theater administrator, and stockbroker. Pierre-Jules-Hetzel, publisher of a family magazine, suggested revising the manuscript of *Five Weeks in a Balloon* to add humor, truncate the science, and provide a happy ending. The book's immediate popularity (1863) launched Verne on a prolific, lucrative career, largely with Hetzel. The first science fiction writer to live by his pen, Verne's books became ever more subtle yet usually lighthearted satires of society and appreciations of science. His most popular, *Around the World in Eighty Days* (1873), was the first Western novel translated into Japanese.

H(erbert) G(eorge) Wells (1866–1946). A lower-middle-class Englishman, Wells attended on scholarship what is now the Imperial College of Science and Technology, for two years assisting T. H. Huxley, Charles Darwin's great disciple. The idea of pattern influenced all Wells's major work, including his early "scientific romances" (such as *The Time Machine*, 1895, and *The War of the Worlds*, 1898), which shaped science fiction. A journalist and essayist throughout his career, his *Outline of History* (1920) attempted to sketch world history in terms of peoples and social forces rather than battles and rulers. As a prominent member of the socialist Fabian Society, Wells argued for a world state, spelling reform, public education, and—against Henry James—the importance of social over psychological truth in fiction. Ever active, he divorced his first wife and had two children by his second, who died, and one each by two of his many lovers.

Virginia Woolf (1882–1941). Woolf, daughter of Sir Leslie Stephen, a prolific writer and editor of Britain's *Dictionary of National Biography*, was part of the famous Bloomsbury group of

London-based intellectuals, which included her sister, Vanessa Stephen Bell (artist); Clive Bell (critic); John Maynard Keynes (economist); E. M. Forster (novelist and critic); Roger Fry (critic who assembled the First Postimpressionist Exhibition, 1910); and Lytton Strachey (biographer of *The Eminent Victorians*, 1918). With her husband, Leonard Woolf, Virginia established the Hogarth Press, which issued *The Standard Edition of the Works of Sigmund Freud*, edited by James Strachey, and brought modern psychoanalytic theory to the English-speaking world, including its avant-garde artists and writers. She was a pioneer of feminism (with a devoted but apparently sexless marriage) and literary Modernism, but each book's completion left her ferociously depressed. After at least two unsuccessful attempts, she died a suicide.

Yevgeny Zamyatin (1884–1937). Zamyatin, the son of a Russian Orthodox priest, became a naval architect and lecturer at the St. Petersburg Polytechnic. A lapsed Bolshevik, he supervised the construction of Russian ice-breakers for 18 months (1916–1917) in Newcastle-upon-Tyne, a sojourn that led to stories bitingly attacking English life and a fluency that resulted in editing collections in Russian of H. G. Wells, George Bernard Shaw, Jack London, and O. Henry while continuing to write his own fiction and essays on the social conditions in Russia. His novel *We* (1920), the first book officially suppressed by the young Soviet Union, was published abroad and inspired many modern dystopias. Unable to publish at home, Zamyatin wrote Stalin (1931) for permission to emigrate. Once permission was granted, Zamyatin went to Paris, where he died. In 1988, during the thaw before the fall of the Soviet Union, *We* headed the list of the first volumes rehabilitated.

Bibliography

Essential Reading:

Asimov, Isaac. *I, Robot*. New York: Random House, 2004. This eutopian composite novel, originally published in book form in 1950, combines fairy tale and technology in classic puzzle tales.

Bradbury, Ray. *The Martian Chronicles*. New York: Bantam, 1984. This lyrical composite novel, first published in 1950, finally offers post-holocaust Earthmen a new chance in a fairyland America set on Mars.

Brown, Margaret Wise. *Goodnight Moon*. New York: HarperCollins, 2005. This delightful, deceptively simple picture book has been a beloved children's classic since it first appeared in 1947.

Carroll, Lewis. *Alice's Adventures in Wonderland and Through the Looking Glass*. New York: Signet, 2000. Taken together, these works (originally published in 1865 and 1872, respectively) form a composite novel that is the acknowledged progenitor of much of the world's best children's fiction. The copious annotations by Martin Gardner highlight Carroll's skill and erudition, which adult readers continue to admire.

Clarke, Arthur C. *2001: A Space Odyssey*. New York: Penguin, 2000. Clarke worked on this novel and the screenplay of Stanley Kubrick's movie of the same name with Kubrick as a sounding board. The result were two 1968 works, a film that changed the meaning of science fiction cinema and a novel that continues to offer humanity ineffable hope.

Esquivel, Laura. *Like Water for Chocolate*. New York: Random House, 1995. Originally published in 1989, this international bestseller subtly blends cooking, romance, family, and Mexico's political history in an irresistible tragicomedy of magical realism.

Gibson, William. *Neuromancer*. New York: Ace, 1986. At its publication in 1984, critics dubbed this novel cyberpunk, a term that instantly rang through our post-industrial culture. Yet no subsequent work has captured cyberpunk's desperate paranoia as well.

Grimm, Jakob, and Wilhelm Grimm. *Household Stories of the Brothers Grimm*. New York: Dover Books, 1963. This edition, drawn from volumes the Grimm brothers published in 1812, 1814, and 1822, includes the translations of Lucy Crane and the illustrations of her husband, Walter Crane, the first person to explore the psychology of book illustration. The tales themselves form a cornerstone of all fantastic literature since they appeared.

Hawthorne, Nathaniel. *Selected Short Stories of Nathaniel Hawthorne*. New York: Fawcett, 1983. Published in the middle of the 19th century, the short stories of this classic author include fables, fantasies, and science fictions, yet they always offer human truth.

Heinlein, Robert A. *The Moon Is a Harsh Mistress*. New York: Orb Books, 1997. This 1966 novel by one of the dominant figures of world science fiction exhibits all his typical virtues and adds a complex character, an artificial intelligence, that makes this fundamentally American novel universal.

Hoffmann, E. T. A. *The Tales of E. T. A. Hoffmann*. Chicago: University of Chicago Press, 1972. Hoffmann's stories, published in the beginning of the 19th century, set the tone for the literary fantastic; popularized a depth psychology that would emerge as the West's dominant self-conception; and presented images, such as "The Sandman," that have multiplied in other works and media.

Hoffmann, Heinrich. *Struwwelpeter*. New York: Dover Books, 1995. First published, with the author's own illustrations, in 1845, this macabre set of warning fables was the most popular European children's book, after Lewis Carroll's *Alice*, in the 19th century.

Juster, Norton. *The Phantom Tollbooth*. New York: Random House, 1988. This didactic yet delightful adventure for youngsters, first published in 1961, is often considered the outstanding 20th-century representative of the line begun by Lewis Carroll's *Alice*.

Kafka, Franz. *The Metamorphosis*, in *Collected Stories*. New York: Random House, 1993. First published in 1915, the plight of the fantastically transformed, alienated viewpoint character has come to be taken as emblematic of the modern condition.

Le Guin, Ursula K. *The Left Hand of Darkness*. New York: Ace, 2000. This 1969 novel, only the second to win science fiction's top two major awards, is a true experimental novel, a milestone of modern feminism, and a probing inquiry into the construction of identity.

Miller, Walter M. *A Canticle for Leibowitz*. New York: HarperCollins, 2006. This classic composite novel, first published in book form in 1959, spans 18 centuries in its quest to understand the relationship between science and spirituality.

Poe, Edgar Allan. *The Portable Poe*. New York: Penguin, 1977. Writing in the first half of the 19th century, Poe produced prototypical works of detective, horror, and science fiction, as well as subtly resonant, fantastic poetry.

Rabkin, Eric S. *Science Fiction: A Historical Anthology*. New York: Oxford University Press, 1983. This thoroughly annotated anthology offers milestones in the development of the genre from the mid-17th to the 20th centuries.

Robbe-Grillet, Alain. *The Erasers*. New York: Grove Press, 1970. When this novel appeared in 1953, it generated the term *New Novel*, a mind-bending subgenre for which this work has remained the crucial prototype, a cinematic, fantastic detective story where myth and realism intersect.

Seuss, Dr. *If I Ran the Zoo*. New York: Random House, 1950. This book, by one of America's most beloved creators of children's nonsense verse and images, comically explores a childhood fantasy of outdoing one's father and conquering the natural and social worlds.

Shelley, Mary. *Frankenstein*. New York: Oxford University Press, 1982. Since its appearance in 1818, this surprisingly erudite work has come to be seen as the first and quintessential science fiction novel, providing perhaps the single most powerful modern myth, that of the escape of untamed science from human control.

Tolkien, J. R. R. *The Lord of the Rings*. Boston: Houghton Mifflin, 2003. This trilogy, first published in 1954–1955, so captured the reading public with its linguistic skill, mythic resonance, fairy tale psychology, and epic confrontation of ordinary folks against extraordinary evil that it changed the climate for fantasy publication ever after.

———. *The Tolkien Reader*. New York: Ballantine, 1986. In the works collected here, including "Leaf by Niggle" (1964) and "Farmer Giles of Ham" (1949), we see Tolkien work his magic on one thread at a time, such as the importance of religion or of democracy.

Verne, Jules. *20,000 Leagues Under the Sea*. New York: Tor, 1995. Since its 1870 publication, this hugely popular novel has exemplified Verne's satire, enthusiasm for science and exploration, and ability to ground the fantastic in present reality.

Wells, H. G. "The Invisible Man," in *Best Science Fiction Stories of H. G. Wells*. New York: Dover Books, 1966. This classic novella, first published in 1897, demonstrates the power of the fantastic to make visible even such invisible human problems as alienation and the need for power.

———. *The Island of Dr. Moreau*. New York: Signet Classics, 1977. This unforgettable fantastic parable, first published in 1896, overtly criticizes imperialism and the misuses of religion while it covertly explores the human traits that drive us to seek power.

———. *The Time Machine*. New York: Tor Classics, 1992. From its appearance in 1895, when it became an instant classic, this parabolic critique of the economics of Victorian England has been an exemplar of the whole field of science fiction.

———. *The War of the Worlds*. New York: Tor Classics, 2005. This 1898 novel has so captured the inherent problems of one group imposing itself on another that it has recurred in countless successful—and notorious—versions in prose, film, and radio.

Woolf, Virginia. *Orlando*. New York: Harcourt, 1993. This 1928 novel, a comic masterpiece by a towering founder of literary Modernism, is both a subtle and fantastic exploration of gender, language, and love in 15 years of a life lived over two sexes and more than three centuries.

Zamyatin, Yevgeny. *We*. New York: Penguin, 1993. Written in 1920, this novel, the first banned by the Soviet Union, is the prototypical modern dystopian fantasy, exploring brilliantly how some of us use modern techniques to enslave the rest at the deepest levels of their being.

Supplementary Reading:

Alkon, Paul. *Science Fiction Before 1900*. New York: Routledge, 2001. This is an excellent, readable discussion of science fiction before the very term *science fiction* existed.

Asimov, Isaac. *The Gods Themselves*. New York: Bantam, 1990. This 1972 winner of the Hugo and Nebula Awards shows Asimov, writing outside his Robot and Foundation series, tackling the issue of how science and scientists work and what that may mean for us all.

Auerbach, Erich. *Mimesis: The Representation of Reality in Western Literature*. Princeton, NJ: Princeton University Press, 2003. This classic (1953), magisterial study argues that "realism" is a conventional style. Chapters 5 and 6 explain and contrast parataxis and hypotaxis.

Bellamy, Edward. *News from Nowhere*. New York: Oxford University Press, 2003. This 1888 book is the most politically influential utopia in American history, spawning more than 400 Bellamy Clubs and a significant run at the presidency of the United States.

Booth, Wayne C. *The Rhetoric of Fiction*. Chicago: University of Chicago Press, 1983. This 1961 classic work of criticism lays out a useful theoretical framework for understanding in detail the manipulation of narrative devices.

Burroughs, Edgar Rice. *A Princess of Mars*. New York: Dover Books, 2005. This 1912 novel added subtle intellectual consistency to pulp science fiction. It is the first volume in the first series of scores of successful works by Burroughs.

Calvino, Italo. *Cosmicomics*. New York: Harcourt, 1976. Calvino's fantastic parables, each based on a single scientific fact, offer superb myths of the human condition.

Carroll, Lewis. *Mathematical Recreations of Lewis Carroll: Pillow Problems and a Tangled Tale*. New York: Dover Books, 1958. In these nonfiction works, published in 1895 and 1885, respectively, we see Carroll the mathematician at play in his professional field.

Cawelti, John G. *Adventure, Mystery, and Romance: Formula Stories as Art and Popular Culture*. Chicago: University of Chicago Press, 1977. This analysis of the common features and diverse pleasures of "formulaic" genres, such as the Western, help explain the power of genres, including science fiction, that build on them.

Clarke, Arthur C. *Childhood's End*. New York: Ballantine, 1987. This work, in print steadily since its first publication in 1953, explores the possibility of human nature allowing for eutopia.

———. "The Nine Billion Names of God" and "The Star," in *The Collected Stories of Arthur C. Clarke*. New York: Orb Books, 2002. These two short stories, originally published in 1953 and 1955, respectively, are among the most reprinted in all of science fiction. Each offers a subtle, provocative confrontation between science and religion.

Defoe, Daniel. *Robinson Crusoe*. New York: Modern Library, 2001. This 1719 classic tale of a lone man's survival is the archetype for the fantasy of taming the world.

Delany, Samuel R. *The Einstein Intersection*. Middletown, CT: Wesleyan University Press, 1998. A post–atomic holocaust world somehow amalgamates mutated humans with the world of ancient myth.

Dunsany, Lord. *The Sword of Welleran and Other Stories*. New York: Dover Books, 2005. First published in 1908, the short stories in this collection support the claim that Dunsany invented the modern fantasy short story.

Freud, Sigmund. *Totem and Taboo*. New York: Norton, 1962. This slender 1913 volume includes a seminal exposition of the Oedipus complex and argues that the ground rules of our cultural world, and their violation, grow from psychological needs.

————. *The Uncanny*. New York: Penguin Classics, 2003. In this 1919 essay, the heart of which is an analysis of E. T. A. Hoffmann's "The Sandman," Freud lays the foundation for a major psychoanalytic understanding of the fantastic.

Frye, Northrop. "Third Essay: Theory of Myths," in *Anatomy of Criticism: Four Essays*. Princeton, NJ: Princeton University Press, 2000. Frye's 1957 *Anatomy* is one of the foundational works of modern critical theory. His discussion of myths is a major contribution to our understanding of how genres develop.

García Márquez, Gabriel. *One Hundred Years of Solitude*. New York: HarperCollins, 2004. This 1967 novel is the best known work of magical realism and of this Nobel Prize–winning author.

Gorey, Edward. *Amphigorey*. New York: Putnam, 1980. Gorey both wrote and illustrated the playfully sinister books first collected here in 1972, each a macabre adult version of what should be children's literature.

Haldeman, Joe. *The Forever War*. New York: HarperCollins, 2003. This award-winning novel from 1974 is a Vietnam-era reworking of Heinlein's award-winning *Starship Troopers* (1959).

Heaney, Seamus. *Beowulf: A New Verse Translation*. New York: W.W. Norton, 2001. This is the foundational epic of English culture, the battles of a hero against a monster and the monster's mother, rendered here in vigorous, modern verse.

Heinlein, Robert A. *Stranger in a Strange Land*. New York: Ace, 1991. This 1961 novel, which bridged science fiction and New Age spiritualism, became a college classic for two decades.

Huntington, John. *The Logic of Fantasy: H. G. Wells and Science Fiction*. New York: Columbia University Press, 1982. This critical exploration of the work of a seminal science fiction writer also offers useful insight into the relationship between science fiction and fantasy.

Jung, Carl Gustav. *Man and His Symbols*. New York: Dell, 1968. First published in 1964, three years after Jung's death, the essays collected here give the most accessible overview of Jung's views of psychology and culture. It is the most prominent depth psychological alternative to Freud.

Kafka, Franz. *Amerika*. New York: Schocken Books, 1996. This novel, published posthumously in 1927, is Kafka's fictional study of America as a possible location for overcoming the alienation of modern culture.

———. *The Trial*. New York: Schocken Books, 1995. This unfinished novel, published posthumously in 1925, presents a modern Everyman caught in the inhuman machinery of modern society.

Landon, Brooks. *Science Fiction After 1900: From the Steam Man to the Stars*. New York: Routledge, 2002. This is a fine, compact, readable overview of its title subject.

Lévi-Strauss, Claude. "The Structural Study of Myth," in *Structural Anthropology*. New York: Basic Books, 2000. *Structural Anthropology* (1958) collects essays that together, formed the basis of a revolutionary way of exploring culture. Chapter 11 uses the Oedipus myth, the Sophoclean original, not the Freudian adaptation, as its prime example.

Lewis, C. S. *The Chronicles of Narnia*. New York: HarperCollins, 2001. Published as separate books between 1950 and 1956, this is the best-loved modern series of Christian children's books.

Lord, Albert. *The Singer of Tales*. Cambridge, MA: Harvard University Press, 2000. First published in 1960, this is the most influential work exploring the relationship between oral and written composition, focusing on fantastic founding epics, such as *The Odyssey* and *Beowulf*.

Lüthi, Max. *Once Upon a Time: On the Nature of Fairy Tales*. Indianapolis: Indiana University Press, 1976. This 1964 study of fairy tales attempts to understand the full range of its subject's psychological, cultural, and aesthetic importance.

Marlowe, Christopher. *Doctor Faustus*. New York: Signet, 2001. First performed in 1594, this play captures the famous image of the man of great learning overreaching and bringing doom.

More, Thomas. *Utopia*. New York: Penguin, 2003. When this work was published in 1516, its title instantly became the name of a genre of fantastic social imagination that stretches from Plato to the present.

Orwell, George. *Animal Farm*. New York: Signet, 2004. This famous 1945 fable uses the warrant of children's literature to create a simplistic yet biting political satire intended for adults.

Ovid. *Metamorphoses*. New York: Oxford World Classics, 1998. This classic masterpiece (c. 8 C.E.) recounts Greek, Roman, and Near Eastern traditional tales of fantastic changes often effected by gods.

Perrault, Charles. *Perrault's Fairy Tales*. New York: Dover Books, 1969. This edition of the 1697 courtly retelling of such classics as "Cinderella" and "Puss in Boots" also has Gustave Doré's famous illustrations.

Plato. *The Collected Dialogues of Plato*. Princeton, NJ: Princeton University Press, 1961. This is a definitive, well-indexed collection of one of the great sources of Western philosophy.

Propp, Vladimir. *Morphology of the Folktale*. Austin, TX: University of Texas Press, 1968. In this 1927 book, Propp reported his discovery of the universal structure of true oral folk tales, many of which we would call fairy tales.

Russ, Joanna. *The Female Man*. Boston: Beacon Press, 2000. First published in 1975, this award-winning novel offers a feminism that contrasts powerfully with that of Le Guin.

Saramago, José. *Blindness*. New York: Harcourt, 1999. This 1995 novel by Nobel laureate Saramago is part fantasy in the tradition of Kafka, part science fiction in the social extrapolative tradition of Heinlein, and all influenced by magical realism.

Stapledon, Olaf. *Star Maker*, in *Last and First Men and Star Maker: Two Science Fiction Novels*. New York: Dover Books, 1968. The deeply poetic 1937 *Star Maker*, which has been called the "one great grey holy book of science fiction," was a bestseller in its time and is now best known as the source for the seeds of hundreds of other novels.

Taylor, Roger, Edward Wakeling, and Peter C. Bunnell. *Lewis Carroll, Photographer*. Princeton, NJ: Princeton University Press, 2002. This marvelous demonstration of the range of Carroll's work as a photographer includes a revealing monograph-length biographical article, as well.

Twain, Mark. *A Connecticut Yankee in King Arthur's Court*. New York: Bantam, 1983. The premise of this delightful time-travel novel (1889) is fantastic, but the action in the past is science fictional, while the satire and romance combine with it all to produce an under-read masterpiece.

Verne, Jules. *The Begum's Millions*. Middletown, CT: Wesleyan University Press, 2005. In this earnest yet charming 1879 book, Verne sets competing French and German visions of the perfect society near each other in the American Olympic Mountains.

Walpole, Horace. *The Castle of Otranto: A Gothic Story*. New York: Oxford University Press, 1998. This short masterpiece from 1764 lent its subtitle to the whole field of Gothic literature.

Wells, H. G. *The Food of the Gods*. New York: Dover Books, 2005. This 1904 novel shows Wells taking a single fantastic novel element and building from it a dramatic critique of society and a portrait of the—let us hope improvable—human condition.

Woolf, Virginia. "Mr. Bennett and Mrs. Brown," in *The Virginia Woolf Reader*. New York: Harcourt, 1984. This important 1924 lecture offers this towering Modernist's view of the differences between male and female writers.

———. *A Room of One's Own*. New York: Harcourt, 1989. This 1929 classic of modern feminism argues for the necessity of real independence of the body for independence of the spirit.

Internet Resources:

Eric S. Rabkin. *Eric Rabkin's Home Page*. http://www.umich.edu/~esrabkin. This site contains links to fantasy and science fiction courses, each of which has further links to supplementary materials in those subjects.

The Internet Speculative Fiction Database. http://www.isfdb.org. This site offers a compendious, although unannotated, listing of modern science fiction writing.

Notes